Authoritarian Party Structures and
Democratic Political Setting in Turkey

Authoritarian Party Structures and Democratic Political Setting in Turkey

Pelin Ayan Musil

Cover by Yonca Duran, reproduced by permission of the artist

First published in 2011 by
PALGRAVE MACMILLAN®
in the United States—a division of St. Martin's Press LLC,
175 Fifth Avenue, New York, NY 10010.

Where this book is distributed in the UK, Europe and the rest of the world,
this is by Palgrave Macmillan, a division of Macmillan Publishers Limited,
registered in England, company number 785998, of Houndmills,
Basingstoke, Hampshire RG21 6XS.

Palgrave Macmillan is the global academic imprint of the above companies
and has companies and representatives throughout the world.

Palgrave® and Macmillan® are registered trademarks in the United States,
the United Kingdom, Europe and other countries.

ISBN: 978–0–230–33752–7

Library of Congress Cataloging-in-Publication Data

Musil, Pelin Ayan, 1981–
    Authoritarian party structures and democratic political setting in
    Turkey / Pelin Ayan Musil.
        p. cm.
    ISBN 978–0–230–33752–7 (alk. paper)
      1. Political parties—Turkey—History. 2. Authoritarianism—Turkey.
    3. Political parties—Turkey—Case studies. I. Title.

JQ1809.A795M87 2012
324.2561′011—dc23   2011023453

A catalogue record of the book is available from the British Library.

Design by Newgen Imaging Systems (P) Ltd., Chennai, India.

First edition: December 2011

10 9 8 7 6 5 4 3 2 1

Printed in the United States of America.

Contents

Figures and Tables

Figures

Tables

Preface

The existing studies assume or treat a nondemocratic party organization as a static and uniform structure, in which national party leaders dominate the local party activists. Moreover, the extant explanations on party structures with no internal democracy focus on the effect of macro-level factors (such as the changes in the nature of democratic competition, political culture, and institutional structure) over the internal strategies of the party leadership. Thus, little attention is paid to the role that local party activists play in such party structures. This study attempts to enhance our understanding of dynamics and factors behind nondemocratic party structures by raising the following questions: *What does intraparty authoritarianism constitute? Is it really a uniform or a static phenomenon as assumed? If not, how can we explain the variance in intraparty authoritarianism? What might be the theoretical and policy implications of such an analysis for democratic development and party governance?*

By conducting a comparative case study of four political parties (AKP, CHP, MHP, and DTP) in four geographically and politically distinct urban districts (*Karşıyaka, Ümraniye, Diyarbakır-Merkez,* and *Tarsus*) within Turkish political system in the aftermath of 2007 national elections, this study identifies four types of intraparty authoritarianism: *benign, clandestine, challenged,* and *coercive.* In order to explain this variance, this study utilizes principal-agent approach, which is modified in two ways. First, as opposed to internally democratic parties, it is the national party leaders (principals) that delegate authority to local party activists (agents) in authoritarian party organizations. Second, the interest configurations between the principals and agents are based on not only *material* but also *ideational* interests. Material interests are those associated with power-seeking aims such as a desire for a position in public office. Ideational interests refer to the shared ideas and values such as ideological attachment, policy interests, or loyalty to the leader. It is argued that interest configurations, which *constitute* the power structures between the national party leaders (principals) and local party activists (agents), vary across space and time. Second, the endogenous and exogenous triggers such as the outcomes of candidate selection processes or electoral defeats have the potential to *cause* a change in the power equilibrium between principals and agents, which might generate a new type of intraparty authoritarianism or an exit to democratic party governance.

Empirical analyses indicate that the agents motivated primarily by material interests are subordinate to intraparty authoritarianism due to the material benefits received from the principals (*benign authoritarianism*). The agents motivated by ideational interests accept the subordination because of their loyalty to the party leader or the party ideology (*clandestine authoritarianism*). That been said, the agents whose interests conflict with the principals as a result of exogenous or endogenous triggers might attempt to shirk from the authority of the principals and object the authoritarian party structure (*challenged authoritarianism*). The authoritarian-leaning principals, in response, may exert coercion over the challenging agents (*coercive authoritarianism*). The success of the challenging agents over the principals depends on the effective use of their *power resources,* such as information, social and economic status, legitimacy, and networking with other agents.

This work, thus, shows that intraparty authoritarianism should be understood as a dynamic and heterogeneous phenomenon, which shows significant degree of variance across space and time. To have a better sense of this dynamic phenomenon, we need to focus on the role of micro-level factors (such as interest configuration and power relationships among principals and agents). With respect to broader implications, the principal-agent relationship must be understood in a different way in authoritarian party organizations where the major responsibility of the local party activists is to fulfill the tasks set by the national party leaders. Therefore, in studying the power structure of authoritarian party organizations, contrary to the conventional understanding, it is useful to assign the role of the principal to the national party leaders and the role of the agent to the local party activists.

Another implication of this study is that exit from intraparty authoritarianism is always a possibility not only because the national party leaders choose to do so, but also because the local party activists have the potential to cultivate new power resources and create power networks against authoritarian party structures. Yet, this possibility arises only when there is a conflict of interests between the agents and principals. Therefore, what causes the rise of such intraparty conflicts (such as electoral defeats, outcomes of candidate selection processes) and what prevents them from arising (such as material benefits, or ideational interests such as leadership loyalty, ideological attachment) must be given further recognition in studying the dynamics of intraparty authoritarianism.

Finally, it must be underlined that even though the arguments of this study are based on a variable-oriented approach (such as intra-organizational variables of internal party democracy) and employ a positivist method, the study bears a significant normative rationale: Despite all the question marks and debates over the necessity of internal party democracy for the overall democratic competition in a political system; it *must be treated* as a desired goal within a political culture like Turkey. Because the channels for society to penetrate into the state has been highly restricted as a result of weak civil society organizations and parties with highly exclusive, state-led structures; internal party democracy is a necessary tool for the development of representative democracy. Thus, this study is the first of its kind in presenting an in-depth explanation for the intraorganizational possibilities of how purely authoritarian party structures can become democratic in time.

Acknowledgments

This book is the product of an extensive period of research that started with my Ph.D. dissertation. Bilkent University provided initial funding and all kinds of academic support to make this research possible. The Support Program of the Scientific and Technological Research Council of Turkey (TÜBİTAK-BİDEB) supported three years of study and research at Bilkent University. The data collection was additionally supported by the Scientific and Technological Research Council of Turkey (TÜBİTAK) through the grant no: 107K349. A Fulbright research fellowship at Georgetown University provided valuable time to conduct the data analysis of this study. Some preliminary outcomes of this research were published in the article I authored, "Authoritarian Party Structures in Turkey: A Comparison of the Republican People's Party and the Justice and Development Party" in *Turkish Studies* (2010, Vol 11, No 2); and I would like to thank Taylor and Francis Ltd. for the reprint permission.

I wish to especially acknowledge many substantial comments on each chapter of this book by Zeki Sarıgil that greatly helped me enrich the theoretical framework of the whole study. I would also like to thank Metin Heper, Ergun Özbudun, Ayşe Güneş-Ayata, Ömer Faruk Gençkaya, Hootan Shambayati, Aylin Güney and the reviewers of the study for many useful comments they gave on the earlier drafts of this book. A special note of appreciation is due to Beren Koramaz, Emine Yönden, and Tuba Durdu for their exceptional assistance during the field research of this project. I also want to express my sincere thanks to Palgrave Macmillan for their support and help during all stages of the production of this book.

Finally, I thank my family and friends; without their constant support, none of this would have been possible.

Introduction

This study provides an explanation for what constitutes an authoritarian party structure, which is a highly undertheorized phenomenon in party politics. An authoritarian party structure or intraparty authoritarianism can be understood as the symmetrical opposition of internal party democracy, a concept that has an important history in political science, grounded in the original work of Robert Michels.[1] Yet, because of the complex relationship between the party in public office, party in central office, and party on the ground,[2] as well as the multifaceted dimensions of internal decision-making systems such as policy determination, candidate selection, and leadership selection processes, what exactly defines an internally democratic party has not reached any consensus so far. Some important measures for intraparty democracy have been the degree of *inclusiveness* of the decision-making processes; *decentralization* and *institutionalization* of party structures.[3] Even though each of these three measures has its own weakness regarding to what degree it can identify internal party democracy; the bottom line in each is that in internally democratic parties, the party on the ground—comprising party members and activists—has certain *power* over the internal decision-making processes. Authoritarian party structures, then, can be understood as structures in which the members and activists *lack* any means of such *power* and are subordinate to the decisions of the party leaders.

The question on "who holds the power in party organizations" has brought divergent hypotheses, starting from Michels, who argues that no matter how democratic the party structure is at the beginning, oligarchy is the inevitable outcome in party organizations.[4] He explains that the effective functioning of an organization requires the concentration of power in a small group of party elite because most decisions cannot be made efficiently by large numbers of people. The party elite in return, uses all means necessary to preserve and further increase its power.[5] Later on, Duverger also accepted that party organizations held such oligarchic features, underlining the institutional factors behind it, such as the characteristics of electoral systems, party systems, and the impact of political regimes.[6]

These essential works by Michels and Duverger raised the attention of many scholars in the study of power in party organizations, particularly in the analyses of changing party types in liberal democracies. The major aim of these studies has been to understand the growing dependency of political parties on state resources and their weakening ties with the society.[7] These studies show that the party elite has begun to gain more autonomy vis-à-vis the party members and activists even though, ironically, party organizations have become more inclusive: Through including more members in decision-making processes, the party elite simply manipulates the less active "ordinary" members in order to swamp the middle-level party activists who are thought to pose the greatest challenge to their dominance in the party.[8] Hence, the real agents of change—the middle-level party activists—in the party organization are prevented from influencing the party decisions. As a result, it is hypothesized that in liberal democracies, the power structure of internally democratic parties are changing in time as a result of the macro developments such as economic growth, mass communications, individualization, which make the parties more dependent on their leaders.[9] Yet, this hypothesis has already produced its counterargument underlining that rather than being divorced from the party on the ground, the party elite has actually become more sensitive to the demands coming from the bottom.[10] This is because the party leaders must also pay attention to their legitimacy in external democratic competition, and such legitimacy can be acquired by internal party democracy.

However, this debate on the power structures of parties, unfortunately, focuses only on one side of the coin. That is, while the question of whether parties are becoming less or more democratic raises divergent hypotheses, the question of whether parties with authoritarian power structures can or cannot become democratic does not receive much attention. While it is possible to see nondemocratic party structures in liberal democracies, in many developing democracies, parties with authoritarian structures outnumber the internally democratic parties. It is because macro-level factors such as the political culture and the institutional structures play a fundamental role in shaping the major pattern within the power structures of parties at their formation. For instance, it is a common perception that parties in many postcommunist states have leader-dependent party organizations because of their weak grounding in civil society.[11] In Latin America, however, parties are labeled as "organizationally thin" due to the low degrees of party membership, which is known as the contingent effect of an illiterate, rural, and "politically unmobilized" segment of the society.[12] In the Middle East, no indigenous tradition of representation existed among political parties, and they dealt less with seizing power than redefining state boundaries and establishing new regimes, which led them to possess leader-dependent structures.[13]

Thus, the studies in liberal democracies mainly focus on effect of macrolevel developments on the transformation of internally democratic parties into more authoritarian structures, whereas the studies in developing democracies focus on how the political culture and pre-democratic legacies have led to the emergence of intraparty authoritarianism. However, in order to measure the effect of macro-level factors, it is, first, essential to understand what constitutes intraparty authoritarianism at the micro level. Rather than treating authoritarian party organizations as uniform and static structures where the party leaders dominate the party on the ground, the power relationship between the two must be studied. Attention must be paid to the role that local party actors play in authoritarian party structures and why they subordinate to their leaders' domination. Such an analysis would also help us to consider whether there is any way back from intraparty authoritarianism toward internal democracy.

Purpose of the Study

The question of whether democratization of party structures is possible would probably be rejected in the very first stage by the advocates of "iron law of oligarchy," who claim that oligarchy is the case for all parties. Yet the "iron law of oligarchy" thesis itself is rooted in a perspective of *change* in understanding the power structures of party organizations. If it is impossible to expect the permanence of democratic party structures, then how can we not expect that parties that are already born with a dominant leader tradition will modify their power structures? The authoritarian party leaders who seek to maintain their power in the party may face challenges against their authority. Then, it is plausible to ask what causes or prevents the emergence of such challenges; and whether it is possible for a challenge to develop into the democratization of the party structure?

Inspired by this puzzle, this study is an attempt to understand the internal mechanisms of authoritarian party structures and question the existing assumptions, which treat intraparty authoritarianism as a static and uniform phenomenon. It asks the following set of questions: What constitutes an *authoritarian party structure* (or *intraparty authoritarianism*)? Are authoritarian party structures *static,* or do they change in *time*? Are they *uniform* structures, or do they show different patterns across *space*? If so, what are the possible patterns across and within authoritarian party structures? What causes the variance in intraparty authoritarianism across space and time? This set of questions will help us to understand the micro-level factors of authoritarian party structures, which have not received as much attention as the macro-level factors such as political culture and institutional framework. Providing explanations to these questions will then help us to understand the transition of the authoritarianism within the party toward internal party democracy.

Relevance of the Study

Political parties are at the heart of democratic competition. Being able to put candidates in legislative or governmental positions by winning elections, parties are marked by a certain dual standing between the state and civil society.[14] To put it more concretely, political parties link the society to the state based on a chain of connections that runs from the voters through the candidates and the electoral process to the officials of the government.[15]

Studying the power structures of parties is necessary in order to see what impact they bring on this strategic function that they have in democratic competition. In fact, how intraparty authoritarianism and internal party democracy affect the democratic regimes has received a significant degree of attention in the literature. The debate between the opponents and advocates of intraparty democracy is rooted in the distinction between the populist and liberal understandings of democracy. The liberals emphasize the virtues of participation and deliberation within parties.[16] Besides, intraparty democracy provides a voice mechanism for voters and party members whose exit option is already available.[17] Against the liberal side, the populists stress the need for a united front and more authoritarianism within parties, which are conducive to structured competition at the systemic level.[18] As Scarrow rightly notes, the reason for the tension in the debate is because the two schools have different concerns: The liberal approach is concerned about the *process* and sees intraparty democracy as an end in itself, while the populist approach is concerned about the *outcome* and sees intraparty democracy as an instrument to help parties offer clear and distinct electoral choices to the electorate.[19] In this respect, according to liberals, intraparty democracy is a goal of the political party, which plays a linkage role between the state and society, whereas according to the populists, existence of intraparty democracy is crucial for a democratic regime to the degree that it effectively serves to the functions of political parties.

Furthermore, the degree of democracy within a party organization shapes the organizational aspects of political parties. For instance, the full inclusiveness of the electorate in decision-making mechanisms leads to a loosening and weak party structure like the parties in the United States.[20] Party cohesion and internal party democracy need to be balanced in line with the needs of the political system. When party leaders are faced with loss of control in the party, they might want to reassert party discipline by undemocratizing candidate selection as was the case in Australian Labor and Liberal parties from the 1950s to the 1970s, Belgian parties in the 1980s and the 1990s, most Dutch parties as well as Austrian People's Party (ÖVP), and Social Democratic Party of Austria (SPÖ) after the 1994 elections.[21]

As a result, internal party democracy or intraparty authoritarianism has an overwhelming significance as an independent variable in democratic politics. This means that providing new perspectives to the study of intraparty authoritarianism as a dependent variable is a very relevant subject to study in political science.

Findings and Arguments

This study shows that an authoritarian party organization has a dynamic and heterogeneous structure based on the interactive power relationship between the central party elite and the local party actors. It reveals that authoritarian party structures show variance across space and time in a given political system. The empirical findings of this study indicate four possible types of intraparty authoritarianism: benign, clandestine, challenged, and coercive. In *benign authoritarianism*, both the local party actors and national party leaders have mutual material gains from the authoritarian party structure. In *clandestine authoritarianism*, the local party actors are not aware of or are indifferent to the domination of the national party leaders. In *challenged authoritarianism*, the local party actors object to the authoritarian party structures. In *coercive authoritarianism*, the party leaders exert explicit coercion or threat over the local party actors who challenge their authority in the party.

In order to shed light on the variance in authoritarian party structures, this study, first of all, underlines the need to treat intraparty authoritarianism as a *relational* phenomenon. In other words, power does not belong to a certain actor within the party but it is rather "relational," taking place between the national party leaders and local party actors.[22] The authoritarian party leader at the national level must take into account the skills, perceptions, and interests of the local party actors because the potential effectiveness of the party leader's power depends on these actors' interests, perceptions, and skills.

In the second step, the study utilizes the principal-agent (PA) model in party structures where interest configurations *constitute* the power relationships between the national party leaders and the local party actors. The study modifies the conventional understanding of the PA model in party politics in two ways: First, as opposed to internally democratic parties, it shows that the delegation of authority is transferred from national party leaders (principals) to local party actors (agents) in authoritarian party organizations, *not* vice versa. Second, it shows that the interest configurations between the principals and agents are based on not only *material* but also *ideational* interests. Material interests are those associated with power-seeking aims such as a desire for a position in public office. On the other hand, ideational interests (shared ideas and values) refer to the interests shaped in *ideational contexts* such as ideological attachment, policy interests, or loyalty to the leader. Due to the different patterns in interest configurations between the principals and agents, this study argues that it is also possible to see a variance in intraparty authoritarianism across space and time. For instance, the agents with material interests are subordinate to intraparty authoritarianism due to the material benefits received from the principals (*benign authoritarianism*). The agents with ideational interests are subordinate to intraparty authoritarianism because of their loyalty to the party leader or the party ideology (*clandestine authoritarianism*).

However, the *endogenous* and *exogenous triggers* such as the outcomes of candidate selection processes or electoral defeats have the potential to cause a change within the power equilibrium in authoritarian party structures, generating new types of intraparty authoritarianism, which may or may not lead to democratic party governance: the agents whose interests conflict with the principals as a result of exogenous or endogenous triggers might attempt to shirk from the authority of the principals and object to the authoritarian party structure (*challenged authoritarianism*). The authoritarian-leaning principals, in response, may exert coercion over the challenging agents (*coercive authoritarianism*). The study argues that the success of the challenging agents over the principals and thus the transition to intraparty democracy depends on how effective their *power resources* are, such as information, social and economic status, legitimacy, and networking with other agents.

In sum, the study shows that the variance in interest configurations between principals and agents (based on the material and ideational interests) has a *constitutive* effect; the exogenous and endogenous triggers have a *causal* effect on the different patterns of authoritarian party structures in a political system.

Methodology

This study is directed by a theory-building research objective and adopts a variable-oriented approach through conducting controlled comparison. A "variable-oriented" approach is concerned with establishing the causal power of particular variables on a certain outcome, and is usually adopted in studies that employ a comparative method.[23] "Controlled comparison" requires that comparison between selected cases be controlled if two or more instances of a well-specified phenomenon resemble each other in every aspect but one.[24] Even though it is extremely difficult to find cases that resemble each other in every aspect but one, George and Bennett argue that this limitation of controlled comparison can be overcome by conducting a "within-case analysis", which focuses not on the analysis of variables across cases, but on the causal path in a single case.[25] According to this alternative approach, the results of individual case studies, each of which employs within-case analysis, can be compared by drawing them together within a common theoretical framework without having to find two or more cases that are similar in every respect but one.[26]

The methodology of this study, thus, combines the features of within-case analysis with controlled comparison. In order to understand the variance in the dependent variable (DV = *intraparty authoritarianism*), this study compares four party organizations by controlling the macro-level cultural and structural variables through focusing on one single political system, Turkey. The selected cases, four political parties in Turkey resemble one another in several aspects because the organizational characteristics of parties are overwhelmingly subject to the provisions stated in the Law on Political Parties in Turkey (No.: 2820). However, the selected parties do not entirely meet the condition of "resembling each other in every aspect but one" because they differ from one another in aspects such as ideology, the styles of the party leaders, and the age of the organization. That is why in addition to the controlled comparison method, this study makes use of the within-case analysis and studies the actors' interests not only *across* but also *within* each selected individual party organization.

Case studies can be of different kinds. The specific kind that this study uses is the plausibility probe. A plausibility probe is a method used to examine whether an untested hypothesis will be strong enough to be tested with even broader, more in-depth inquiries.[27] For the purpose of this study, the untested hypotheses are listed as follows:

1. Differences in *interest configurations* within party structures and/ or the rise of certain *endogenous and exogenous triggers* lead to a

variance in intraparty authoritarianism *across* and *within* party organizations.

2. It is possible to see a transition from intraparty authoritarianism toward intraparty democracy (a) when a *conflict of interests* arises between the authoritarian party leaders and local party actors, and (b) when the latter cultivates effective *power resources* against former.

An *interest configuration* within a party structure is the one taking place between local and national party actors and shaped by two types of interests: material interests (i.e., desire for power) and ideational interests (i.e., ideological attachment, sense of community obligation). The difference in the types of interests among major party actors (party leaders and local actors) brings varying *interest configurations* within party structures, which may eventually affect the internal power relationships. Alternatively, the examples of *exogenous triggers* are electoral defeats or victories, the emergence of new parties or disappearance of old ones in the system; whereas, some examples for *endogenous triggers* are the outcomes of candidate selection processes, the resignation of party leaders or other key party actors. Finally, *power resources* of the local party actors are defined as informational advantage, legitimacy, social and economic status, and networking.

Plausibility probes are rooted in data and reasoning. To put it differently, the purpose is to establish the validity of the central propositions for further inquiry. As emphasized by Eckstein, plausibility probes involving attempts to estimate the potential validity of a hypothesis "are especially important where non-empirical probes yield very uncertain results, and there is also reason to use them, as additions to others, as cheap means of hedging against expensive wild-goose chases, when the costs of testing are likely to be very great."[28] In this respect, the causal value of the independent variables in this study (interest configurations, exogenous and endogenous triggers, power resources) has been analyzed in 16 relationships between the party leaders and local party actors, based on 91 in-depth interviews. The 16 relationships are derived from *four* parties and their local branches from *four* different districts in Turkey (The rationale behind the selection of the districts, which are *Karşıyaka*, *Ümraniye*, *Diyarbakır-Merkez* and *Tarsus*, is explained in details in the section titled "Methodological Notes on the Field Research" in chapter 5 on page…). Based on its validity, the hypothesis of this study needs to be tested in broader frameworks in future studies.

Country Selection: Intraparty authoritarianism is an undertheorized political phenomenon. Yet, why is it studied in Turkey? The formation of the first political parties in Turkey followed a top-down, elite-driven transition to democracy, paving the way for the leaders' dominance as the major characteristics of power structures within parties. The authoritarian characteristics of the first party organizations were adopted by their successors later on. These characteristics even became institutionalized through the adoption of Law on Political Parties. Özbudun asserts:

> The Turkish political parties law, adopted in 1983 by the military regime, is probably the most detailed of its kind in Europe. It contains not only party prohibitions, but also extremely detailed regulations on party organization, registration, membership, nominations, discipline, and party finance. Consequently, all Turkish parties have very similar organizational structures imposed upon them by the law.[29]

Furthermore, the literature on party organizations in Turkey well recognizes their authoritarian characteristics, yet the question of "what exactly constitutes it" needs to be studied with micro-level analyses. Such analyses have been neglected in Turkey as Sayarı once pointed out:

> The organizational dimension of political competition in Turkey has received surprisingly little attention despite its obvious relevance for understanding party behavior. Undoubtedly, much more systematic research is needed before we can begin to answer questions concerning the degree of organizational centralization, the nature of authority relationships between leaders and sub-leaders, the level of involvement in party activities, or the functional relevance of organizational work for the success in the elections.[30]

Some monographic studies on the organizational characteristics of political parties in Turkey do exist.[31] Yet, there are very few studies that compare the authoritarian characteristics of party organizations in detail, and these studies do not focus on the dynamism and heterogeneity of intraparty authoritarianism.[32] Therefore a contemporary, comparative study of party organizations with an emphasis on intraparty authoritarianism in Turkey can provide a good laboratory to theorize authoritarian party structures. It is an ideal, representative case where intraparty authoritarianism is embedded in the political culture and the institutional framework (i.e., the Law on Political Parties).

Selection of Parties: The selected parties in this study are the Justice and Development Party (AKP—*Adalet ve Kalkınma Partisi*), the Republican People's Party (CHP—*Cumhuriyet Halk Partisi*), the Nationalist Action Party (MHP—*Milliyetçi Hareket Partisi*), and the Democratic Society Party (DTP—*Demokratik Toplum Partisi*).[33] Representing four major ideological trends, these parties held parliamentary office between the years 2007 and 2011. During the six-month period when the research was implemented between September 2007 and February 2008, these were the main parties that had certain influence over the party system, pursuing identical goals such as being able to influence the public opinion and being successful in the electoral competition. For the sake of the research objective, the parties that relatively had a lesser amount of influence on public opinion such as the Motherland Party (ANAP—*Anavatan Partisi*) and Democratic Left Party (DSP—*Demokratik Sol Parti*) were eliminated from the study. Since the major electoral defeat of these parties in 2002 elections, their role in the political system has diminished, and thus their organizational structures have become very unstable, leading to constant resignations by the party leaders and attempts for unification among parties.[34] In this respect, these cases would not provide healthy analytical results for studying the authoritarian party structures in Turkey.

Roadmap

This study is structured in the following order: chapter 1 reviews the existing explanations for intraparty democracy and intraparty authoritarianism, aiming to provide a definition of both concepts. It shows the weaknesses of the present explanations in studying authoritarian party structures: In the studies on liberal democracies, the focus is mainly directed on the macro-level explanations for why and how internally democratic parties gain authoritarian features in time but not vice versa. In developing democracies, the main focus is attributed on the effect of two macro-level factors—mode of transitions to democracy and the legacies of the pre-democratic regimes—on the power structures of parties. Thus, none of the two bodies of literature provides an adequate explanation for the micro-level dynamics of intraparty authoritarianism. This chapter, then, elaborates the potential micro-level causes of intraparty authoritarianism such as party ideology or leadership styles, and shows that they fall short in explaining the possible variance in intraparty authoritarianism across space and time.

Chapter 2 provides the literature review on authoritarian party structures in Turkey with the aim to show the weaknesses of the existing explanations of intraparty authoritarianism in Turkish politics. The explanations in Turkish politics mainly focus on the role of political culture and institutional framework regarding why the parties show authoritarian features, yet these explanations treat intraparty authoritarianism as a very static and uniform phenomenon. Furthermore, the chapter analyzes the role of party ideologies and leadership styles on power struc-tures and concludes that these explanations are not sufficient to under-stand the variance *within* authoritarian party structures.

In order to construct a theoretical framework for intraparty authori-tarianism, chapter 3 discusses the advantages of utilizing the PA theory in party politics (i.e., providing an explanation for dynamism and change in hierarchical structures). The chapter further outlines the need to modify the theory in order to shed light on intraparty authoritarianism: First, contrary to the conventional understanding, it argues that the role of the principal should be assigned to the party leaders and the role of the agent to the local party actors. Second, it argues that the materialistic bias of the PA theory needs to be restored through integrating the role that ideas and values have in shaping interest configurations between the principals and agents. In this respect this chapter shows that the interests of the party actors can be either material (i.e., desire for power) or ideational (i.e., loy-alty to the leader and ideology).

Chapter 4, through the modified PA theory, provides a theoreti-cal model that explains the possible variance that authoritarian party structures show across time and space: it first shows that the extent of ideational or material interests pursued by principals and agents molds different types of *interest configurations* within authoritarian party structures (i.e., strategic, nonstrategic, and hybrid interest configura-tions). Since the interest configurations *constitute* the power structure of party organizations, the different types of interest configurations lead to a variance in intraparty authoritarianism. Second, it justifies the causal impact of exogenous and endogenous triggers, such as electoral defeats or the outcome of candidate selection processes, on the vari-ance in authoritarian party structures: these triggers conflict of interests between principals and agents. Then, depending on how effectively the *power resources* were used by the agents, it leads to an exit from intra-party authoritarianism.

Chapters 5 and 6 provide the empirical validity of the arguments given in the previous two chapters in the case of Turkey. Based on 91 in-depth interviews, conducted right after the 2007 national elections with the local party actors from selected parties and districts, chapter 5 reveals the obser-vation of four patterns of authoritarianisms—*clandestine, benign, coercive, challenged*—across and within parties in Turkey. The responses of the local party actors on the open-ended questions like "whether they think the last candidate selection process was inclusive in their party," "whether they have ever taken any opposing action against their leaders," or "whether they think their party structure is democratic or not" help to identify these patterns across and within authoritarian party structures in Turkey.

Chapter 6, in order to explain this existing variance in intraparty authoritarianism in Turkey, first shows how the relationship between principals and agents is constructed in Turkish party structures contrary to the conventional PA approach to party organizations. Second, through analyzing the interest types of the local party actors and the conflicts between principals and agents, it explains the observed variance across and within parties. It shows that through taking part in a power network against intraparty authoritarianism, the CHP local actors in districts *Karşıyaka* and *Ümraniye* came closest to exit from intraparty authoritarianism, yet failed to do so due to the lack of effective power resources (i.e., lack of grassroots support and personal attributes of the faction leader).

1

Existing Explanations on Intraparty Authoritarianism

This chapter aims to provide a review of how intraparty democracy and intraparty authoritarianism are explained so far. It first provides the definition, and second reviews the macro- and micro-level causes of these two power structures. Finally, the chapter evaluates the limitations of the literature in understanding intraparty authoritarianism.

What are Intraparty Democracy and Intraparty Authoritarianism?

The power structure of a party is usually characterized by the relations between the three faces of the party organization: party in public office, party in central office, and party on the ground.[1] The "party in public office" comprises the elected members of the party in parliament and/ or government. The "party in central office" and "party on the ground" together constitute the extraparliamentary branch. The party in central office is understood as the national leadership of the party organization, which in theory, is organizationally distinct from the party in public office.[2] Yet, this theory is mainly derived from the evidence acquired from party organizations in liberal democracies. The experience in newly developing democracies shows that the party in public office and central office has more overlapping features, in other words, the same group of party elite may control power both in central and public office.[3] However, the party on the ground represents the rank-and-file of the party, comprising of ordinary party members as well as the party activists who play a more extensive role than the members at the grassroots level.[4]

In the literature, extending greater influence to the party on the ground in decision-making processes is generally understood as promoting internal party democracy.[5] On the other hand, if the party leaders in public or central office gain the influence over the party organization, it is authoritarianism that is extended. Yet, before outlining what describes such influence, there is a need to outline the key decision-making processes within the parties.

Decision-Making in the Party Organization

There are three major decision-making processes within party organizations: candidate selection, selecting party leaders, and defining policy positions.[6] *Candidate selection* is usually known as the central defining function of a political party in a democracy.[7] It gives important clues about the democratic or authoritarian features of party organizations. Are primaries held? Is it all members of the party organization or only members from administrative boards that can join the primaries? Who determines the eligibility for being a candidate? Are choices limited by party rules (are there any quotas)? Similar to candidate selection, the choice of alternative methods for the *selection of party leaders* sometimes reflects another dimension of intraparty democracy.[8] The questions like "who may participate as a selector," "are there limits on who may stand as a candidate for leadership in the internal election" are important measures of whether the party behaves in a democratic manner or not. Because the selection of the leader is important for the party's image, there may be conflicts about how to set the rules.[9]

Another decision-making process in the party organization is based on *determination of party policies*. There may be party policy committees that aim to aggregate different viewpoints from the party, for instance, by introducing consultations or collecting comments. Or, the policy determination process simply may not take into consideration the majority of party members' opinions. Whether a party has a democratic nature can be demonstrated by understanding if the policies have been developed in cooperation with all party members who are supposed to represent the party in whole. For instance, the UK's Labour Party in 1997 went through a significant internal democratization process through including members, unions, and local party organizations into the policy-making processes.[10] Similarly, Australian Labor Party has a strong commitment to have the policy-making processes as inclusive and participatory as possible.[11]

Internal party democracy or authoritarianism can be observed in these three processes of decision-making within party structures. The greater the influence of the party on the ground over these processes, the more democratic the party is considered. The lesser the influence, the more authoritarian the party is.

Inclusiveness, Decentralization, and Institutionalization

What identifies the influence of the "party on the ground" over the processes of candidate selection, selection of party leaders, and policy determination? The literature usually outlines the terms *inclusiveness, decentralization,* and *institutionalization* in referring to such influence in internally democratic parties. Therefore, according to this literature, it would be right to assume that the lack of these phenomena alternatively results in the lack of such influence and thus intraparty authoritarianism.

Rahat and Hazan elaborate the importance of *inclusiveness* in candidate selection.[12] In candidate selection, the "inclusiveness" feature takes into account two dimensions: candidacy and the selectorate. In terms of candidacy, the questions such as "can anybody present him/herself as a candidate in the candidate selection process?" and "what are the requirements for being a candidate?" show to what extent the criteria for candidacy are inclusive of party members. The selectorate, on the other hand, is the group that selects the candidates and the more this group is inclusive, the more democratic the organization is. Usually if the selectorate consists of the whole electorate, it is considered to be the most inclusive, and if it consists only of a nonelected party leader, it is considered to be the most exclusive.[13] Among these two, the composition of the selectorate is argued to be the most vital and defining criteria for internal party democracy.[14] As long as the more important and powerful selectorate continues to be a restricted and small party elite, one cannot speak of a substantial degree of democracy inside the party. It is because, no matter how inclusive the candidacy requirements are, the limited selectorate will still have the full control over the final results.

Yet, some scholars argue that *inclusiveness* does not always enhance, but impedes internal party democracy.[15] From time to time, the party elite chooses inclusiveness as a strategy to strengthen its position, relying on the fact that the less active party members can be manipulated to suppress the middle-level party activists who are thought to pose the greatest challenge to their dominance of the party. Having party decisions made by direct postal vote of the full membership, rather than allowing them by the party congress is an important example for how this strategy works.[16] In this way, the role of party activists who represent the actual initiators of change is marginalized in decision-making processes. Thus, a high degree of inclusiveness may ironically strengthen the influence of the national party elites over the party organization.

Along with inclusiveness, *decentralization* is another term related to the access to control over decision-making mechanisms within a party. Decentralization can be either *territorial*—when local selectorates nominate party candidates, or *functional*—when it ensures the representation of social groups such as trade unions, women, and minorities.[17] In decentralized parties, the national party elite probably meets much less often and tends to be focused more on coordination and communication than on providing definitive guidance to the party.[18] However, the role that decentralization plays in the internal democratization of parties is not always positive, either. If the selectorate consists only of a small group of people, then decentralization can only mean that the control of decision-making mechanism passes to a local oligarchy from the national oligarchy. In contrast, some centralized parties may ironically have very democratic features: the party leaders may choose internal party democratization through membership-wide ballots in a way to weaken the power of local party activists who might manipulate membership rolls to their own advantage.[19]

Finally, *institutionalization* is another term used in describing the influence of the party on the ground over the decision-making processes. Parties with high degrees of intraparty democracy are generally highly institutionalized because they need rules that define who is eligible to participate and what constitutes victory in internal contests.[20] Randall and Svasand argue that there is a consensus among internal actors on the party's functional boundaries and procedures for resolving disputes.[21] Thus, in institutionalized parties, the decision-making is entrenched in the rules and regulations rather than being dependent on the arbitrary choice of party leaders. However, party institutionalization may not also go hand in hand with internal party democracy, either. The rules and practices of a party organization may alternatively favor the power of the national party elite over the key decision-making processes. In other words, "highly institutionalized structures are not necessarily internally democratic ones...institutionalized parties that are not internally democratic may be more difficult to reform than are those with less well-entrenched rules and practices."[22]

In sum, even though inclusiveness, decentralization, and institutionalization all seem to identify some evident characteristics of internally democratic parties, the literature also points to the dangers of using these terms in referring to intraparty democracy. It is because, under certain conditions, each one of them has the potential to impede the influence of the party on the ground over the decision-making mechanisms and on the contrary strengthen the role of the national party elite. Yet, among the three, *inclusiveness* of the selectorate is the most determinate factor in democratizing party structures as long as the selectorate also possesses the necessary *checks and balances* in the party. As Mair argues, including more party members in formal decision-making procedures may end up in the strengthening of the party leadership unless these powers are given to individual members together with the tools to organize internal opposition.[23] Thus, inclusiveness dimension must be accompanied by access to internal checks and balances such as the power to remove leaders; otherwise it may result in a decreasing role and influence of the party on the ground.

Rather than focusing on the more complex and vague position of decentralization and institutionalization in internal party democracy, this study simply acknowledges that it is *inclusiveness* accompanied by *checks and balances* that internal party democracy accounts for. In *internally democratic parties*, the party on the ground (both members and activists) is included in the decision-making processes and able to oppose or remove the party leaders in central and public office when they deem it necessary. However, in *authoritarian parties*, the party on the ground is excluded from the decision-making processes and is subordinate to the power of the party leaders both in central and public office.

Causes of Internal Party Democracy and Intraparty Authoritarianism

Any student of party politics studying the power structure within political parties can easily see that the literature exceedingly focuses on the effect of structural and cultural factors over the internal power balance of party organizations. One side of the literature is mainly devoted to understanding the evolutionary change of the power structures of parties in liberal democracies on the questions of whether and why the party on the ground is losing their influence over the internal decision-making processes.[24] There are two opposing hypotheses in this regard: one hypothesis, which is grounded in the original work of Michels, is that the party on the ground within party organizations is losing its control as the party in public office seeks more autonomy in making the central party decisions.[25] The second hypothesis is that, rather than being divorced from the party on the ground, party leaders have become even more sensitive to the demands of their members, strengthening their role in the party,[26] in other words, parties are becoming even more democratic. The other side of the literature elaborates the power structures of parties in developing democracies with an aim to understand the reasons for the emergence of party structures where the influence of the party on the ground is comparatively weaker.[27]

The common ground of both bodies of literature is the effort to understand the reasons for the rise of authoritarian features within party structures at the macrolevel.[28] The following two sections analyze these existing explanations and show that these explanations are not helpful in understanding what constitutes intraparty authoritarianism and its variants at the microlevel.

Explanations in Liberal Democracies

The existing power structure of political parties in liberal democracies is known as the outcome of an evolution of party organizations. As Katz and Mair argue, in liberal democracies, organizational evolution of parties has been reflective of a dialectical process in which each party type generates a reaction, stimulating further development, leading to another party type and thus to another set of reactions.[29] It is widely recognized that each of the four party types; "cadre," "mass," "catchall," and "cartel" or "modern cadre" parties is transformed as a reaction to one another, following a macro-level change in the political environment.[30] The types of parties are distinguished based on the question of who holds the internal power over the organizational structure.

The nineteenth century is known as the era of *cadre (elite) parties*, the "first political parties emerged in proto-democratic systems with suffrage limited to a small privileged class of the more propertied male population."[31] They are characterized as the network of local notables who elected themselves for public office, in other words, they are an "agglomeration of local parties rather than a single national organization."[32] The central authority and control is weak as the parliamentary caucus easily dominates the party on the ground that is constituted of the notables' local supporters. Because the elite party at the national level is the alliance of local parties on the ground, the crucial decisions in cadre parties are usually made at the local level. Therefore, the decision-making process in cadre parties is of a decentralized feature. Yet they are highly exclusive of broad segments of the society and intraparty democracy is almost nonexistent in cadre type of parties.

Mass parties are the parties of social integration, aimed to integrate the socially excluded groups such as the working class to the political arena.[33] In other words, the individual representation in cadre parties is replaced with the representation of the social masses that emerges in mass parties.

The internal balance of power then shifts to the masses, composed of a wide spectrum of committed members, such as the party on the ground, while the central party office acts on behalf of the party members' interests. It is the sectoral representation in mass parties that accompanies the idea of internal party democracy, justifying the submission of those elected to the public office to the decisions made in the democratic extra-parliamentary organs of the party.[34] Since the party on the ground, in theory, controls the party in central office and in public office, mass parties are known to be democratic organizations. Yet, in practice, ideological rigidity, the internal training of the members and recruiting the elite may make party competition unlikely.[35] According to Michels, bureaucracy, by design, is hierarchically organized to achieve efficiency, and the effective functioning of an organization therefore requires the concentration of much power in the hands of a few. Those few, in turn, will use all means necessary to preserve and further increase their power, undermine the democratic character of the organization and lead to oligarchy.[36] Hence, as Carty and Cross notes, "in theory the relationship between the party in central office and on the ground was 'symbiotic'; in practice, Michels taught us that power was heavily vested in the party's central office."[37]

According to this evolution paradigm in liberal democracies, when a number of structural factors lead to the decline of mass parties, the rise of a new party type is observed: *catchall party*, in which the party in public office is solely directed by the electoral imperative.[38] This type begins to dominate the party politics, after an increase in the use of leisure time, the development of welfare states and mass communications, and a transformation of attitudes toward political parties leads to an overwhelming decline in the number of party members (markedly expressed in both absolute numbers and as a percentage of the electorate in 1990s).[39] As the parties grew to be less dependent on the grassroots support of the party members, the newly developed communication devices, then, becomes the most important bridge between candidates and voters in catchall parties.[40] The party in public office conceives democratic politics as a competition between a team of leaders and internally seeks for control of the party on the ground. That is why, at the heart of the catchall party, there is a fragility reflecting the unsettled relationship between the party in public office and party on the ground.[41] So long as the party on the ground is satisfied with the prospect of electoral victory—either because party loyalty is strong or there are great differences in the policies that the alternative governments would propose—there may not be a significant tension between the party on the ground and the party in public office.[42] It is when one of these conditions erodes; the tension rises between the two in a heightened form.

As a result of the unsettled tension between the party on the ground and the party in public office, Katz and Mair hypothesize that a *cartel* is tacitly formed among the ruling parties, which brings together the fourth and the last type of party emerging in western democracies.[43] In this model, the tension between the party on the ground and the party in public office gets settled in favor of the latter, which moves toward a cartel in order to liberate itself from the party on the ground. The party leaders in cartel parties, who take politics as a profession, deal with the problems of government with technical and professional expertise and find more consistent resources—such as state subventions—for party campaigning. This brings together a desire for autonomy by party leaders from those who are "more inclined to see the problems of government in ideological rather than in managerial terms."[44] When the desire for autonomy by the party leadership is challenged by the democratic organizational impulse within the party, it may lead to two possible outcomes. First, the party in public office can strengthen its position by choosing internal party democratization as a strategy, through extending the level of inclusiveness in decision-making processes such as policy determination or candidate selection. Second, the party can adopt a stratarchical form. Stratarchical organizations are based on the principle of a division of labor in which different and mutually autonomous levels coexist with one another, and in which there is a minimum of authoritative control, whether from the bottom-up or from the top-down.[45] In this way, "the local party will become essentially unconcerned about any real input into the national party (and vice versa), and will devote itself primarily to politics at the local level."[46] Stratarchical solution to the internal tension inside the cartel parties, thus, causes an alienation of the party branches from one another.

The Katz and Mair paradigm, thus, assumes that the political parties in their final stage of evolution are no longer democratic institutions since the internal rules of the last party type, cartel party, are designed to foster either the "manipulation" (inclusion of passive party members) or the "isolation" of their members (stratarchization); leading to a democratic dead end.[47] Yet, these studies do not admit that cartel parties are entirely based on authoritarian structures. Democratic practice within cartel parties still continues, however it is the function of internal party democracy that changes. It becomes a manipulative tool to strengthen the autonomy of the party elite. Still, as long as the party on the ground loses its control over the decision-making processes vis-à-vis the party elite, this study acknowledges these structures as being closer to intraparty authoritarianism than internal party democracy (more reasons, below).

There are two major limitations of the party change literature in understanding the power structure of political parties in liberal democracies: first, the effort is focused on understanding the change within the power structures mainly through explaining the interests and behaviors of the party elite (particularly in public office), almost without emphasizing the role of the interests and behaviors of the party activists and members within this development. It is argued that "internal party democratization" is henceforth possible only through the "choice" of the party leaders who aim to legitimize their power or receive certain electoral benefits through giving voice to their members. Yet, assuming a party organization as democratized because the party leaders have chosen to do so is already problematic. The same party leaders can alternatively choose to exclude the party members from the decision-making structures. There is limited explanation on the role that the interests of the local party actors play in the power structures of parties. In fact, that is why this study acknowledges the definition of internal party democracy in which the party members and activists have the necessary tools to oppose the decisions of the national party leaders.

Second, this literature mainly elaborates the questions of whether and why the party leaders (in public office) are gaining more influence over the decision-making mechanisms vis-à-vis the party on the ground. Therefore what is questioned is the evolution of internally democratic parties toward more authoritarian structures, but not really vice versa. In this respect, the question of whether the existing authoritarian party structures can exit to intraparty democracy has not truly received the attention of scholars. Thus, once a party develops into an authoritarian structure, whether it can regain its democratic practices (e.g., competitive leadership elections, inclusive policy-making, and candidate selection processes) still remains to be a puzzle. In this respect, this study is an effort to understand this often neglected opposite direction of change within the power structures of party organizations.

Explanations in Developing Democracies

The literature on the power structure of party organizations in newly democratizing states underlines the different experience of intraparty authoritarianism compared to liberal democracies: contrary to the parties in Western Europe, in developing democracies, intraparty authoritarianism emerges at the time of *party formation* rather than *party change*.

The organization of the first internally democratic parties, mass parties, was initiated by the existing social groups to represent the interests of a particular segment of the society in liberal democracies. However, many of the parties in recently established democracies had an institutional, rather than societal origin.[48] Different transitional paths to democracy had different effects on the varying types of parties. A prominent study in this field belongs to Ingrid van Biezen who shows that while the Western European democracies have followed a path from competitive oligarchy to democracy, the new democracies in Southern and Eastern Europe have followed divergent trajectories including both "inclusive domination" and "closed domination" in Dahl's terms.[49]

The predemocratic regimes in Southern Europe were classified as being authoritarian, and in Eastern Europe, they were classified as totalitarian regimes. In this respect, the political power in predemocratic regimes in Southern European countries approximated more to a closed domination, whereas Eastern European countries approximated more to an inclusive domination.[50] Since the free political organization was prohibited both under the authoritarian and totalitarian regimes, party formation in these newly established democracies was not accomplished until the first elections that the parties had the opportunity to organize.[51] Therefore, in Eastern and South European democracies, political parties emerged as weakly institutionalized entities, comprising of weak links with the society and low level of organizational loyalty among politicians. In Eastern European case, parties had a low level of popularity and small party membership as a result of the lack of social cleavages, weak grounding of parties in civil society.[52] The elite-driven nature of democratic transitions particularly led to the formation of top-down, centralized party organizations. Therefore, it is a common perception that parties in many postcommunist states have weak, leader-dependent organizations.[53]

Gunther and Diamond stress that nearly all of the existing typologies of parties are derived from the studies of West European parties over the past century and a half.[54] Therefore, they create a new typology of parties inclusive of the cases drawn from third-wave democracies. The main distinction within this typology is based on the "organizationally thick" and "organizationally thin" parties. They argue that the origin of the "organizationally thin" parties that show a great deal of authoritarian features and low degree of party membership was the *contingent effect* of an illiterate, rural, and "politically unmobilized" segment of the society. This type of party evolution was observed in the twentieth century of Latin America.[55]

Rustow, comparing the Middle Eastern parties with the European cases, stresses a common ground on what was experienced in all subregions of Europe: all in all, it was a struggle between the representative assemblies and the royal power, and the former was what was missing in the Middle East region's path to democracy:

> Representation came to be considered a general civic right rather than a corporate class privilege [in Europe], and the partisan contest spilled over

from the chambers of the legislature to the public at large. Throughout the European cultural realm, party organization thus has become a universal and durable instrument of modern politics under democratic and even under totalitarian regimes...In the Middle East, there is no indigenous tradition of representation. Medieval political theory in Islam was preoccupied with the personal qualifications of the ruler and with the precepts of sacred law derived from scripture and precedent.[56]

Furthermore, in the Middle East, parties had their origins in protest against occupying powers and absolutism rather than in voting alignments within assemblies. They dealt less with seizing power than redefining state boundaries and establishing new regimes, and usually this effort takes place under the leadership of elite cadres. Due to the weakness of social groups, parties in the Middle East are also considered to have had organizationally thin, leader-dependent structures at birth.

In contexts where social groups do not constitute the basis of parties, political patronage and clientelistic ties between the leaders and the followers play a functional role in creating political participation, as observed in Latin America and Eastern Europe. Even though the neoclassical theory of political patronage sees patronage as a product which political parties supply to satisfy the demands of their voters, there is also the evidence that the demands of the voters are largely determined by the kind of incentives that were offered to them when they were first mobilized.[57] In this respect, whether interests are aggregated along class, territorial, functional, or individual lines depends on how politicians decide to allocate rents.[58] Then, politics begins to look like the interaction of supply and demand side of clientelism in time. Even though both sides may be subject to change as a result of independent structural developments in the political system,[59] the clientelistic genesis of political parties gives a clear advantage to the central party office, which is, in most of the newer democracies, already born as the most dominant party element. The predominance of the central office is observable in the personalized networks around party leaders. As Biezen points out:

> Even in parties where the selection process is formally carried out according to a bottom-up procedure, the national executive often enjoys—in practice and by party statute—the ultimate authority to veto candidates or to decide on their rank order on the party lists. Moreover, the influence of the national executive on the selection of candidates also frequently extends to the selection of public officeholders on the local and regional levels.[60]

The main reason for the dominance of the central party office is derived from the different structural development that the developing democracies followed, compared to the liberal democracies. While the introduction of public funding in Western Europe contributed significantly to parties' shifting orientation from society toward the state, in the newer democracies the linkage with the state came immediately in the wake of democratization, leaving parties embedded in the state from the very beginning. The extensive availability of and dependence on public funds has not only created strong party-state linkages, but also further centralized the locus of power within the party.[61]

Due to a lack of party institutionalization, the central party office has the desire to reduce the potentially destabilizing consequences of emerging intraparty conflicts that are an inevitable byproduct of the context of weakly developed party loyalties.[62] Therefore, an extensive level of party discipline is preferred against intraparty democracy by the central party office whose predomination illustrates that it is intraparty authoritarianism rather than intraparty democracy that characterizes most party structures in third-wave democracies. Thus the bottom line of the literature in the party politics of developing democracies is that intraparty authoritarianism is embedded in the political culture and institutional framework of the newly built democracies.

The major limitation of the literature on the party politics of developing democracies is that it does not go further than explaining the macro level causes of intraparty authoritarianism. The parties may be formed with authoritarian characteristics as a result of the historical legacies or the nature of democratic transitions, however, why do they preserve their authoritarian character? Is it not possible to expect the development of internal party democracy within these organizations in the future? In other words, this literature does not explain the possibility of change.

Furthermore, intraparty authoritarianism in this literature is considered as a phenomenon in which party leaders in central or public office own the power resources and control the whole party structure; and to a lesser extent deal with the demands and reactions of the party on the ground. To some degree, the existing clientelistic ties may seem to explain how the party activists keep being satisfied, but even in the most clientelistic parties, material resources of the party leaders are not always sufficient to win the submission of the party members and activists; particularly when they are in opposition.[63] Thus, the reasons for the subordination of party members to the power of the national party elite are not entirely elaborated at the micro level.

Yet, some scholars do underline the importance of micro-level factors on power structures of parties, which are party ideology, leadership styles, and some exogenous events like electoral defeats. The following sections analyze these factors.

The Role of Party Ideology

There are three main reasons for the correlation between ideology and organization among political parties:[64] First, ideology might have direct cause on the organizational structure: belief in the leader's dominance and belief in democracy are two contrasting ideological positions, that can explain why a party organization has an authoritarian or a democratic structure. Second, the ideological platform of the party may appeal to specific social groups in the system, whether a well-organized working class or a wealthy, elite segment of the society. The social group, characterizing the ideology of the party may be effective on the organizational structure as well. Third, the relationship between ideology and organization may be the result of historical path dependency. Members of the same ideological family may resemble each other organizationally because of the structural conditions that affect their formation.

The most prominent example for the relationship between ideology and organizational structure is found in Duverger's famous "contagion from the left" thesis. He links leftist ideology to the conditions of origin, stressing that parties which have come into being outside parliament generally represent the leftist ideology and tend to be more centralized than parties arising within the electoral and parliamentary cycles because the leftist parties, due to their membership requirements are focused on controlling dues-paying party members.[65] Some opponents, however, argue that green and left-libertarian parties are most likely to emphasize democratic themes because such parties often want to transform the political order, and show how alternative models of political organization might work.[66] Parties on the center-right, contrary to leftist parties, relies more on donations from business groups rather than membership dues, expect little activity from members, depend more on charismatic leaders.[67]

In the light of these discussions, it is possible to see that the role of party ideology, as an explanation for internal party democracy or authoritarianism, treats the power structure of parties as something static and uniform, assuming that once the specific power structure is constructed upon the organizational goals, it remains still and homogeneous. In this sense, it does not consider the possibility that there might be different degrees of ideological attachments and varying interests among the party members and activists.

The Role of Leadership Styles

Two individuals with access to the same resources may exercise different degrees of power because of different motivations: one of them may use his resources to increase his power; the other may not.[68] Party elites with different motivations may bring different styles of leadership to the parties.

There are different approaches to leadership styles in organizations, which can be helpful in understanding the internal workings of political parties, identifying what the goals and motivations of the party leaders may be. One approach is based on the distinction between "task-oriented style" and "interpersonally oriented style" introduced by Bales in 1950 and developed further by other leadership researchers such as Hemphill and Coons as well as Likert.[69] According to this approach, "task-oriented style" is defined as a concern with accomplishing assigned tasks by organizing task-relevant activities—such as electoral mobilization. The task-oriented leader clearly provides targets, timelines, technical support, and advice but little focus on team members as individuals requiring support. On the contrary, "interpersonally oriented style" is based on maintaining interpersonal relationships by tending to the followers' morale and welfare. This style of leadership results in strong engagement of the followers, feeling valued and important; yet it may result in lowered output if focus is too much on providing support for nonwork related personal issues.

Another distinction is between transactional and transformational leadership. Transactional leadership was described by Burns as motivating followers primarily through contingent reward or punishment based exchanges.[70] Typically, the main focus of transactional leaders is on setting goals, clarifying the link between performance and rewards, and providing constructive feedback to keep followers on task.[71] In contrast, transformational leadership involves developing a closer relationship with the members, based more on trust and commitment than on contractual agreements. Transformational leaders help followers to see the importance of transcending their own self-interest for the sake of the mission and vision of their group and/or organization. By building followers' self-confidence, self-efficacy, and self-esteem, such leaders are expected to have a strong, positive influence on followers' levels of identification, motivation, and goal achievement.[72]

Based on these arguments, one can come to the inference that the task-oriented style and the transactional style of leadership contain authoritarian features: they can lead to increased absenteeism due to the lack of appeal to the subordinates' expectations while at the same time using reward or punishment to ensure compliance to leader's directions and expectations. On the other hand, "interpersonally oriented style" and "transformational style" of leadership, tend to provide more democratic organization, as the leaders tend to communicate more with their members and use participation to engage them in organizational issues.

Apart from these leadership styles, smaller number of studies did actually distinguish between leaders who behave democratically and behave autocratically. This dimension of leadership, ordinarily termed democratic versus autocratic leadership or participative versus directive leadership, followed from earlier experimental studies of leadership style[73] and has since been developed by a number of researchers.[74] Yet, the major limitation of *leadership styles* as an explanation for the power structures within parties is that, just like observed in party ideology, it treats the "subordinate group" as one homogenous entity. It assumes that all members are likely to respond to the leadership styles in the similar way and falls short in understanding that they actually might have different type of interests. Therefore, focusing on leadership styles in understanding intraparty authoritarianism might provide limited comprehension of why the party members and activists subordinate to the national party leaders.

Exogenous Political Conditions and Events

Some studies have shown that whether a party is represented in the government or in the opposition has an impact on the general pattern of its power structure.[75] One of the most important resources of the party elite in cartel parties is the control over party wealth, sustained from the state subventions. The regular subventions that the parties receive from the state provide the party elite the ability to purchase the submission of the party members. Therefore, as long as parties can access government resources, the party elite can use appointments, patronage, and rewards in a much easier way to control the behavior of local party activists and maintain party unity. In this sense, the core source of control for parties in government is the access to state subventions.

Yet, in times of opposition, the party elite may more easily be challenged because the access to financial resources is restricted. The lack of resources needs to be compensated with the valuation of effectiveness, control of productivity, structured demands, and the patterning of legitimation in the party.[76] In this respect, the *party infrastructure* becomes the party elite's core source of control either by reform or active implementation of the party rules on the ground.[77]

The relationship between the party elite and the party on the ground is less conflictual when the party is in government than when it is in opposition, due to the availability of party's external material resources. That is why when cartel parties are in government, they possess more anti-democratic features: satisfying the demands of the local party activists through a patronage system, the party elite aims at keeping the real issues off the political agenda and operates with an exclusive class of inside participants, and a set of rules structured to disadvantage, if not completely shut out, challengers to that class of participants.[78] Intraparty democracy is more likely to take place when the party is in opposition; as cartel parties need to deal with the tension inside the party through making organizational changes due to the scarcity of resources, such as enhancing the voice of the local activists in the party.

In addition to the effect of being in government or in opposition on party structures, electoral defeats or victories are also considered as some effective exogenous events, which can affect the power structure in parties. An electoral defeat or a victory can simply erode or promote the "legitimacy" of the party elite's authority due to having failed or succeeded to realize the common goals of the organization. In fact electoral defeats have a major impact on democratizing party structures. Examples are various: affected by the loss of presidency to Richard Nixon and following a disastrous 1968 party convention, the Democratic Party in the United States adopted a *Mandate for Reform* to clean up its act as well as broaden its appeal; the new rules were intended to give the grassroots party member a direct voice in the presidential nominating process, and to reduce the influence of the party elites.[79] Similarly, the defeat of the Labour government by Thatcher's Conservatives in 1979 in Britain led to a new arrangement for electing the party leader, weighting toward the party's affiliated trade unions.[80] Furthermore, most parties in Canada experimented several reforms such as adopting quotas for women and youth in party leadership conventions, as a result of societal pressures to make conventions more representative and reduce the perceived democratic deficit.[81]

This study acknowledges the role that these exogenous factors play over the power structures. Yet, it emphasizes that how these factors change the power structures at the micro level needs further clarification. For instance, does internal democratization of an electorally defeated party come as a choice of the party leaders who believe that they need to strengthen their legitimacy? Or is it the outcome of a challenge coming from the bottom, that is local party activists and members? Besides, in addition to exogenous factors, this study also stresses the significance of endogenous triggers, most specifically, the "outcomes of candidate selection processes" that are likely to cause intraparty conflicts between party leaders and local party actors in authoritarian party structures.

Evaluation

Intraparty democracy and intraparty authoritarianism are two opposite power structures within political parties. In the former, it is the influence of the party on the ground—activists and members—that control the power structure. In the latter, the party on the ground is subject to the dominance of the party leaders that are either in public or central office. This study acknowledges that the influence of the party on the ground over the decision-making processes is determined by the degree of *inclusiveness* of the selectorate in key decision-making mechanisms and the availability of the *checks and balances* through which party activists can oppose or remove the top party leadership when necessary. Even though decentralization and institutionalization are also associated with internally democratic parties, they remain insignificant without the existence of these two conditions; therefore it is better to elaborate internal party democracy with *checks and balances* and the *inclusiveness* dimension. On the opposite end, this study identifies intraparty authoritarianism with the *exclusiveness* of the selectorate and the *lack of tools* for the party members and activists to *oppose* or *remove* the leaders.

However, what constitutes or causes intraparty authoritarianism remains to be a vague issue in the literature due to the less attention given to the micro-level dynamics of party structures. The analysis of macrofactors such as the changing nature of democratic competition in liberal democracies mainly focuses on the internal strategies of the national party leaders to dominate the party activists and members who have become a burden for their autonomy in the party structure. In the literature of developing democracies, on the other hand, it is only the macrolevel factors such as the historical legacy of pre-democratic regimes, political culture, or institutional framework, that are analyzed for the causes of intraparty authoritarianism. In a way, neither side of the literature questions whether authoritarian party structures can become democratic in time.

Yet, is it right to treat intraparty authoritarianism as a static phenomenon? The activists and members are the weak party actors in hierarchical party organizations; but cannot the weak actors cultivate *power resources* to challenge the authoritarian behavior of the leaders?

Furthermore, all factors analyzed in the study of power structure of parties (including the micro-level factors such as party ideology or leadership styles), assume authoritarian party organizations as uniform structures. The distinction between the middle-level activists and the ordinary party members within the composition of the party on the ground is well highlighted, but it is assumed to be the only existing variance. The difference between the interests of the activists and the ordinary members are certainly an important one affecting the power structure but these interests—either the interests of the party activists or the members—may also vary across *space* and *time* within a political system. Therefore, the strategies of the party leaders may also diverge in response to this variance. In this respect, one of the aims of this study is to understand whether such heterogeneity exists within authoritarian party structures.

This study highlights that in order to understand what *constitutes* the authoritarian power structure within party organizations; there is a need to study internal *party governance*. In a way, this study acknowledges what Panebianco once said:

> [Power] manifests itself in an "unbalanced negotiation" in a relation of *unequal exchange* in which one actor receives more than the other...One can exercise power over others only by satisfying their needs and expectations; one thereby paradoxically submits oneself to their power. In other words, the power relation between a leader and his followers must be conceived as a relation of unequal exchange in which the leader gets more than the followers, but must nonetheless give something in return.[82]

Despite Panebianco's analysis, it is surprising to see that power is treated as something owned by the party elite in authoritarian party structures. There is a need to treat it as a relational phenomenon and pay attention to the internal governance processes between the party leaders and the local activists.

2

Intraparty Authoritarianism in Turkey

The comparative studies have shown that the skills, strategies, and choices of political leaders are critically important in explaining democratic transitions and consolidations as well as breakdowns.[1] Turkey is one of the countries where political leaders have played a paramount influence in shaping the societal, political, and economic evolution of a country in its path to democracy. As the founding father of the Republic and the first political party—Republican People's Party (CHP— *Cumhuriyet Halk Partisi*), Mustafa Kemal Atatürk initiated a cultural revolution, aimed at modernizing Turkey through a radical program of secularization and social change in the 1920s and the 1930s. His successor, İsmet İnönü, played the most important role in personally shaping the transition from an authoritarian one-party regime to multiparty politics and thus to electoral competition in the second half of the 1940s. The personalities of these two prominent leaders in Turkish political history, thus, have been the focus of many systematic analyses.[2]

Apart from these two prominent names in the democratic development of Turkey, several studies on Turkish party politics emphasize that the party leaders coming after Atatürk and İnönü, have been responsible both for the achievements and the shortcomings of Turkey's experience with democratic politics.[3] The reason for the important position of leaders' decisions and choices in Turkish politics is summarized by Sabri Sayarı as follows:

> The importance of leaders in shaping political outcomes in Turkey stems largely, though not exclusively, from the near absolute control that they exercise over party organizations. By controlling the nomination of candidates in the elections, serving as the principal gatekeepers in the distribution of political patronage, and enjoying extensive authority (such as

legal means to abolish local party units that oppose the central executive leadership and expel dissident party members from the organization), party leaders have managed to amass a great deal of personal power at the expense of organizational autonomy.[4]

Thus, authoritarian structure of party organizations—subordination of the local party actors to the decisions of the party leaders—is a long-lasting and well-known phenomenon in Turkey. It is further elaborated under the labels of "oligarchical tendencies" of parties, "ineffective operation of intra-party democracy," "highly disciplined leadership," and "overly centralized structures."[5] Besides, the party leader acts as the leader of both the central executive office and the parliamentary group in almost all Turkish parties. Özbudun gives an example on the nature of the relationship between the central party office and party in public office as follows:

> Article 28 [of the law on political parties] stipulates that the decisions concerning a vote of confidence or no confidence in a minister or the council of ministers can be taken only by the party's parliamentary group.... although legally speaking the parties' central executive committees do not have the power to take binding decisions on matters of vote of confidence, in practice both organs work together closely and both are dominated to a large extent by the party leader.[6]

However, leaders' dominance in party structures is treated as a given fact, directing the studies on party politics to be mainly focused on the politics of party leaders in Turkey. It is widely accepted that local party organizations do not exercise any influence in the nomination and the adoption of party programs. Nomination process is run under the monopoly of the party central executive committee with oligarchic tendencies. For instance, Rubin states that:

> In general, the parties have no significant internal democracy. Leaders who make bad mistakes in government or elections survive. Corruption does not lead to a political fall.[7] Ideas are not generated within parties where debate is discouraged. Obedience rather than competition governs the parties' political culture.[8]

Due to the accepted nature of the dominance of party leaders, little attention has been paid to the analyses of power structures of parties in Turkey; for example whether there is a way out from authoritarian party structures or whether authoritarianism ever shows variance across and within parties.[9] Such an analysis, however, would be useful to understand the chances of the development of intraparty democracy in a context where macro factors such as political culture and institutions produce the dominant leader tradition. After all, the reasons for "why party members and activists choose to subordinate to the decisions of the party leaders" have neither empirically nor theoretically been well elaborated in Turkish politics.

The first section of this chapter, discussing the constraints on leadership opposition or removal within party structures, shows that intraparty authoritarianism is a phenomenon embedded in the political system of Turkey. The second section reviews the macrolevel causes of authoritarianism within parties: *Turkish political culture* and the *Law on Political Parties*. These reviews show that the macro factors are not sufficient to explain the possibilities of *change* within authoritarian structures. The third section reviews the other possible microlevel causes of intraparty authoritarianism such as *leadership styles*, *party ideology*, and *local politics*, yet shows that these factors fall short in providing an explanation for dynamism and heterogeneity in authoritarian party structures. Finally, the chapter concludes by emphasizing that there is a need to pay more attention to the interactive relationship between the party on the ground (local party organizations) and the party leaders in understanding intraparty authoritarianism.

Constraints on Leadership Removal and Internal Opposition in Turkey

Party leader election, as discussed in the previous chapter, is one of the significant decision-making processes in party organizations. Analysis of how party leaders are internally elected indicates the degree of democracy or authoritarianism within party structures. The possibility of leadership removal through intraparty elections points to the existence of internal party democracy to a certain extent. The scarcity of the number of leadership removals within party structures in the lifespan of the Republic of Turkey, thus, can be regarded as an adequate proof for the embeddedness of intraparty authoritarianism in its political system.

The party leader is elected by secret ballot by a majority of delegates attending the national party convention in most parties in Turkey. However, since the loyalty and the votes of a sufficient number of delegates are already secured through their preselection at district and provincial conventions, the reelection of the party leader is generally assured.[10] Opponents of the party executive who nevertheless succeed in being elected as delegates are often in the minority. Hence, it is extremely difficult to launch a successful challenge against the incumbent leadership.

Table 2.1 shows the tenure of major political parties and their leaders before the 1980 military coup in Turkey, which reveals that leadership change through intraparty elections is not observed within parties with only one exception, the 1972 intraparty elections within the CHP. The constraints on leadership removal is due to the incumbent central party organizations' control over the general procedures and the outcome of the party leader elections since the provincial party conventions, where the delegates to the national party convention are chosen, are usually under

Table 2.1   Leadership change in the major parties of Turkey in the pre-1980 era

Party name	Party tenure	Party leader(s)	Have intraparty elections ever led to leadership change?
Republican People's Party (Cumhuriyet Halk Partisi CHP)	1923–1981	**Atatürk** (1923–1938) **İnönü** (1938–1972) **B. Ecevit** (1972–1981)	**Yes.** Ecevit's election—After Atatürk's death, Inönü led the CHP. In 1972, Ecevit won the party leadership against Inönü in intraparty elections. Ecevit and the CHP were banned from politics following the 1980 military intervention.
Democratic Party (Demokrat Parti—DP)	1946–1960	**Menderes** (1946–1960)	**No.** The DP was closed down by the 1960 military intervention and Menderes was executed.
Justice Party (Adalet Partisi–AP)	1961–1981	Gümüşpala (1961–1964) **Demirel** (1964–1981)	**No.** The AP was established as the successor of the DP. Demirel became the leader following Gümüşpala's death. Demirel and the AP were banned from politics following the 1980 military intervention.
Nationalist Action Party (Milliyetçi Hareket Partisi—MHP)	1969–1981	**Türkeş** (1969–1981)	**No.** Türkeş and the MHP were banned from politics following the 1980 military intervention.
National Salvation Party (Milli Selamet Partisi—MSP)	1972–1981	**Erbakan** (1972–1981)	**No.** Erbakan and the MSP were banned from politics following the 1980 military intervention.

Note: The party leaders whose names are written in bold had the highest influence on Turkey's experience with democracy, compared to others.

the control of a clientelistic network which aligns itself with the dominant faction within the central party organization.[11]

The leadership change within the CHP in 1972 can be considered as one of the rare instances of intraparty democracy in Turkey. İnönü, who served as the CHP party leader for 34 years, was removed from his position through internal party elections in 1972. There were two major reasons for this change: an important exogenous shock on the Turkish political system—the military memorandum in 1971—as well as the nature of the allocation of power sources within the party organization. With regards to the allocation of power sources, the secretary general position within the CHP was a strong institution, paving the way for the rise of strong secondary leaders, who could challenge the party leadership.[12] Therefore, a number of challengers against Inönü's policy positions arose from time to time.[13] Yet they were easily eliminated from the party; due to the authoritarian leadership style of İnönü. When Ecevit was the secretary general, though, the 1971 military memorandum caused a major divide in the party on a specific policy position, which was 'to be' or 'not to be' on the side of the newly established government supported by the military.[14] The faction supporting the secretary general Ecevit's position against the newly established government, soon gained power against Inönü's faction and led to this leadership change. Yet, under Ecevit's leadership, the party constitution was changed in a way to eradicate the significance of the secretary general position in the party.[15] The party, thus, continued with an authoritarian pattern.

The military coup in 1980 closed down all political parties, banning their leaders from politics. In 1987, the ban on the leaders and in 1992 the ban on the parties were removed. Table 2.2 shows the return of all major party leaders from the pre-1980 era—Demirel, Ecevit, Erbakan, and Türkeş—back to politics in 1987.

With the two exceptions of intraparty elections—the Motherland Party (ANAP—*Anavatan Partisi*) in 1991 and the Democratic Society Party (DTP—*Demokratik Toplum Partisi*) in 2007—no democratic leadership change was observed in the post-1980 period, either. Even though the case with the ANAP is based on a leadership crisis, it can be considered as an instance for intraparty democracy because there was a certain challenge against the authoritarian trend in the party, which ended successfully. The ANAP, established as a new party in the post-1980 era, was dominated by Özal to such an extent that when he left the party leadership in 1989 to become the president of Turkey, a smooth transition to a new leadership was hardly expected. His personal influence on the party was still paramount even after he left.[16] Yet, Özal's departure from the party did change the power balance in the party. Although the candidate

Table 2.2 Leadership change within major parties in the post-1980 era

Party name	Party tenure	Party leader(s)	Have intraparty elections ever led to a leadership change?
Motherland Party (ANAP)	1983–...	**Özal (1983–1989)** Akbulut (1989–1991) **Yılmaz (1991–2002)**	**Yes. 1989.** Özal became the president of Turkey, which led to a change in the ANAP leadership. Yılmaz's leadership was not supported by Özal. Yet, the intraparty dynamics led to Yılmaz's election against Akbulut.
True Path Party (DYP)	1987–...	Tuna (1983) Avcı (1983–1985) Cindoruk (1985–1987) **Demirel (1987–1993)** **Çiller (1993–2002)**	**No.** The DYP was established to appeal to the support base of the AP. After the removal of the ban on ex-party leaders, Demirel was brought back to the party. Being elected as the president of Turkey in 1987, he left his place to Çiller.
Social Democratic People's Party (SHP)	1985–1995	Gürkan (1985–1986) **E. İnönü (1986–1993)** Karayalçın (1993–1995)	**No.** The party was established by an agreement between Gürkan and E. İnönü. İnönü ended his political career in 1993, and Karayalçın was elected as the new leader. The party was closed after joining the CHP in 1993.
Democratic Left Party (DSP)	1985–...	R. Ecevit (1985–1987) **B. Ecevit (1987–1988)** Karababa (1988–1989) **B. Ecevit (1989–2004)**	**No.** Following the 1981 closure of the CHP and the political ban on Ecevit, Ecevit's wife founded the DSP in 1985. After the removal of the ban, Ecevit became the leader of the party. Losing the 1988 elections, he left the party but shortly after, came back in 1989.
Welfare Party (RP) followed by the Virtue Party (FP), Felicity Party (SP)	1983–2001	Türkmen (1983–1984) Tekdal (1984–1987) **Erbakan (1987–1998)** Kutan-FP(1998–2001) Kutan-SP (2001–2008) Kurtulmuş (2008–2010)	**No.** The RP was established as a successor of the MSP. After the removal of the political ban on Erbakan, he became the RP leader. The party was closed and Erbakan was re-banned from politics by a court decision in 1998. The RP was followed by the FP but it was also closed in 2001. The traditionalist faction in the FP founded the SP under the leadership of Kutan, Erbakan's loyal friend.

Party	Years	Leaders	Democratization effect?
HEP (1990–1991) DEP (1991–1994) HADEP (1994–2003) DEHAP (2003–2005) DTP (2005–2009) BDP (2008–...)*	1990–...	Işıklar (HEP) **Zana (DEP)** Bozlak (HADEP) Bakırhan (DEHAP) **Türk**, Tuğluk - Ayna, Demirtaş (DTP) Kışanak, **Demirtaş (BDP)**	**Yes. 2007.** The ban on the leaders of these pro-Kurdish parties made the democratic intraparty leadership changes hardly possible. Yet, in 2007, the division between the radical and moderate factions (between Türk-Tuğluk, and Ayna-Demirtaş) within the DTP did cause a change in the party leadership.
Republican People's Party (CHP)	1992–...	**Baykal (1992–1995)** Çetin (1995, seven months) **Baykal (1995–1999)** Öymen (1999–2000) **Baykal (2000–2010)** Kılıçdaroğlu (2010–...)	**No.** Baykal had formed a faction within the SHP against İnönü. After the removal of the ban on previously banned parties in 1992, Baykal became the leader of the newly established CHP. He resigned in 1995 and 1999 but returned back to party leadership without any challenges against his power until 2010 when he resigned from leadership.
Nationalist Action Party (Nationalist Work Party until 1993) (MHP)	1983–...	**Türkeş (1987–1997)** **Bahçeli (1997–...)**	**No.** Right after the political ban on Türkeş was removed, he was re-elected as the leader of the MHP in 1987. Following his death in 1997, Bahçeli became the leader of the MHP.
Justice and Development Party (AKP)	2001–...	**Erdoğan (2001–...)**	**No.** Founded in 2001, the AKP leader Erdoğan had previously acted as the leader of the modernist faction within the FP. Winning the 2002 and 2007 general elections with a very high margin, the AKP has become the single government party.

Note: The party leaders whose names are written in bold had the highest influence on Turkey's experience with democracy, compared to others.

*These are the ethnic-based pro-Kurdish parties, subject to closures by court decisions, which outline that the parties cause a divisive threat to the Republic. Yet, the final one, the BDP, is currently represented in the parliament.

he supported after he left had the highest chance to acquire the party leadership; in intraparty elections, Yılmaz, who served as a minister in Özal's government, successfully challenged Akbulut, who previously had the secondary role in the party as he was one of Özal's loyalists. It was indeed in the 1992 leadership elections that Yılmaz even won a bigger victory within the party. As ANAP was defeated in the October 1991 general elections, Özal had taken an active campaign against Yılmaz's leadership. Yılmaz did his best to get over Özal's pressure on the party and create his own authority,[17] and re-won the party leadership in the 1992 intraparty elections against Özal's candidate.

The intraparty democracy case for the DTP in 2007 intraparty elections was also a consequence of external shocks in the system. Many pro-Kurdish parties, represented by the DTP and its predecessors have been considered as anti-system parties by the bureaucratic center of Turkey.[18] These parties have been subject to the highest number of closures in Turkish political history, because of the claim that they have organic ties with the Kurdish terrorist and separatist organization—the PKK. The party is claimed to consist both of a moderate wing, close to solving the Kurdish question on a democratic basis and of a radical wing, which is on the side of more separatist values. Even though this distinction between the two sides is not a clear-cut one, the 2007 intraparty elections within the DTP caused a great public attention when Aysel Tuğluk and Ahmet Türk, known as the moderate party leaders of the party were removed from the leadership. According to the DTP constitution, the party leadership is represented by two party leaders based on gender equality; one male, one female.[19] In the 2007 leadership elections, Tuğluk and Türk on the moderate side, who were blamed to pursue 'passive' and 'consensual' politics in the parliament, were replaced by Selahattin Demirtaş and Emine Ayna on the radical side.[20] The triggering effect on this leadership change was the 2007 election results. The results were considered as a failure because most of the votes in the DTP's strongest support base, the Southeastern Anatolia populated with Kurdish citizens, moved to the AKP. Furthermore, as a pro-Kurdish party, the DTP, for the first time, was able to form a party group in the parliament on its own.[21] The party's hold of the public office as well as a certain degree of loss in the votes from the Southeast altered the balance of power in the party. Unsatisfied with the moderates' passive performance in the parliament, the radicals offered more concrete policies to its grassroots in line with the party's ideology, which helped the radicals to come to power.[22] However, Demirtaş had to resign due to his arrest soon after he was elected, leaving his position back to Türk on the moderate wing.

Apart from the leadership changes within the CHP, ANAP and DTP, the parties in Turkish political system did not experience democratic intraparty elections. These three instances can be considered as exceptions of internal party democracy since the dominant party leaders in the party organizations were replaced through internal party dynamics in party conventions represented by the party delegates. However, such changes neither indicate nor cause intraparty democracy in the long-term. Still, the most important "inclusiveness" dimension of internal party democracy particularly during the candidate selection and policy-making processes, remains to be concentrated in the hands of the party leaders. Second, the intraparty competition in the three examples took place as a result of exceptional exogenous triggers (i.e. military memorandum) and endogenous developments (i.e. leadership crisis) in the political system, rather than arising during the routine state of affairs. That is why, party organizations in Turkey, in essence, have leader-dependent, authoritarian structures.

Macrolevel Factors of Intraparty Authoritarianism in Turkey

The literature in Turkish politics provides two major macrolevel explanations for the embeddedness of intraparty authoritarianism in the political system of Turkey: the impact of political culture and the institutional framework.

The Impact of Political Culture on Party Structures

The context in which a party is born is critical for the type of party structure, and that party leaderships cannot be seen independent from the institutional and structural elements. There is a need to understand the political and social context in which parties were born. Rather than following a break from the society with a move toward the state as in old democracies, the parties in Turkey were already born within the state and detached from the society. This gap between the state and the society is known as the center-periphery rift in Turkey,[23] which indicates the long-lasting conflict between a "nationalist, centralist, laicist, cohesive state elite" and a "culturally heterogenous, complex, and even hostile periphery with religious and anti-statist overtones."[24] In Turkey, it was largely the political parties that represented the periphery.

The party formation in Turkey was similar to the path that the authoritarian regimes followed in transition to democracies. It is the combination of both contextual and genetic factors that have led to the dominant type of party organization, in which leaders' domination plays a central role. As Rustow notes, since the decline of the Ottoman Empire, "politically active Turks have displayed an instinct for discipline, a readiness to provide followership" which then set the basis of the nature of party development in Turkey.[25]

As the Republic was established in 1923 by Mustafa Kemal Atatürk, the construction of the state produced new goals and new plans to be conducted. These goals were "military defense of independence (1919–1922); establishment of a new state (1923–1928); legal and cultural reforms (1926–1933), state sponsored industrialization (1930 off)."[26] These goals were to be initiated by the state elite, who were also the party elite within the CHP, the first political party of the Republic, formed around Atatürk's leadership.

The organizational structure of the CHP in the one-party system (1923–1946) reflects the authoritarian characteristics of the new regime.[27] The relationship between the party center and the party's local organizations was highly restricted. While the instructions of the central party elite could easily reach the local organizations, the demands and reactions of the local organizations were hardly conveyed to the party center.[28] The party congress, composed of provincial party leaders, was convening only for the sake of expressing the party strength and praising the work of the central party organization.[29]

Even though the one-party era witnessed the formation of two other parties, the CHP was unquestionably the only dominant organization in governing the new Turkish state. Both the Progressive Republican Party *(Terakkiperver Cumhuriyet Fırkası)*, and the Free Republican Party *(Serbest Cumhuriyet Fırkası)* were organizations founded (in 1924 and 1930 respectively) to legitimize their leaders' opposition against the CHP's and Atatürk's authority in the political system. It was the party leaders that organized the party bases in a top-down manner. Yet, both parties were eliminated from the political arena on the grounds that they challenged the CHP's and therefore the Republic's objectives toward reaching the western ideal. According to Dodd, it was because, Atatürk, in principle, accepted party competition, but not if it went too far, in other words, not if it led to group interest at the expense of the society's general interest. The general interest meant, according to the state elite, finding the best policy for the transformation of the Turkish society from a medieval structure toward modern Western civilization.[30]

The dominant position of the central governmental elite (military officers and civil servants) within the CHP became consolidated,[31] which allowed the party to play a key role in the establishment of a responsible, though not a responsive political system in Turkey.[32] It represented the bureaucratic center of the regime and resembled the cadre type party, with members comprising of high-level bureaucrats and local notables. Moreover, the key positions in the party belonged to the members of the military and state bureaucracy. It was rather difficult to make any changes in the composition of the party membership as the elite structure of the party was vastly closed to any external links with the agrarian society.[33] In the one-party era, thus, the party organization was a tool through which the state elite initiated their political reforms. It was after the transition to multiparty era that political parties mainly functioned to win elections, recruitment of candidates for office, serving more to the institutional functions of political parties.

The two fundamental features of Turkish political culture; first, *nonautonomy* of political parties vis-à-vis the bureaucratic state elite—particularly the military—and second, *clientelism* played the most important role in consolidating the authoritarian party structures in the multiparty era. Both of these features were grounded in the long-lasting center-periphery rift in Turkey.[34] With regards to *nonautonomy*, the political parties, representing the periphery, were dependent on the center, which was mainly constituted of the military and the bureaucratic elite. In other words, the role of the parties was to function in democratic politics in line with the principles of the new Republic.[35] It was when they failed to do so that the military intervened in party politics in 1960, 1971, and 1980. The military, in this respect, inherited Atatürk's approach to political parties: party competition was necessary for democracy, but not if it led to group interest at the expense of general interest. The organizational development of political parties was, therefore, interrupted when they were closed down by the military interventions, which aimed to reorganize the society in line with the principles of Atatürk.

On the other hand, as no influential social groups existed following the transition to multiparty politics, it was *clientelism* that played a functional role in the development of political participation in Turkey.[36] The center-right parties, the Democratic Party (DP—*Demokrat Parti*) in the 1950s, and its follower the Justice Party (AP—*Adalet Partisi*) in the 1960s developed a wide network of particularistic interests in this sense.

During the 1950 elections, the DP successfully appealed to the peripheral grievances against the CHP's centralist, bureaucratic single-party rule.[37] The general practice that the DP leadership employed was to mobilize provincial local notables who had influence over local religious groups as a strategy to influence the constituencies who were suffocated by the CHP's elitism. The party soon became popular particularly among the craftsmen and peasantry, offering promises in rural development as well as leaning toward the religious segments of the society.[38] The DP leader, Adnan Menderes used political patronage as an important means in his exercise of the party and government, especially when rewarding his supporters and punishing his critics. The rewards at the local level meant appointing or securing the election of his supporters to the chairmanship of the local party organizations as well as offering career opportunities or financial help to the followers. Conversely, he denied the similar rewards and marginalized the role of those who opposed his leadership.[39] In other words, Menderes exercised power within the DP in an increasingly personalized manner.

The DP's heir, the AP had a strong party organization. The AP leader Demirel was particularly skilled in building patronage networks. He distributed patronage to his allies, whether they were relatives or friends, rich or poor. However, those who were not Demirel's supporters were discriminated against, both within and outside of the party organization. In addition to the relationship that the local organizations of the AP established with smallholder peasants and land-owning villagers in several parts of the country,[40] the party also had a connection with various Islamic communities and leaders. This involved a process of exchanging votes and political support for access to public resources and protection against threats from the state and secular forces.[41]

The clientelistic politics was adopted by many party leaders later on, following the tradition in the DP and the AP. The religiously oriented parties, National Order Party (MNP *Milli Nizam Partisi*), National Salvation Party (MSP—*Milli Selamet Partisi*), and Welfare Party (RP—*Refah Partisi*) led by Erbakan starting from the 1960s to the late 1990s have developed an extensive grassroots clientelistic network, not only by offering its members material benefits such as fuel, food, and various commodities but also creating a personal atmosphere of closeness, affection, and companionship.[42] In the post-1980 era, the True Path Party (DYP—*Doğru Yol Partisi*), the ANAP, and even center-left parties originating from the CHP have been dominated by the leaders' patronage network, the party apparatus becoming ineffective and weakened like almost all other parties in Turkey, with rising clientelism, widespread corruption. Thus, clientelism in Turkey is a long-lasting phenomenon, leading the majority of party members see their membership as a means to obtain personal, sometimes quite small, sometimes very substantial, benefits from their parties, particularly when they happen to be in government.

In sum, it can be noted that the organizational development of political parties in Turkey did not take place as a result of a politically influential civil society, which was the case in Western democracies. Rather than representing a dual standing between the state and society, political parties were established largely autonomous from social groups in Turkey.[43] The first political party, the CHP, represented the state elite's interest, which was at the same time considered as the general interest of the society. The parties coming after the CHP were expected to function in the similar way, however they were rooted in the periphery, a heterogeneous, weakly organized society. Even though the state elite's belief in democratic norms facilitated Turkey's transition to democracy at the systemic level,[44] authoritarian party structures dominated the multiparty era due to the lack of political activism and party leaders' investment in clientelistic ties.

Institutional Framework

The Law on Political Parties (SPK—*Siyasi Partiler Kanunu* No: 2820) regulates the establishment and organization of political parties in Turkey. The activities of political parties were regulated by the Law of Associations until the mid-1960s. In 1965, the first law on political parties was adopted within the framework of the 1961 constitution. The current law is the outcome of the 1982 constitution, which was enacted after the 1980 military intervention. Several studies criticize the SPK and show it as a reason why parties cannot experience a healthy organizational development in Turkey, underlining that the law strengthens the hierarchical party model and leaves little room for intraparty democracy.[45]

The SPK has three main effects on the rise of authoritarian party structures. Firstly, it makes the parties dependent on state revenues and creates a cartelization effect.[46] As the parties in government have the power to distribute and use the state resources, the assumption that the parties in power have the greatest access to the state financial resources and donations from groups becomes stronger. Cartelization in this sense firms up the stateness of the parties.[47] Even though there are examples of cartelized parties in which internal party democracy still plays an important role in Western democracies (such as the ability of party members to oppose or remove the party leaders); the cartelization of parties in a democratizing state like Turkey has a concrete impact on intraparty authoritarianism. Established already isolated from the party on the ground, cartelization strengthens the antidemocratic nature of party organizations since the party leaders tend to care less for their accountability towards the party members than for trading on the state resources.

The SPK's second negative effect is that it promotes the exclusiveness of the process of candidate selection in political parties. The current practice in almost all parties in Turkey is to have candidates selected by the central executive committee, where the weight of the party leader is paramount.

According to the SPK, it is up to the central party committee to decide whether to organize primaries at the local level or to use the method of central voting in determining the candidate lists for the parliament.[48] Many parties, in this respect, choose to determine candidates based on the central party organization's decision, which restricts the rights of the local party members to participate in the organization's decision-making process. Thus, the SPK leaves the most significant function of political parties, candidate selection, in the hands of the party leader.

Thirdly, it regulates all the organizational characteristics of the parties, limiting the alternative models of organization and encouraging a single type hierarchical party model, which all political parties must be subject to.[49] Parties consist of party conventions and elected executive committees at the national, provincial, and district level. The smallest unit of the party organization, whose convention methods are codified by the law, is the district party organization (ilçe teşkilatı). The 1960 military intervention in politics closed all the subdistrict level party organizations (ocak ve bucak teşkilatları), which had played an important role between 1946–1960 in the local activities of parties regarding the mobilization of masses. The district party organizations, after 1960, became the main units that constituted the link between the provinces and towns at the local level. Just like in typical cadre parties, this change particularly strengthened the position of the local elites in the districts, who tended to follow the orders of the central party organization.[50]

Almost in all party structures, it is common to see that the district party elites control the membership registration at the local level, which is a highly problematic issue in Turkey.[51] Keeping their membership records in district organizations, parties submit the membership list to the Office of the Chief Public Prosecutor of Republic (OCPPR—Yargıtay Cumhuriyet Başsavcılığı) and inform the changes in every six months. Despite the OCPPR's close inspection, membership figures of parties are unreliable. For instance, the ANAP received less votes than its registered members in the general elections of 2002.[52] The loose membership status is an advantage for the local party leaders at the district level, who can easily raise and reduce the membership registry numbers during the local party conventions, using their clientelistic ties. Even though they are formally elected in the party conventions, due to the malfunctioning of the delegate selection process, they can hardly be replaced through democratic conventions. The similar process is repeated in higher levels of the party organization, such as the provincial party conventions whose delegates are largely determined under the influence of the provincial party leaders and the national conventions whose delegates are controlled by the national party leaders in practice.[53] Similarly, the factions that arise in the conventions mostly reflect the disputes related to personal power struggles, rather than on policy-related issues. Yet, if the party's position on major ideological or policy-related issues is challenged, the party leader often has the power to marginalize the role of the opponents in the parties.[54]

Thus the SPK made parties more dependent on the state and personalized networks rather than on the grassroots. The law is an outcome of the Turkish political culture and sets the institutional background of intraparty authoritarianism through its effects based on cartelization, exclusiveness of the candidate selection process and the hierarchical party model. However, this institutional framework is not exogenous to intraparty authoritarianism in Turkey since it is the party leaders who interpret the law in an anti-democratic manner and show reluctance in reforming it.

Microlevel Factors of Intraparty Authoritarianism in Turkey

While the institutional framework and the political culture of Turkey as two major macrolevel factors provide important explanations for the emergence and consolidation of authoritarian party organizations in the political system, they fail to shed light on their dynamic and heterogenous structures. In other words, they fall short in trying to understand the possibilities of change within intraparty authoritarianism. Yet, is it not possible to expect a change or a variance among these party structures? Are they forever confined to such authoritarianism? Thus, in order to explore the possibilities of change, there is also a need to pay attention to the microlevel explanations of intraparty authoritarianism in Turkish politics.

At the microlevel, *party ideology* and *leadership styles* play an important role in shaping the power relationship between party leaders and the local party activists. The leadership styles of party leaders generally tend to be controlling any potential conflict in the party organizations. Not only the leaders control the leadership elections, they are also in command of the key intraparty decisions, both in candidate selection and policy determination processes.

The impact of party ideology on internal party dynamics is elaborated to a lesser extent in Turkish politics than on leadership styles since personalism is known to play a much more significant role in shaping the power structures of parties. The reason why the effect of personalism on the party power structures seems to be larger than party ideology in Turkey is that almost in all political parties in Turkey, the party leaders are the founding leaders of their party organizations.[55] Yet, apart from personalism, some studies do reflect on the right-wing and center-right parties in which the ideology leads the members and activists to perceive their leaders as charismatic and therefore to subordinate to their decisions such as in the AKP, the MHP, and the religious parties.[56]

Between 1923–1946, since the establishment of the Republic until the transition to multiparty era, the two successive party leaders of the CHP, Atatürk and İnönü considered national unity as a prerequisite for democracy and initiated a cultural revolution through the channels of the CHP, which represented the bureaucratic center in that era. In his analysis on the CHP's party membership during the single-party era of the Republic, the CHP leadership aimed to attach larger segments of the society to the party, yet their aim was not to mobilize the society. The administration had an idea about who should be made a member and who should be prevented from becoming a member of the party as it was assumed that an uncontrolled widening of the party base could pose a threat to the reforms that the party was undertaking.[57] However, the massive rise in the number of the party membership from 697.046 to 1.512.719 between the years 1936 and 1941 indicates that the CHP central elite aimed at widening its support base.[58] The aim of the party elite was to offer an incentive for the population to take an interest in the CHP's activities, which were related to widening the cultural revolution in the society.[59]

İnönü was indeed a rationalistic democrat and acted in an authoritarian manner only when conditions made it necessary.[60] After all, İnönü himself initiated the transition to multiparty politics in Turkey in 1946. Yet, after Atatürk's death in 1938, he assumed the title of "national chief" and "permanent leader of the CHP" because he was going to start opening the political regime while consolidating republican reforms.[61] He thought that when he was the leader of the party, he was unrestricted to initiate his own views and beliefs.[62] At the same time, he was ready to step down if the party members lost their confidence in him.[63] That is how the leadership change within the CHP occurred in 1972: when Ecevit and his faction gained control in the party, İnönü stepped down and resigned. Yet, until Ecevit, the list of İnönü's challengers whose political careers came to rapid ends was a long one.[64]

Menderes, the leader of the center-right DP, formed during Turkey's transition to multiparty politics, displayed an extraordinary power and authority. Personalization of power and political patronage was apparent in his leadership style. The DP's national executive committee, which played a major role before 1950, gradually became submissive to Menderes's own decisions.[65] Having gained 53 percent of the national vote in 1950, Menderes obtained a significant political resource to authoritatively direct his actions on his subordinates. Authoritarianism derived from similar motivations was observed with Özal, during his leadership of the ANAP (1983–1989)[66] and with Çiller when she was the leader of the DYP (1993–2002). Ecevit, the second leader of the CHP following İnönü defended democratic values while creating the opposition faction against İnönü. Yet, when he became the leader of the CHP, his command of the party appeared to follow the traditional model of Turkish political leadership, maintaining a close control of the party organization and not easily accepting criticism from within.[67] In fact, after the ban on the political leaders was removed in the post-1980 era, he established his own party, the DSP, accepting no internal opposition, which Ayata calls "minimal party organization."[68] Ecevit's choice to act in an authoritarian way is known to stem from his concern about extreme left-wingers infiltrating the party organization, which he experienced during the first years of his party leadership within the CHP.[69]

Demirel, the leader of the center-right AP, known as the successor of the DP, was also an authoritarian leader, relying on his patronage network that eased the subordination of the party members to his decisions. He had already inherited a party organization, interwoven with a clientelistic ties, which he made use of during his leadership of both parties—the AP (1961–1980) and the DYP (1987–1993).[70]

Baykal, who became the leader of the CHP in 1992, pursued a leadership style, based on "unquestioned loyalty to the leadership," marginalizing the role of local party organizations in decision-making processes both in candidate selection and in programmatic or ideological debates.[71] Whenever there is an evident rise of voice that questions Baykal and his leadership circle, the means to control this voice is highly coercive. He also refrained from having intraparty elections and tried to minimize the functions of the party organization.[72]

In terms of ideology, even though the CHP presents itself as a center-left party, it is far different from the programmatic social democratic parties with centralized mass structures in Western Europe.[73] In the post-1992 era, the party ideology represents an uneasy combination of three legacies, which are far from having been integrated into a coherent whole:[74] the first legacy is that of modernization which the CHP initiated in the single-party period of the early Republican era. It emphasizes nationalist, centralist, laicist, and populist political platforms. The second legacy is that of democracy because it was under the CHP's leadership that competitive politics had been introduced. The third legacy is the social democracy adopted by the party in the late 1960s. Depending on the circumstances, specific events and developments, party leaders adopt positions that are more in line with one or another of these legacies.

Therefore, one can conclude that ideology, as a micro factor, does not have an effect on the power structure of the CHP.

Within the right-wing parties such as the nationalist Nationalist Action Party (MHP—*Milliyetçi Hareket Partisi*) and the religious parties established under the leadership of Erbakan—MNP, MSP, RP, ideology seems to have an important impact on intraparty authoritarianism together with the leadership styles. In 1960s, the MHP was formed by Alpaslan Türkeş who merged the legacy of the Turkist movement with a nationalist-conservative discourse, founded on an anticommunist fanaticism.[75] Türkeş was not only the founder of a party with a nationalist ideology, but also deemed as the originator of the MHP's main principle called the Nine Lights Doctrine (*Dokuz Işık Doktirini*). As a leader, he gained the devotion and faith of the party members as he was considered to be the man who revived and renovated the idealist movement (*ülkücü hareketi*) and turned it into a party organization. In fact, he was declared *Başbuğ*, (the Turkish word for *Führer*) in the 1967 national convention of the party.[76] At the time, Türkeş, displayed authoritarian tendencies not only for dealing with "the communist threat" effectively, but also for rendering Turkey a strong country in the shortest possible time.[77] Even though he somewhat changed his style after 1980; the loyalty to the leader prevailed in the party structure, without leading to any major challenges to intraparty authoritarianism within the MHP.

Bahçeli was elected as the leader of the MHP after Türkeş's death in 1997 in the party convention. He was known as a leader with a moderate image than Türkeş.[78] Some rank-and-file in the party continued to have far right tendencies; however, Bahçeli's authoritarian leadership played a helpful role in preventing these tendencies from surfacing so that the party could maintain its pro-system credentials.[79] However, due to a strong emphasis on the "leader" and deep ideological attachment to the party among the MHP activists, one would not expect to see a challenge against the leader's authoritarianism in the party.

Erdoğan, the leader of the AKP, has a very charismatic personality in the eyes of his voters and even some voters of other parties.[80] After all, Erdoğan has been very popular since he was a candidate for mayor of Istanbul in 1994.[81] In terms of ideology, for some observers, the AKP represents the transformation of political Islam into "new Islamism", which was formed through the transformative impact of democratization and economic liberalization.[82] For some other observers, the AKP as a coalition of conservative democrats initiates the withdrawal of Islam from political sphere to the social and individual sphere.[83] In its discursive positioning, the AKP is also argued to be on the centre-right, balancing the more rightist elements in its electoral base with its emphasis on democracy.[84] In a recent study identifying the psychological ties between the parties and voters, it has also been observed that economic satisfaction and political Islam such as a desire for a Shari'a based religious state emerged as the two important sources in determining the ties of the AKP with the voters.[85] All in all, Islam (while not certain whether it is political Islam or not) forms a significant dimension of the AKP's ideology. In terms of the organizational power structures, parties with religious references are usually identified with authoritarian characteristics such as loyalty to or faith in the leader. The most noticeable ones among these are the extremely religious parties known as the "devotee" or "fundamentalist" mass parties.[86] Yet, the AKP certainly differs from these extreme examples and interprets Islam in a more progressive way. In fact, Erdoğan, while founding the party, made it straight that the AKP members should not unquestionably obey or worship leaders. Abdullah Gül who acted as the second influential leader of the party also stated that the AKP central team would be open to criticisms unlike what they had experienced in the RP where the decisions were made by the dictatorial leader.[87] However, it did not last long for the AKP leadership to transform the party organization from a democratic to an authoritarian structure since the changes in the AKP constitution in 2003 strongly signaled the oligarchization of the party. Yet, due to the influence of religious elements in the party ideology as well as the charismatic leadership of Erdoğan one would expect to see a proto-hegemonic type of authoritarianism within the AKP where the rank-and-file hardly questions the authority of the party leader.[88]

Finally, the DTP and its predecessors, DEP, HEP, HADEP, and DEHAP have derived their values from their pro-Kurdish stance. In order to understand the ideology of these pro-Kurdish parties, it is important to note that the unitary state in Turkey has always been suspicious towards the issue of ethnicity. The most important recent factor for this suspicion has been the rebel Kurdistan Workers' Party (PKK) and its aim of founding an independent Kurdish state.[89] The threat of territorial loss has increased the repressive policies of the state officials against the pro-Kurdish parties, because there were reservations on the potential bonds that they had with the PKK. Four successive parties (HEP, DEP, HADEP, DEHAP) were closed by the Turkish Constitutional Court and thousands of pro-Kurdish party members were sentenced to jail.

The current ideology of the DTP is shaped by these contemporary events. As Watts defines, the united goal of the party is dedicated to:

> …providing greater freedom and security for public and collective expressions of Kurdish cultural and political identities, primarily but not exclusively within the framework of a single but decentralized Turkish state. In

particular, pro-Kurdish activists seek the right to publish, broadcast and teach Kurdish in public schools and to form Kurdish cultural and political associations; amnesty for the PKK and its fighters, substantial economic development in the Kurdish regions of the southeast; and governance-related demands involving devolution, decentralization or regional autonomy.[90]

Withstanding the closures and charges imposed by the various branches of the Turkish state, the DTP activists have formed a united front against its competitors in the political arena, no matter the intraparty conflicts are likely to occur at the top leadership level. The party leaders are aware that much of the electoral support base is voting for the party because they see it as surrogate PKK, and there are continual struggles between them over how closely to work with this organization.[91] However the DTP activists perceive their party as a united organization fighting for Kurdish rights in Turkey, which is likely to encourage their loyalty to the party and its ideology. In return, this type of loyalty to the party ideology has the potential to contribute to the centralization and authoritarianism within the party since the grassroots activists usually tend to have faith in the decisions made by their leaders on their behalf.

As a result, the party ideologies and the styles of the party leaders have a considerable impact on generating the submission of party members and activists to the authority of party leaders in Turkey. Yet, in understanding party authoritarianism, these two factors treat the party on the ground as one homogenous entity as if the reactions or the loyalties of each local party actor or organization would be similar. Moreover, they also neglect the fact that changing external conditions might affect the behaviors and internal strategies of the party actors in *time*.

Evaluation

This chapter has revealed that the Turkish political culture and the institutional framework have formed party structures of a highly authoritarian nature in Turkey. The top-down establishment of party organizations largely autonomous from society, the nonautonomous nature of the political parties from the bureaucratic center, and clientelism culture had a great impact on the power structures. However, these two macro factors fall short in explaining what really constitutes intraparty authoritarianism in Turkey. While they explain the causes for the formation and the rise of authoritarian party structures; they do not shed light on the potential variance across and within political parties. Similarly, they do not elaborate on whether it is possible to see future chances of intraparty democracy within these structures. Rather, these explanations assume intraparty authoritarianism as a static and uniform phenomenon as if the party leaders possess the party organizations.

The leadership styles and party ideology as microlevel factors, on the other hand, clearly influence the authoritarian structure of parties, but these explanations do not question how a change from authoritarianism to democracy might occur within parties. The explanations on leadership styles focus mainly on the authoritarian behaviors of the party elites in Turkey. Party ideology only explains why the party members tend to be loyal to their leaders (i.e. charismatic domination), especially in right-wing and center-right parties such as the MHP, the AKP and the religious parties.

Explaining intraparty authoritarianism requires an analysis of intra-party governance, which is a dynamic process at the microlevel, taking place between the national party leaders and the activists from various local districts. Even if leaders are motivated to act in an authoritarian manner, they have to respond to the demands of the party on the ground or find a way to control these demands. The analysis of intraparty governance, thus, will release us from considering authoritarian party structures as an unchanging, given fact and help to understand the variance in intraparty authoritarianism or even possible occurrences of intraparty democracy. A principal-agent approach to party governance, in this respect is introduced as the most suitable tool in the next chapter.

3

A Principal-Agent Approach to Intraparty Authoritarianism

Chapter 1 has defined the internally democratic or authoritarian party structure, and underlined that intraparty authoritarianism is treated as a uniform and static structure, in which the party leaders in central or public office dominate the party on the ground. Chapter 2 has outlined the embedded nature of intraparty authoritarianism in the political culture and institutional framework in Turkey, and the authoritarian leadership styles of the party leaders. Although the political culture and institutional structures, as macro-level factors, may shape intraparty authoritarianism (as in the case of Turkey), variance in intraparty authoritarianism, based on the complex web of interests between the party leaders and activists can be expected. In order to understand the possible exits from intraparty authoritarianism in such a political context, therefore, one should not consider intraparty authoritarianism as something static and uniform. What is the role of the party on the ground (local party actors) in this authoritarian structure? Why does the party subordinate to the authoritarian party leadership?[1] Do the party activists ever attempt to change the status quo? How do the party leaders control the potential challenges to their authoritarian position within the party? What are the chances for exit from authoritarianism?

In order to shed light onto these questions, this chapter approaches intraparty authoritarianism as a relational phenomenon derived from the relational theory of power.[2] In other words, intraparty authoritarianism is treated not as something that belongs to a certain actor (i.e., the party leader) but rather as a relational phenomenon. This will help us understand the fact that intraparty authoritarianism contains multiple *interdependent* actors. These multiple actors are engaged in a *hierarchical governance process* that shapes the authoritarian party structure and the variance in it. The sole authority is vested in the hands of the party leadership, yet, the local actors have their own interests and goals that may lead them to challenge the authority of the party leaders. To develop and explain this argument, this study employs the principal-agent approach.[3] In other words, it will be possible to explain the variance in intraparty authoritarianism in a given political system when the relationships between national and local actors are analyzed through the principal-agent approach.

This chapter is organized in the following order: The section "Intraparty Authoritarianism as a Relational Notion" situates the concept of "intraparty authoritarianism" on the relational theory of power. It discusses that an authoritarian party structure consists of multiple interdependent actors molded in an unbalanced power relationship. The section "Governance as Hierarchies" argues that this unbalanced power relationship takes shape within hierarchical party governance, based on the interaction of a multiplicity of actors influencing each other in governing the party. The section "Principal-Agent Approach and Intraparty Authoritarianism" introduces the principal-agent approach, explaining that the substance of this hierarchical party governance is derived from the delegation of authority. In other words, the national party leaders (NPLs) delegate their authority to local party actors (LPAs) to act for benefit of the party at the local level. Yet, potential conflicts may arise between the party leaders and the self-interested LPAs. In assigning the principal and agent roles to the party actors, this section underlines the overwhelming difference between the liberal democracies and developing democracies, as discussed in chapter 1. It is argued that the conventional application of the principal-agent approach to party politics needs to be modified while studying authoritarian party structures. Finally, the section "The Role of Ideas and Values in the PA Approach" outlines the need to integrate the role that values and ideas play in shaping individual preferences, and thus, proposes the construction of a principal-agent model comprising both of *ideational* and *material* interests.

Intraparty Authoritarianism as a Relational Notion

The implicit treatment of power as though it were an attribute of a person or group is a repeated flaw in common conceptions of power. This treatment often deals with research questions such as "Who are the power holders?" This certainly is a problem in studying political parties with authoritarian structures as well, since it often directs the attention on *party leaders* as power holders, rather than on *party organizations* in the competitive political system. Understanding authoritarian parties in this form foresees an *intransitive* power relation within their structures. The statement that "the party leader has power" is incomplete, unless we specify "over whom". In other words, power must be treated as a property of the social *relation*; not as an attribute of the actor.[4]

In a power relationship, it is important to specify who is influencing whom and with respect to what. Dahl describes his "intuitive idea of power" as "A has power over B to the extent that he *can get* B to do something he would not otherwise do."[5] As Baldwin argues, *a relational concept of power* assumes that power is never inherent in the properties of A, but rather inheres in the actual or potential relationship between A's properties and B's value system.[6] In other words, A must take into account B's values, perceptions, and skills because the potential effectiveness of A's power depends partially on B's values, perceptions, and skills. If B's perceptions, values, and skills make it impossible for A to influence him, then potential power would never have been attributed to A in the first place.[7]

In intraparty authoritarianism as well, the party leader has the power over the LPA, because the values, perceptions and skills of the local actor allow the party leader to influence him. In this respect, power becomes relational in intraparty authoritarianism. While there is one NPL, there are *multiple* local actors, and they may differ from one another in their skills, values, and perceptions. Then, it would be plausible to expect differences in the patterns of power relationships among these actors due to the expected differences in the local actors' skills, values, and perceptions.

The ability of the actors to exert more power on the other actors is based on the notion of *power resources*. Dahl defines power resources as the "*means* by which one person can influence the behavior of other persons."[8] As Baldwin explains, the problem with this definition is that, it does not explicitly state that the means by which one actor can influence the behavior of another depends on *who is trying to get whom to do what*.[9] He argues that the only way to determine whether something is a power resource or not is to place it in the context of scope and domain.[10] In other words, a power resource is determinable only in terms of its use. The owner of a power resource in one scope and domain might have difficulty in converting this resource into another one in another scope and domain. However, there are some resources that are most likely to be effective in most situations, and most people over most scopes would rank these sources high.[11] The most well-known high-ranking power resources comprise of categories such as patterns of social standing, distribution of wealth, access to legitimacy, popularity, and control over sources of information.[12]

In political parties, or most recently in the cartel party, control of the *financial sources* probably constitutes the highest level of power resource for the party leaders in public office. This is a common aspect of cartel parties, which are highly capital-intensive and subject to receiving state subventions. Yet, the catchall parties usually combine both capital and labor intensive characteristics in which membership dues still play a certain role in financing parties.[13]

Legitimacy is another power resource of the party leader in public office. The party organization with all its members and activists expects the leaders to pursue effective activities in order to achieve the collective goals of the organization, usually labeled as policy-seeking, office-seeking or vote-seeking goals.[14] Here, the power resource of the party leaders then becomes what Parsons calls "valuation of effectiveness, control of productivity, structured demands and the patterning of legitimation."[15] In order not to face with challenges inside party, the NPLs must take into account the demands of the LPAs.

For the LPAs, *access to information* is an important power resource vis-à-vis the NPLs. With knowledge of the economic and social situation of their local constituencies, the members of the local party organizations can keep track of all the voter records at the local level. The LPAs, particularly, have an advantage over the NPLs who cannot be as knowledgeable as they are on the local voting behavior, as well as the needs of the society. Based on their proximity to the electorate, some LPAs, such as the local party leaders, may even be more respected than the NPLs at the constituency level. The *social status* of the LPAs may even bring more power to the local party organizations.

The LPAs also have the potential to come together and form factions, which bring forth the possibility of *networking* among each other, in other words, they can create power networks. A "power network" is defined as two or more connected power-dependence relations.[16] The creation of a power network, such as a faction within the party, being another advantage of local party organizations, may alter the power structure of the party.

Finally, the political *skill* of the actors can be treated as another power resource.[17] It is an important fact that individuals of approximately equal wealth, social status, knowledge, or access to authority may differ greatly in interests and power due to the varying degrees in skills. All actors in the party organization—NPLs, LPAs, and local party members (LPMs)— can be considered to possess these resources deriving from personal characteristics. In some instances, the lack of "skills" is treated as a major cause for the failure of converting potential power into actual power. In other words, it may be argued that the political actors who possess all significant power resources may fail to actualize their power just because they do not know how to use them. However, as Baldwin convincingly argues, emphasis on skill in conversion processes makes it all too easy for the power analyst to avoid facing up to his mistakes.[18] Therefore the probability of successful conversion, in other words, *skills*, must be included in estimating the *capabilities* or the *power resources* of the actors.

"Governance as Hierarchies"

Based on the existence of different interests and the availability of divergent power resources, there may be varying power relationships between the national and the local party actors. Therefore, we might see, even in authoritarian party structures, an ongoing negotiation, and a bargaining process between these party actors on maintaining and sustaining their interests. It is this internal bargaining or negotiation process that *governs* a party organization, or directs the behavior of the party organization (such as in candidate selection or policy-making processes as discussed in chapter 1). Even though, party organizations consist of *hierarchic* structures in which some actors (i.e., local party activists) are subordinate to the power of the others (i.e., national leaders), these actors are nevertheless engaged in an interactive *governance* process, the outcome of which might constitute different types of intraparty authoritarianism or intraparty democracy. The nature of party organizations is, thus, similar to Moe's description of hierarchy with its emphasis on two actors:

> The authority relation is not characterized by command or fiat, as classical organization theorists suggest, but rather is two-way. The subordinate has a zone of acceptance within which he willingly allows the employer to direct his behavior. Thus the nature of authority relation and whether or how well it works depend upon both parties to the agreement.[19]

In fact, *governance as hierarchies* is an often dismissed but the oldest form of governance structure; it supposes that the state, distinctly separated from and superior to the society, governs society vertically by the imposition of law and other forms of regulation.[20] Yet, the national-level government or another institution may seek to impose control, but there is a persistent tension between the wish for authoritative action and dependence on the compliance and action of others.[21] It outlines a kind of organizational structure, based on the routinization of a relationship in which subordinates accept the authority of the superiors.

Intraparty authoritarianism also implies an interactive process of governance, the nature of which depends on how the subordinate and dominant party actors have come to agree on the form and substance of their relationship. The relationship between the NPLs and the LPAs starts with the local actors' acceptance that they must be subject to the authority of the party leaders. The substance of this relationship resembles the principal-agent model in which the NPL (principal) permits and directs the LPA to act for her benefit at the local level. The LPA (agent), then, has a primary duty to act for the benefit of the party leader. Yet, the "principal" and "agent" roles are usually assigned in the opposite way in internally democratic parties, the reasons of which will be explained below.

Principal-Agent Approach and Intraparty Authoritarianism

The principal-agent (PA, hereafter) approach to governance is a prevalent theory in the studies of "governance as hierarchies." It has been adopted by the economists as a means to understand the market activity, and has also been an insightful tool to comprehend public bureaucracy, particularly the U.S. congress and the institutions of the European Union.[22] The PA relationship is based on an actor (designated as the agent) who acts on behalf of, or as representative of the other (designated as the principal) in a particular domain of decision problems. The main puzzle in this relationship is that the principal directs his/her agents through contracts or other arrangements to act for his/her benefit; yet the notion that one will solely operate on behalf of other's benefit contradicts the *fundamental economic principle of self-interest.* In other words, the agents have incentives to pursue their own interests and to "shirk" from the principal. When the conflicting interests are accompanied by imperfect information about an agent, the principal cannot completely control his/her agent's performance.[23] Therefore, the PA approach underlines the significance of *informational advantage* of the agents over the principals since *information* constitutes an important high-ranking power resource as explained before.

The PA approach also has a significant value in understanding the conventional power structure of party organizations, based on the *delegation of authority* from the party on the ground to the party in central and public office. Yet, in authoritarian party structures, as the following pages will show, the delegation of authority is forwarded from the top party leadership to the LPAs. Before explaining this model, yet, there is a need to revise the major assumptions of principal-agent models.

Four Fundamental Issues of the PA Approach

Analysis of the relationship between agents and principals in an organization deals with four main issues. First, *why do the principals need to delegate their authority to agents?* The principal may simply need to hire agents to use their skills, knowledge or time that s/he does not have. The PA approach is therefore functionalist. Keohane's theory of international institutions,[24] for instance, outlines that states as principals agree to adopt certain institutions to lower the transaction costs of negotiations and monitor compliance to international treaty obligations. Pollack, in his explanation of the institutions of European Commission (EC), adds another reason, stating that it helps to adopt regulations that are either too complex to be debated by principals or require credibility of a genuinely independent regulator.[25]

Second, *how do the agents find the opportunity for discretion if they are bound by the contracts made with the principal?* The theory assumes that the principal remains in a disadvantaged position unless s/he has the sufficient information to evaluate the agent's performance. Since the agent is likely to have more information about itself than the principal, it is not difficult for the agent to create an opportunity to shirk. Furthermore, the "difficulty in monitoring the actions of the subordinates, asymmetric information in the form of expertise, or transactions costs in overturning the actions of subordinates all can give agents some opportunities for discretion".[26]

Third, *what control mechanisms do the principals, as rational actors, adopt, anticipating the possible shirk of their agents?* There are both administrative and oversight procedures to prevent the possibility of the agency shirking. The former brings a legal limitation to the agents' scope of activity by setting the rules of the contractual relationship, whereas the latter allows the principals to monitor agency behavior and apply positive or negative sanctions. The oversight procedures are two types: The first one is the "police-patrol oversight," in which the principal actively monitors the agency behavior with the aim of remedying and detecting any violations. The second one is "the fire-alarm oversight" in which the principals rely on the third parties such as civil society organizations or interest groups to monitor agency activity.[27]

Finally, there is a wide range of discussion on the question of "*is it the principal or the agent that controls power in a given structure?*" The first argument is that the agent becomes the central figure in exercising authority, completely making his/her own choices, entirely unconstrained by the principal. This view is also known as the "run-away bureaucracy thesis" and is explained by the impossibility of the principals' having any kind of effective monitoring mechanisms over agents.[28] The run-away bureaucracy thesis is countered by the "congressional dominance school," which argues that effective monitoring of the agency actions is not the only means of controlling agency behavior. It can well be substituted with a variety of institutions and incentive systems.[29] In fact, "institutions—whether in the form of incentive systems, explicit and implicit contracts or rules—evolve and survive to partially mitigate, if not solve, these problems".[30] Therefore according to this argument, the primary control is always in the hands of the principal due to the existing institutions, rules, and regulations.

Conventional Usage of the PA Approach in Party Governance

The usage of the PA approach in the studies of party organizations is unfortunately limited to the cases mostly from Western democracies where it is intraparty democracy that has originally been dominant in the power structures of parties. This limitation leads to a taken-for-granted manner in attributing the principal and the agent roles to party actors. In this respect, based on the threefold relationship among the party on the ground (LPAs), party in central office, and party in public office, the PA model is conventionally applied to party organizations as shown in figure 3.1. According to figure 3.1, party representatives in public office work as the agents of the extraparliamentary party organization—constituted both of the LPAs and the central party office. Meanwhile, within the extraparliamentary party organization, the party on the ground is the principal of the party in central office.

According to this delegation approach, the extraparliamentary party organizations have a formal internal party selection mechanism. The LPAs select those individuals as leaders for the central party office that

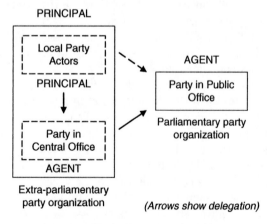

Figure 3.1   Conventional understanding of principal-agent relations in internally democratic party organizations.

are considered most likely to achieve the party's collective goals—such as policy-seeking, office-seeking, or votes-seeking goals.[31]

However, the extraparliamentary party organizations delegate their authority to the party in public office and exercise their influence both via the internal party mechanisms and via the institutions and mechanisms of the parliamentary chain of delegation. Müller argues that the latter form of party control can take two forms:[32] (1) the institutionalization of party rights in public rules (such as the constitution, the electoral law, and the parliamentary rules of procedure) and (2) the party's giving directions to public office holders who in turn use their institutional rights to make other public office holders behave according to the party line. The delegation of authority from the extraparliamentary organization to the party in public office is shown with two different arrows, one originating from the LPAs (party on the ground) and the other from the central party office. This implies the inclusive nature of the candidate selection process, which gives equal strength to the national and the local party organizations in determining their agents in the parliamentary office.

If the delegation link between the LPAs and the party in public office gets weakened in time (as shown with a dashed link), it makes the central party office stronger in determining the candidates, yet intraparty democracy continues to exist as long as the local actors have the power to control the central party office's decisions. In this respect, what matters most for the continuity of intraparty democracy is *the strength of the delegation link between the local party actors and the party in central office so that the party on the ground has the necessary checks and balances to control the decisions of the central party office.* As Cox and McCubbins argue, political parties have leaders (central office) in order to overcome the dilemma of collective action because they (1) internalize the collective interest of the party and (2) monitor their fellow partisans.[33] This means that there is internal competition for the position of central party office and that incumbents can be held accountable if they fail to act in the collective interest.[34]

The emergence of the mass parties in response to decline of the cadre parties reflected the origin of such a PA structure in political parties: The NPLs were the elected agents of the party members, who acted as the principals that control the organization and try to hold the party leaders accountable for their actions.[35] Mass parties, which were initially formed to represent the working classes' right to vote in Western democracies,[36] by nature required a formally articulated party organization on the ground and a strong central office acting as its agent to coordinate the local branches.[37] The PA model in mass parties can be regarded as a tool in understanding why the agents, party leaders, tend to shirk from their main responsibilities. In fact, what Michels proves with his "iron law of oligarchy thesis" is the supremacy of the agent (central party office) over the principal (LPAs) as a result of the incompetence of the masses to deal with the complex organizational structure, and a skillful professional leadership that acts to preserve its power.

For the students of party politics, the shift from mass parties to catchall and cartel parties in Western democracies further implies that the role of the LPAs as the principal in parties is diminishing in a more striking way. The party leaders are recruited for their valuable skills—"to reason, persuade, bully, inspire, rally, intimidate, mediate, and so on," which provides them a major source of power to dominate the principals.[38] Thus, the agents are becoming more skillful, professionalized politicians with the control of power switching from the hands of the central party office to the party in public office. The party in public office legitimizes its authority by presenting itself as the agent of the LPAs within catchall parties.[39] The state-dependent cartel parties emerge when the governing party in public office frees itself from the expectations and demands of its followers, which means that almost full domination of the agent over the principal is realized. The desire for autonomy by the professionalized party elite becomes a greater motive than following the demands of the party members. The party elite, thus, chooses to distribute selective incentives (appointments) and solidary incentives (group identification) to the principals when in power; and deals more with the organizational demands when in opposition.[40]

Yet, intraparty democracy, particularly the leader selection process in the party, is an important control mechanism for the party members relating to how the leader is recruited and how he can be removed. However in cartel parties, this process can well be in command of the party leaders, who are eager to manipulate the democratic processes for greater autonomy. An example is Britain where the shift of power from trade union activists to the due-paying members in the electoral college resulted in the clandestine autonomy of the party leadership in the Labor Party.[41] Furthermore, even though the factions have the power to replace leaders they deem not suitable for the party, due to high transaction costs such as bringing the electoral college together in terms of time, effort, finance, and MPs' mobilization costs; the leaders' replacement is overwhelmingly difficult within the party.[42] In this respect, the cartel party model depicts that the agents have begun to dominate the principals' control mechanisms.

The "agency dominance" view in party organizations has received a number of criticisms by those who argue that the party members, representing the principal, still rule in the party.[43] At the empirical level, Detterbeck finds out that the local and regional party units still have an influence on the national party organization in Germany, Denmark, and

Switzerland.[44] At the theoretical level, the argument that the party leaders have become divorced from the internal principals (members, activists) as well as external principals (voters) does not stand on a strong rational micro-foundation since the cartel party thesis disregards the party members' option of exit:

> If party activists have the exit option and can form new parties,...they either keep party leaders responsive to their preferences or withdraw to other parties, thus realigning the political convictions of leaders and activists within the same party through the exit of dissenters.[45]

Thus, the debate between principal versus agency dominance is still continuing, based on the evidence of organizational change across parties in the context of liberal democracies.

Modifying the Conventional PA Model for Intraparty Authoritarianism

In political contexts like Turkey, where intraparty authoritarianism is embedded in the political culture and institutions of a system, it is more useful to consider the PA relationship in the reverse order. In such contexts, where parties are established in a top-down manner through elite-driven transitions to democracy, it is the NPLs that control the party organization as a whole. In this respect, the party in central office—the main principal of the party organization—delegates its authority both to the LPAs and to the party in public office to fulfill certain tasks on its behalf (see figure 3.2). The LPAs act as the agents of the party leaders to perform the given tasks in line with the party goal. For the office-seeking and vote-seeking parties, the party leaders assign the tasks of campaigning or organizing at the local level to the LPAs. With respect to candidate selection, it is up to the party leaders, again, whether to include the LPAs and LPMs in the process of determining the candidates. As Scarrow outlines, LPMs are important for the party organization because parties often look to members to provide more concrete types of aid, such as donating money or time to campaign efforts.[46] Thus, NPLs may delegate their authority to the party activists in order to achieve the goals of the party organization.

In authoritarian party structures, the PA relationship between the extraparliamentary party organization and the party in public office is also different from democratic party structures. The main reason for this difference is the different established mechanism that allocates the state resources to the parties. For instance, in many postcommunist and south

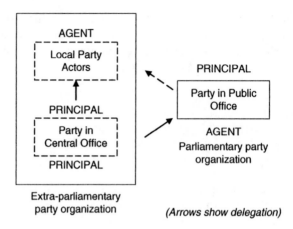

Figure 3.2   PA model in authoritarian party structures.

European political systems, it is empirically validated that state support was introduced when most parties were still in an initial stage of party formation and therefore usually lacked alternative organizational resources, thus, public funding was always likely to play a critical role in these political systems.[47] The locus of power is found within the extraparliamentary executive rather than in the party in public office because newly emerging parties were created from within the party in public office, or would acquire parliamentary representation (and often also government responsibility) almost immediately after their formation.[48] In this respect, it is the party in central office that acts as the principal of the party in public office, but they work very closely in practice and together act as the principal of the LPAs. The party in public office can be regarded as the agent of the party in central office but as the principal of the LPAs. The delegation link between the party in public office and the LPAs is the reversal of the link seen in liberal democracies. However, compared to the party in central office, the party in public office has a weaker tie with the LPAs (represented with a dashed arrow line in figure 3.2).

Such an approach to the PA model in political parties with authoritarian structures can be an important tool to understand the power relationship between the local and national levels of the party. How do the LPAs (agents) find opportunity for discretion? What are the control mechanisms that the party leaders (principals) employ to prevent the possible shirking of the LPAs (agents)? The proximity of the LPAs to the grassroots level and the potential to provide time and effort for party success can have rationally anticipated effects to win the elections according to the party leaders. Yet, the party leaders cannot effectively reach the grassroots constituencies so they are dependent on the information, effort, and skill of the LPAs who can assist in the mobilization of masses. The effort, knowledge, and skills of the LPAs provide them with power resources that can be used against the authoritarian behavior of the party leaders in time.

Thus, there is an interactive power structure based on the relationship between the party leaders (principal) and the LPAs (agents) who exchange resources and know-how. The nature of the contract between the agent and the principal as well as the changing degree of resources and knowledge that they both separately possess may generate different patterns in power relationships, and thus a variance in intraparty authoritarianism.

The PA Approach and the Goals of the Party Actors

If the power structure of a party is constituted in a top-down manner at its very formation and becomes institutionalized in this form, the roles of the principal and agent simply work in the reverse order. Party in central office (sometimes together with the party in public office) acts as the principal delegating its authority to the LPAs. In order to understand how the PA approach explains the expected variance in intraparty authoritarianism, as well as, the possible exits from it. First, there is a need to clarify where to locate the NPLs among party in central and public office. Second, there is a need to define "LPAs" and emphasize the distinction between LPAs and LPMs. Third, it must also be understood what the goal and interests of each actor are, and why these interests are expected to be different for them.

In authoritarian party structures, taking into account the close and complex relationship between the party in central and public office,[49] it may be better to refer to the principals as "national party leaders" who dominate *both* offices. These offices are subject to the goals and interests of the same leaders as long as they are dominated by the same leaders. However, the LPAs (party on the ground) comprise both of LPAs and LPMs. Thus, the delegation of authority between national and local levels of the party organization usually takes place among three party actors: NPLs, LPAs, and the LPMs. The LPAs are the leaders and agents of mobilization at the local level whereas the LPMs form the more passive dimension of the LPAs. The LPAs are closer to the national party organization and thus more aware of the party dynamics at the national level. The LPMs are more distant and usually more eager to show obedience to the party leaders.[50]

The goals and interests of the party actors, particularly NPLs, are mostly associated with the organizational goals of the party, which is categorized into three groups: vote-seeking, office-seeking, and policy-seeking goals.[51]

A vote-seeking party is originally based on Down's theory of electoral competition, in which parties are seeking to maximize electoral support for the purpose of controlling government.[52] An office-seeking party seeks to maximize, not its votes but its control over political office. Whereas office-seeking and vote-seeking goals may overlap since vote maximization also leads to office benefits, an office-seeking party has been defined mainly in the study of government coalitions in parliamentary democracies.[53] In this sense an already elected party represented in a government coalition may aim to maximize its control of public office. A policy-seeking party, similar to the office-seeking parties, is evolved from coalition studies, aiming to maximize its effect on public policy while in government.

In a party structure in which the party leadership is the principal and the LPAs are the agents both the LPAs and the LPMs are the agents of the NPLs interested in achieving the collective goal of the party. However, the PA model can be applied to the relationship between the LPMs and the LPAs. Considering the hierarchical nature of authoritarian party structures, the LPAs also delegate their authority to the LPMs, the authority to represent the organizational interests at the grassroots level.

The nature of the PA relationship between the national and local levels of party organization in an authoritarian structure is depicted in figure 3.3. The NPLs assign certain party tasks to the LPAs who are the local party chairs, members of local executive boards, or other influential activists. If the vote-seeking goal dominates the party organization then the LPAs are asked by the NPLs to fulfill their tasks to this end. During electoral campaigns, for instance, such tasks are maintaining voter records, knocking on doors, initiating phone banks, organizing

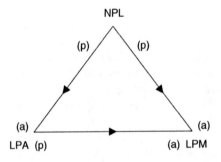

NPL = National party leaders, LPA = Local party activists,
LPM = Local party members
(p) = principals, (a) = agents

Figure 3.3   Principals and agents in an authoritarian party organization.

local social events, and so on.[54] If the goal of the party is to determine and implement policies in the institutions to which the party gains access, the LPAs can be asked by the NPLs to initiate such policy determination and implementation processes at the local level. The LPMs, however, are the passive agents of both the NPLs and the LPAs and their major duty is to represent the interests of the NPLs and the LPAs in general. In this respect, it is the LPAs rather than the LPMs that are the *real agents of change* within a party organization. Thus, in order to analyze the possibilities of change in an authoritarian party structure, *one must rather focus on the power relationship between the LPAs and the NPLs.*

Agency Losses, Agency Costs in Authoritarian Party Structures

According to the PA approach, it is expected that agents shirk from the authority of the principals because all individuals are rationally directed by their own self-interests in determining their behaviors. Thus, it is expected that the LPAs tend to shirk from the authority of the NPLs unless their interests overlap with the interests of the NPLs.

The occurrence of the act of shirking by the LPAs can be considered as a challenge to the authoritarian structures, which may lead to agency losses and agency costs in the organization. The NPLs—the principal— have to apply certain control mechanisms to prevent the LPAs' act of shirking. The possible shirking of the agents derives from the conflict of interests between the principals and the agents as well as the informational advantage of the agents over the principals.[55] The informational advantage of the LPAs over the NPLs has been made clear by stating that they are more knowledgeable about their constituencies and their own acts. Therefore, the NPLs are always in a disadvantaged position, lacking sufficient information about the performance of the agents. Yet, what causes the presence of conflictual interests between the LPAs and NPLs in a party organization? Why and under what conditions does such shirking occur? If the act of shirking does not occur, why does it not so?

The intraparty conflicts may arise from the conflicts between the policy-seeking, the vote-seeking, and the office-seeking goals of different party actors. In many studies, the NPLs are presumed to be rational actors or *entrepreneurs*[56] who engage in party leadership out of self-interest rather than altruism. According to this presumption, they are primarily motivated by office benefits; and the vote-seeking goal is instrumental for them as it leads to public office. They may also be interested in policy-seeking behavior, but this is because only policy-oriented individuals can hold leadership positions in the first place. The LPAs, however, may vary in their preferences over policy and office benefits; in this respect the preferences of the activists have a *constraining effect* on the party leaders' office-seeking behavior because the party leaders must take into account the interests of the local actors within the party in order to uphold the public office.[57]

The LPAs who are supposed to spend effort for the success of their party but possess different interests, may well take advantage of their informational superiority to shirk from the NPL's authority. Rather than following the goals set by the NPLs and the party organization at the local level, the LPA may pursue to promote their own interests—such as creating their own bonds with the LPMs and the potential voters who would support their status rather than the status of the NPLs. In this sense, they can be a challenging force against the NPLs. Furthermore, there is a certain transaction cost for the principals in monitoring the activities of the agents. The agenda of the NPLs, particularly the elected top officials are usually loaded with the current political affairs, which makes it extremely difficult for them to keep track of every local agent in local constituencies.

Then, *what control mechanisms do the principals, as rational actors, adopt, anticipating possible shirk of their agents?* Within the administrative procedures, the party statutes already limit the scope of the activities of the LPAs as agents, and there are discipline mechanisms in case their activities go beyond the legal framework. However, due to the transaction cost in following each agent's compliance with the rules, the principals may also seek oversight procedures. They may impose *ex post* negative sanctions for the agents who act beyond the scope of their activity by posing a threat of expulsion from the party, or they may provide *positive sanctions* or material rewards—such as offers for seats in the public office or simple monetary benefits.

Yet, internal party dynamics form, by nature, some subtle control mechanisms for the NPLs without making it necessary for them to directly evaluate the performances of the LPAs. First, the benefits of the LPAs may well be in line with the benefits of the NPLs. The success of the party in elections not only helps the central leaders to be elected for governmental offices, but it also helps the local leaders to be elected for public offices or to rise to higher positions within the party. Being listed as candidates for members of the parliament can automatically motivate the LPAs to perform their tasks well. The LPMs, similarly, can have relations with higher-level elected officials if their party manages to win the elections. Second, Weingast argues that "the existence of readily observable agency costs does not imply that a particular arrangement fails to serve the principal's interests better than alternative arrangements."[58] In other words, an agency cost may be compensated with other advantages that more than outweigh it. For instance, the expulsion of a local party leader who tends to shirk from the NPL's authority is a certain agency cost; but it may help the NPL to change his/her strategy toward other local party leaders with future potential's shirk, which may be more advantageous for the NPL's power in the party.

All these probabilities in the course of the relations between the principals and the agents in the party are likely to generate variance in intraparty authoritarianism, which will be elaborated in detail in the next chapter. They will also shed light on the last question of the PA approach with respect to its application to authoritarian party structures; "*is it the principal or the agent that controls power in a given structure?*" showing that is hard to adopt a static stance on this issue. The variance in intraparty authoritarianism somehow shows that the dominant position of the national leaders over the power structure of a party can well be challenged across time and space. Thus it is possible to find a third way between the opposing views. The possible influence of the LPAs over their principal—NPLs might depend on the efficacy and credibility of the control mechanisms that NPLs utilize, which may vary over time, from one context to another.[59] First, each LPA, coming from different backgrounds and local contexts, may have a different approach to the rules of the NPLs, some complying with them, others deviating from them. As a response, the NPLs change their tactics as well. Second, the power resources of the LPAs may also show variance from one local context to another. Third, the LPAs may shirk from the certain policy issues or party decisions adopted by the NPLs whereas in others they may follow the line of the NPLs.

The Role of Ideas and Values in the PA Approach

One major weakness of the PA approach in political studies is that it has a very materialistic foundation. The behavior of the principals and the agents is assumed to be shaped only through material interests. If the theory is applied in this materialistic way to the relations between the party actors within the party organization, it will vastly neglect the significant role that values and norms play in constituting the interests of the major party actors. PA theory is, for instance, criticized for overlooking factors associated with organizational culture. Jones underlines the neglect of important noncontractual aspects of bureaucratic relationships, where control may rest on organizational culture as on the PA contract.[60] He states that "people in organizations identify emotionally and cognitively with operating procedures, and this nonrational process compounds the disjointed adjustment behavior in bureaus."[61] Brehm and Gates also have noted "the overwhelming importance of attributes of the organizational culture" in their study of supervision/control over police behaviors.[62]

Understanding the causes of conflicts between the actors' interests in party organizations requires to take into account not only the *material interests* such as desire for power or wealth, but also ideational interests derived from ideas, norms, and values, because they can have a *constitutive* rather than a *constraining* effect on the actors' preferences. With the term *ideational interests*, what is meant is the actors' concerns shaped within norm-guided social contexts.[63] It foresees that actors do not interact only in material world but in a sociocultural environment. In other words, the structures lead actors to redefine their interests and identities in the process of interacting.[64] In this sense, defining the party leaders only as office-seeking actors,[65] who are constrained by the preferences of the LPAs and LPMs can bring about misleading causal analyses. The policy-seeking behavior of the party leaders can also take place, not because their office-seeking interests are constrained by the policy-seeking activists, but because the preferences' of the activists have begun to constitute their own interests (i.e., leading to the formation of ideational interests). Similarly, the office-seeking behavior of the party leaders may influence the originally policy-seeking activists' interests and lead them to become more interested in officeseeking.

In fact, the activists' interests are already known to be of an either ideational or a material type. The theories of organizational incentives emphasize that the actions of the party activists do not only originate from material interests. The most famous categorization of organizational incentives is the one that distinguishes "material incentives" (tangible rewards that have a monetary value or which can be translated into rewards that have such a value), "solidary incentives" (intangible rewards that derive from the act of participation itself, such as an opportunity to socialize, gain social prestige, or a sense of belonging to an organization) and "purposive incentives" (intangible rewards that are derived from the stated ends of the organization, such as achievement of public policy objectives) among the party actors.[66] These incentives allocated to party activists, in fact, form the nature of their interests—ideational or material. Furthermore, Eldersveld elaborates the interests of the party actors with the term "motives" in two categories: personal and impersonal.[67] The personal motives basically indicate a desire for recognition, interest in making friends, and impersonal motives are about sense of community obligation, or a desire to influence public policy. Due to the existence of motives derived from the actors' ideas and values together with material motives, the PA approach with a purely materialist approach would be insufficient to explain the reasons for "conflict" or "nonconflict" situations, "agency shirking," and the control mechanisms in the party organization. Thus the materialistic approach of the PA theory must be integrated with the possible values and ideologies (such as ideational interests) that the agents and the principals possess in addition to their material interests in order to explain the variance in intraparty authoritarianism.

Conclusion

The main purpose of this study is to see what constitutes intraparty authoritarianism and its potential variance across space and time. In order to explain the causal mechanism for this variance, this chapter has argued that intraparty authoritarianism must be treated as a relational phenomenon. In other words, authoritarianism does not belong to a certain actor within the party organization, rather it should be understood as a power relationship. This study shares the view that power is a relational phenomenon and the authoritarian party leader at the national level must take into account the interests, values, and skills of the LPAs because the potential effectiveness of the party leader's power depends on these actors' interests, values, and skills.

The power relationship between the NPLs and the LPAs takes place during the governance of the party organization through a system of *delegation of authority*. In governing the party organization, the NPLs as the strong power-holders delegate their authority to the weak power-holders—the LPAs—to fulfill certain tasks at the local level in line with the goals set for them. This leads us to study the power relationship within the authoritarian party structures through a *principal-agent* framework, which is a form of governance that is *governance as hierarchies*. Yet, it must be noted that allocating the role of the principal to the NPL and the role of the agent to the LPA is contrary to the conventional understanding of the PA approach in party politics. This contrast is because the conventional PA approach in party politics has mostly been adopted in the studies of democratic party structures in liberal democracies. Yet, this chapter has argued that the PA model must be applied in a reversed form to understand the causes of variance in authoritarian party structures. There are three reasons: First, it introduces the *informational advantage* of the agents, the LPAs, as an important power resource vis-à-vis the principals, the NPLs, so that a challenge to intraparty authoritarianism may occur. Second, it emphasizes the potential *conflict of interests* as a major reason for why the local activists tend to shirk from the authoritarian rule of the party leaders and challenge the existing power structure. Third, it provides an explanation for how the party leaders as the principals may have to cope with the LPAs through introducing control mechanisms such as administrative and oversight procedures, positive, and negative sanctions. Furthermore, it also explains how the interests of the principals and agents may overlap, and therefore may not lead to any change within the power relationship.

Still, the PA approach in general lacks a constructivist perspective, neglecting the role that ideas and values might play in shaping the interests of the actors. Therefore, the PA approach needs to pay attention to ideational interests that equally mold the behavior of the actors as material interests. This approach will also clarify why conflict of interests are present in some power relationships whereas they are absent in others, as the next chapter will explain.

4

Understanding the Variance in Intraparty Authoritarianism

The aim of this chapter is to specify, first, the core mechanisms—the types of interest configurations—that *constitute* different patterns of power relationships between the party actors; and second, the factors—exogenous and endogenous triggers—that *cause* a change in this mechanism. In this respect, this chapter seeks to explain the variance in intraparty authoritarianism, using Wendt's "constitutive and causal theorizing" techniques.[1]

According to Wendt, constitutive theorizing has the objective to account for the properties of things by reference to the structures in virtue of which they exist. Constitutive theories, therefore, are static and seek to show how the properties of a system or a structure are constituted.[2] In other words, they take snapshots of existing systems or structures in an effort to explain how systems are constituted rather than explaining dynamic processes. As such, constitutive questions usually take the form of *how possible?* or *what?*: What constitutes the power relationship between the party actors? How is it possible that different power relationships can exist within a party structure? What are the different types of interests that the principals and the agents have in the authoritarian party organization? How do the different types of interests shape intraparty conflicts?[3]

Causal theorizing, on the other hand, explains dynamic processes or changes in the state of a variable or a system. Causal factors are independent of and prior to the transitions themselves; hence the terminology of independent and dependent variables is often used in causal theorizing. Causal theorizing answers questions of the form *why?* and, in some cases, *how?*[4]: Why does a variance in intraparty authoritarianism occur? How do the power relationships between the party actors change?

Through the use of causal and constitutive theorizing, this chapter explains the rise of four types of authoritarian party structures: *clandestine, benign, challenged,* and *coercive.* In *clandestine authoritarianism,* the LPAs are not aware of or indifferent to the domination of the NPLs. That is why the LPAs in this type of authoritarianism have no motive to change the power structure. In *benign authoritarianism,* the LPAs are subordinate to the power of the NPLs due to the material benefits that they receive from the authoritarian party structure. That is why, even though they are aware of intraparty authoritarianism, they do not take initiative to change the power structure. In *challenged authoritarianism,* the LPAs object to the authoritarian party structures as a result of the rise of conflicts between their interests and the interests of the NPLs. In this type of authoritarianism, the LPAs either take initiative or have the motive to create change. Finally, in *coercive authoritarianism,* the NPLs exert explicit coercion over the LPAs who challenge their authority in the party.

Because interest configurations *constitute* the power relationships within party organizations, the variance in interest configurations leads to two types of intraparty authoritarianism during the status quo, clandestine or benign. Depending on the nature of the exogenous and endogenous triggers in the political system, yet, it is possible to see a challenged and a coercive type of authoritarianism, because these triggers *cause* a change in the power equilibrium of party structures. In fact, some of these triggers may bring transitions from authoritarianism toward democratic party governance, as the next sections will elaborate.

Interest Configurations in Party Governance

The office-seeking, policy-seeking, and vote-seeking interests of political parties[5] are based on a party's position within the external competitive environment. In other words, these are the organizational interests or aims of a political party. These organizational interests may overlap with the party actors' (leaders, activists, members) own interests, yet they may not necessarily have to be the same with personal-level interests. As Panebianco rightly asserts:

> A plurality of aims are often pursued within an organization, sometimes as many as there are actors in the organization. The so-called organizational aims, therefore, either simply indicate the result, *the complex effect which derives from the simultaneous pursuit of particular aims by the different actors* (and in that case it would be equivocal to define such an effect as an "aim"), or else they are but abstractions lacking empirical evidence.[6]

Chapter 3 indicated that the interests of the party actors, even the party elite, need not be *material.* In other words, to some degree, their interests may also be shaped by ideas, norms, and values. In this sense, the interests can also be *ideational*. Yet, the interests of the party elite are usually elaborated as being overwhelmingly material. In other words, it is argued that the true objective of an organization's leaders is not to pursue the manifest aim for which the organization is established, but rather the organization's survival and together with it, the survival of their own power positions.[7] In this sense, the materialistic tendency of the party elite is often taken-for-granted. Even when party elite pursues policy-seeking aims, it is argued that it is not because they care for those policies, but rather it is because there are organizational constraints that they have to take into account in order to maintain the survival of their position.[8] Yet, it is unrealistic to consider any party actor having only materialistic interests. Even in authoritarian party structures, the principals (i.e., NPLs—national party leaders) and the agents (i.e., LPAs—local party activists) may have both ideational and material interests, which bring about a major difference in the power relationship between the agent and the principal within the party.

Distinguishing the interests of party actors as *ideational* and *material* is also helpful to clarify the confusion between purposive (or ideological) and solidary motives in the often-referred Clark-Wilson categorization of membership motivations.[9] The assignment of questionnaire items according to the Clark-Wilson categorization does not show consistency in several studies.[10] For instance, some researchers consider the "sense of community obligation" as a purposive (ideological) motive, while some locate it in the solidary category.[11] Conway and Feigert assign "party loyalty" to the purposive category, whereas most others label it as a solidary motive.[12]

This study elaborates the *ideational interests* of party actors as interests derived from shared ideas, values and norms, which constitute the identities and consequently the interests and interactions of such actors in the organization. Some examples for ideational interests are:

- An interest enhancing the actor's status in the community
- Strong loyalty to the party
- Loyalty to party leadership
- Concern for public issues
- Sense of community obligation
- Making social contacts and friends

The material interests, on the other hand, are purely derived from an individual-level cost-benefit calculus, such as:

- Search for power and influence
- An interest in being appointed to a government office

- An interest for running for public office
- Being close to influential people
- An interest for finding a job

Whether the party actors have ideational or material interests, molds the interest configuration among the agents and principals within party organizations. Figure 4.1 shows the different interest configurations between the principals and the agents in authoritarian party structures based on these ideational and material types of interests. In this respect, the figure shows that not only the interests of the LPAs (agents), but also the interests of the NPLs (principals) may vary between material and ideational types.

Strategic interest configuration: In a strategic interest configuration, both the principals and agents are primarily motivated by material interests. The behavior of the actors in the party is initially motivated by self-defined preferences, which consist of access to political power and public office. NPLs (principals) behave in an authoritarian manner in decision-making processes because their desire for power or holding an office is more dominant than their ideational interests. In general, the office-seeking or vote-seeking interest of the party organization overlaps with the material interests of the party leaders because they can have access to power only by achieving electoral success, which maintains the organization's survival. On the other hand, in this type of configuration, the agents (LPAs) with material interests in the party organization do not necessarily take the party rules and the decisions of the principals for granted. They conform to the decision of the principals only if it increases

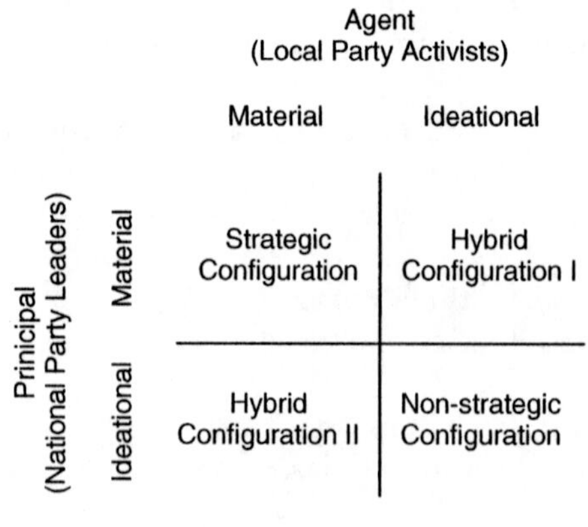

Agent
(Local Party Activists)

	Material	Ideational
Principal (National Party Leaders) — Material	Strategic Configuration	Hybrid Configuration I
Ideational	Hybrid Configuration II	Non-strategic Configuration

Figure 4.1 Interest configurations in an authoritarian party structure.

their political utility and on the condition that the costs of compliance are less than the costs of opposition.

It is a purely zero-sum game between the principals and the agents, in which the principals utilize a number of control mechanisms to win the submission of the agents to their authority. The administrative procedures—the discipline mechanisms already outlined in the party bylaws—may not be sufficient to control the possible shirk of the agents due to their informational advantage. Instead, providing *ex ante* positive or *ex post* negative sanctions is a convenient method. Positive sanctions (rewards or promised rewards) are important resources by which the principals affect the behavior of their agents. Appealing to the material interests of the agents, the positive sanctions are useful tools to help agents increase their utility, promising certain benefits in the power structure. These positive sanctions are also, in Panebianco's words, selective incentives, which are benefits that the party leadership distributes only to some of the participants and in varying amounts.[13] Another control mechanism is to impose *ex post* negative sanctions, in the form of a threat of marginalization in the power structure of the party. The negative sanctions may become actualized and turn into negative incentives,[14] such as imposition of coercion or repression over the local actors whose interests conflict with the party leaders' interests.

Hybrid Interest Configuration I: In this type of interest configuration, while the party leaders aim to seek power in the party and therefore materially motivated, the behavior of the local party actors is shaped by their ideational interests. This type of configuration is commonly observable in many party structures as it is often argued that party activists tend to be more policy-oriented or attached to the party ideology than the party leaders who are more office oriented.[15] Members who are heavily motivated by nonmaterial incentives, and are committed to the party ideology, may be less likely to be willing to compromise on issues.[16] They may also be the most likely to drop out if the party leadership does not take the policy positions that they favor, compared to the other members who are motivated by material incentives. The members with material incentives are more likely to remain involved even if their party takes policy positions that they do not fully support, as their incentives for involvement remain less affected.[17]

In authoritarian party structures in which the party leaders have material interests such as desire for power and public office, the policy-oriented activists do not necessarily constrain the behavior of the party leaders, since the leaders would rather choose to marginalize the role of these activists than decentralizing policy decisions or ensuring their accountability towards them. It is because the costs of any action that constrains their decision-making behavior would be higher than facing with agency costs. In this respect, it is reasonable to expect that the policy-seeking activists whose interests conflict with the party leadership choose the exit option from the party organization, and do not create a challenge to intraparty authoritarianism. However, apart from being policy-oriented, the ideational interests of the party members may also be concerned with "enhancing social status" or "loyalty to the party leader or ideology." Such interests have a great potential to serve to the material interests of the party leaders who seek to consolidate their power in the party. Activists' loyalty or interest in enhancement of their social status can be used in a *strategic* way by the party leaders. The distribution of collective incentives to these ideationally motivated party activists, then, keeps them loyal to the authoritarian behavior of the party leaders and becomes functional for the realization of the party leaders' power-seeking goals.

Hybrid Interest Configuration II: In this type of interest configuration, the party leaders have ideational, the activists have material interests. The motivation of the party leaders to behave in an authoritarian way does not need to originate from power-seeking aims. Party leaders, in many contexts, have to deal with the efficiency-democracy dilemma of their party organizations.[18] In this sense, they may choose to maximize efficiency at the expense of intraparty democracy. To maintain their authority, they may use positive and negative sanctions to appeal to the materially motivated agents as outlined in the strategic type of interest configuration. Therefore, the outcome of this type of configuration can be expected to be similar to the outcome in *strategic interest configuration*.

Nonstrategic Interest Configuration: Within this type of interest configuration, both the party leaders and the party members have ideational interests. The authoritarian behavior of the party leaders is, again, derived from their norms and values rather than power-seeking aims such as efficiency versus democracy. The activists are ideationally subordinated to the decisions of the party and the party leader. In this respect, the outcome of this type of configuration can be expected to be similar to the outcome in *Hybrid Interest Configuration I*.

The differences in the interest configurations collectively show that *it is the interests of the agents that matter for the potential variance* in the power structure of authoritarian parties. Authoritarian party leaders, either motivated by material or ideational interests, tend to repress or conceal any potential conflict within the party, yet, they have to take into account the types of interests in order to identify the true control mechanism for the potential shirk of the agents.

The Observable and the Latent Conflict in the Party Organization

The national party leaders—NPLs must take into account the interests of the local party activists—LPAs as a matter of the interactive power relationship between them. The potential effectiveness of the power of the NPLs, in other words, depends on the interests of the LPAs. The difference in the ideational and material type of interests among the LPAs affects the nature of conflicts and consequently the power structure of the party organization, which is to be explained now.

The conflicts between the NPLs and LPAs can be either *observable* or *latent* in the party organization, which can be analyzed through Lukes' study on "three faces of power."[19] The observable conflict may take place either on actual or potential decision-making processes. When the actual decision-making processes lead to the emergence of an observable conflict, the conflict is exhibited in the actions of the party actors, and thus can be discovered by observing their behavior. The NPLs, then, exert their decision-making power over the LPAs and this type of power is visible through their *behaviors*: They can impose positive or negative sanctions. This is exactly how the first face of (one-dimensional) power is exercised.

When there is an observable conflict on *potential* issues rather than actual ones, the party leaders may choose to "confine the scope of decision-making to relatively *safe* issues" and therefore exert their non-decision-making power.[20] In other words, decisions are prevented from being made on potential issues over which there is an observable conflict of interests.[21] The party leaders need to spend a certain effort to prevent potential conflicting issues from becoming actual. This is how the second face of (two-dimensional) power is exercised. The positive and negative sanctions are still important mechanisms that the party leader uses since the conflicts are observable.

It is when the conflicts are *latent* that the party leaders do not require using the control mechanisms to maintain their authority in the party. In other words, the conflicts can be prevented from arising in the first place, through distributing collective incentives to the ideationally motivated local party actors. This can be realized through *manipulation*, which makes conflict latent or unobservable and therefore the subordinate group is unaware of what its real interests are. According to Lukes,[22] this is the exercise of the often-neglected three-dimensional view of power. Lukes accepts the fact that it is difficult to identify the process or mechanism of the three-dimensional power.[23] Yet, he outlines its three distinctive features: Such an exercise, first, involves inaction rather than (observable) action. In other words, the failure to act in a certain way may well have specifiable consequences. These consequences can be identified by considering that the actions in question would have led to the appearance of a political issue. Second, the exercise of power is held unconsciously. In other words, one may be unaware of the real motive or meaning of the other's action. And finally, power is exercised by collectives, such as groups or institutions. Thus, organization itself becomes the most important source for the exercise of the three-dimensional power in modern age. Galbraith has once noted that:

> When an exercise of power is sought or needed, organization is required. From the organization, then, come the requisite persuasion and the resulting submission to the purposes of the organization.[24]

Defining it as "conditioned power," Galbraith explains this type of power as the one, which is exercised by changing beliefs. The individuals are unconscious of their submission to a power because they submit through persuasion, training, or social commitment to what seems natural or right. The submission reflects the preferred course; yet, the fact of submission is not recognized.[25]

These features of the three-dimensional view of power have, in fact, been implied in Katz and Mair's cartel party hypothesis, though not explicitly accepted.[26] Intraparty democracy has lost its meaning through the exercise of the three-dimensional view of power since the party elite is capable of manipulating the belief of the rank-and-file. Thus, introducing intraparty elections does not challenge their authoritarian position. In line with this hypothesis, the "Hybrid Interest Configuration I" is illustrative of the exercise of the three dimensional power. LPA who possess ideational interests such as loyalty to the party ideology, enhancement of their social status, or simply loyalty to the party leader can easily be manipulated via collective incentives. In this respect, the authoritarian party structure may be *clandestine*, in which the local activists are unconscious about the exercise of power. As the conflicts are made latent, there is certain inaction in a situation where the action in question would be to pose a challenge to the authority of the party leaders.

If the conflicts are observable between the party actors, in other words, if it is the one or two-dimensional view of power that is exerted by the party leaders, however, the authoritarian party structure becomes *benign.* The positive or negative sanctions provide the means to repress these conflicts. The local activists with material interests as stated in the "Strategic Interest Configuration" may be aware of the intraparty conflicts and tend to react to these conflicts. However, within this type of authoritarian party structure, the party leaders win either through threatening appropriate adverse consequences (negative sanctions) or by the offer of rewards (positive sanctions).[27]

Explaining the Change in the Power Relationship

There is power equilibrium in the authoritarian party structure when the interest configuration based on the distinction between the ideational and material interests establish the status quo and constitute the major pattern in the power relationship, which is either *clandestine* or *benign.* Yet, under what conditions does the interest configuration change? When does a (new) conflict occur? How does the agent—LPA—tend to shirk from the authority of the principal?

The literature on institutional change emphasizes the significance of both the endogenous and exogenous factors, which are expedient in explaining the change in the power structure of parties as well.

The Role of Exogenous and Endogenous Triggers

The change in the party structure can be the consequence of exogenous or endogenous developments in a political system as well as a combination of both. Many substantial political shifts in policies, regimes or systems are explained by exogenously led developments such as wars, financial crises and environmental disasters;[28] which constitute *critical junctures* that alter the equilibrium in a path-dependent continuity.[29] Such external shocks bring new actors, ideas, and goals to the forefront and can produce a dynamic change.[30] Yet, the exogenous factors are not sufficient to explain the transformation of politics in the absence of such shocks. To demonstrate this argument, the focus of analysis also shifts to the examination of "endogenous events" that are developments internal to the institution itself as a potential source of change.[31] Such events bring opportunities of change in the existing institutional structures when learning experiences of the agents lead them to challenge the "shared" institutional template; or when the new conflictual ideas of the key actors question the existent frame.[32]

Exogenous and endogenous factors are not necessarily at odds with each other. As illustrated in some seminal studies, not all exogenous shocks lead to change, even in extremely important shocks.[33] This makes the patterns of response by the actors to the external developments extremely important because only the developments that carry certain meanings for these actors lead to a change.[34] Thus, in some cases, the triggers for change might be exogenous; yet, it may also be the endogenous factors that shape the process of political change. As Williams asserts in his analysis of policy change;[35] while the spark that starts policy change processes can be exogenous to the existing subsystem, policy change itself is still largely influenced by factors normally thought to be endogenous to the subsystem, the policy goals, and strategies of the key actors. For instance, while factors associated with globalization fall under the category of exogenous developments, their effects on a policy system might create endogenous triggers in the long term such as entrance of new actors or new goals into the policy-making process.

Furthermore, the actors' responses do not need to be based on rational calculations of interest since such responses may also be shaped by ideational interests. If new "cognitive scripts" are constructed by the actors in a way that new institutional moral values are legitimized; the key actors can question the existent frame through mediating new and conflictual ideas.[36] This type of adjustment, in return, can bring about transformative political change through operationalizing institutions, which gives effect to the new frame. As Carter persuasively argues, the concepts, "framing" and "operationalizing" are important analytical tools to understand the mechanisms of change.[37] The concepts indicate two sequential processes: Through "framing," the actors create an identification (and resolution) of the new dilemmas and tensions that have internally arisen either due to exogenous or endogenous triggers. In other words, *they begin to question the existing frame.* "Operationalizing," on the other hand, gives effect to the new frame, based on the extent of new institution building. The processes of "framing" and "operationalizing" by the actors initiate political change.

The change in the power structure of political parties can also be based on exogenous and endogenous triggers that the political system produces. The endogenous triggers may come in the form of death of the party leader, corruption scandal, outcomes of candidate selection processes, appointment of new powerful local actors, etc. The exogenous triggers also come in various forms such as, loss in an election, entrance of a new party into the system, or disappearance of an old one.[38] However, stating that such developments can bring about a change in the power structure of the parties is not sufficient to understand the change unless it is specified how they influence the internal mechanisms of the party organization. For instance, electoral defeats, as one of the most well-recognized external factors, vital for the organizational structure of the parties, can affect the patterns in power relationships within parties because they simply erode the legitimacy of the ruling party elite's authority due to having failed to realize the common goals of the organization. The position of a party may shift from being in government to being in opposition due to the electoral defeat. As Bolleyer has argued, in times of opposition, the party leaders may more easily be challenged by the local party actors because their access to financial resources/state subventions is restricted.[39] In other words, the local party actors begin to question the existing frame. The capital, which is the primary power resource of the party leaders, needs to be replaced with the valuation of effectiveness, control of productivity, structured demands, and the patterning of legitimation in the party. Operationalizing occurs, when the party infrastructure becomes a core source of control by the party leaders either by reform or active implementation of the party rules on the ground. The exogenous and endogenous developments, therefore, can bring a change in the interest configuration of the party organization, which makes adaptation necessary for actors against these shocks. Figure 4.2 summarizes the relationship between interest configurations, exogenous/endogenous developments, and the power relationship within parties. Interest configuration provides a *constitutive* explanation for the power relationship between the LPAs and the NPLs. The third variable 'exogenous and endogenous developments' has, on the other hand, a *causal* depth because it appears to lead to the rise of a new type of intraparty authoritarianism.

The exogenous and endogenous developments act through interest configurations. Therefore, the causal priority belongs to the presence of exogenous and endogenous triggers in explaining the *change* in the power relationship between the party leaders and the local activists.

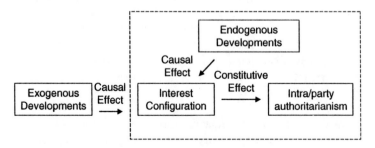

Figure 4.2   The effect of interest configurations and exogenous and endogenous developments on intraparty authoritarianism.

Mechanisms for Change: Balancing Operations

The exogenous and endogenous developments may trigger new tensions and dilemmas within the party organization. Yet, how is it possible that the *weak actors,* LPAs—local party activists start challenging the authority of the *strong actors,* NPLs—national party leaders in the party structure? How is it possible for the weak ones to question the existing frame and operationalize change in the status quo situation of intraparty authoritarianism, which is maintained either through *clandestine* or *benign* means by the strong ones?

Emerson's explanatory framework of "balancing operations" is a useful tool to understand the structural changes in power-dependence relationships within a party.[40] In his analysis, the unbalanced power relationship may change for the advantage of the weaker side in four ways, which he calls "balancing operations." According to his analysis, the tension involved in this kind of relationship can be reduced in two ways; either through 1) cost reduction, or 2) balancing operations.[41] Cost reduction is a process involving change in values (personal, social, economic), which reduces the pains incurred in meeting demands of a powerful other. Yet, these adjustments do not necessarily alter the imbalance of the relation. The weak actor, here, continues to be submissive to the strong actor redefining her/his moral values with appropriate rationalizations and shifts toward group attachments. In other words, suppose that a LPA with material interests is unhappy about his submissive role in the party because he does not receive any material benefits from the authoritarian party structure. Therefore, a shift from material to ideational interests would help this actor in reducing his costs of being a submissive actor. In other words, he can nonetheless continue to be the weak agent of the party leader, with an interest in enhancing his friendship circle rather than taking part in party decisions; such as sociability. In this sense, cost reduction, does not change the nature of the equilibrium in the power relationship.

Yet, *balancing operations* take place through the changes in the variables that define the structure of the power relationship. Emerson outlines four types of balancing operations.[42] His analysis will be illustrated in the power relationship between the LPAs and the NPLs in an authoritarian party structure:

1. In the first type of balancing operation, the weak actor reduces motivational investment in goals mediated by the strong actor. This is called motivational withdrawal. In this case, the weak actor loses some of his/her interest in the collective game under the impact

of frustrations and demands imposed by the strong actor. The weak actor, in other words, begins to deny and move away from the dependency on the strong actor. The weak actor's motivational orientation and commitment toward different areas of activity will reflect this process. With respect to the principal-agent (PA) approach, this is the point where the *agency shirking* starts. No matter how the rules and procedures outline the duties and responsibilities of the LPAs, the rise of a conflict in the interests between the NPLs and the LPAs may lead to the motivational withdrawal of the LPAs, altering the unbalanced power-dependence relationship.

2. The second type of balancing operation takes place when the weak actor cultivates alternative sources for gratification of the goals mediated by the strong actor. As outlined in chapter 3; information, money, enhancement of status, networking are important potential power sources for the LPAs.[43] In fact, the informational advantage sets the fundamental basis of the PA approach,[44] where LPAs are the most knowledgeable of their constituencies and their own actions. Still, economic well-being or social status are two other power resources that the agents can generate. These resources may help the LPAs win the submission of the loyalty of the party members and voters in their constituencies, increase their popularity, thus their power vis-à-vis the NPLs. In other words, the collective goal of the party organization, that is to attract voters, is maintained through the sources of the LPAs rather than of the NPLs.

An awareness or increase in the alternative power resources of the LPAs, therefore may alter the power balance in the authoritarian party structure. Another alternative power resource that can be generated, yet, is the possibility of *networking* among the agents. The agents may form and extend the network through allying with other agents who are also dependent on the principals.[45] In other words, new networks can be formulated by the formation of new relationships. The tensions of unbalanced relation between the strong NPL and the weak LPA_1 as well as the weak LPA_2 will make LPA_3 and LPA_4 ready to form new relationships, with an additional weak LPA_5 and LPA_6, until it leads to a new *faction* in the party. The lengthened network may move the unbalanced relations toward a new balance as these agents strengthen the position of the new faction vis-à-vis the NPL.

3. This situation takes us to the third type of balancing operation, which is coalition formation against the strong actor. That is, a balance can be maintained through collapsing the two relational

networks into one group-person relation with the emergence of the collective actor. Therefore, while the second type of balancing operation reduces the power of the strong actor through the creation or awareness of alternative sources, the third type increases the power of the weaker actor through collectivization.[46]

4. Finally, in the fourth type of balancing operation, the weaker member's power increases to such an extent that s/he is able to control the formerly more powerful actor through increasing the latter's motivation in the newly formed power relation. This is normally accomplished through giving him status recognition in one or more of its many forms such as an increase in the degree and a change in the type of positive sanctions or rather a voice in the decision-making process. In authoritarian party structures, the accomplishment of the fourth type of balancing operation by the local party actors paves the way for intraparty democracy because it means that the necessary checks and balances have been maintained against the power of the national party leaders.

However, not all initiatives for balancing operations are successful. Besides, the possibility of balancing operations arises only when (1) there is a conflict of interests between the weak and strong actors (which are the LPAs and the NPLs in an authoritarian party structure); (2) there are effective power resources that weak actors can utilize. That is why, the success and possibility of balancing operations is dependent on the scope, domain, and time; which also brings a variance in intraparty authoritarianism.

Variance in Intraparty authoritarianism Across Space and Time

The variance in intraparty authoritarianism is based on the scope and domain as well as the timing of the power relationship. The next two sections will evaluate these two factors.

The Scope and Domain Factor

In explaining the nature of a power relationship and any possible changes that such relationship can go through, both scope and domain must be specified.[47] It is of crucial importance to recognize that power may rest on various bases, differing not only from culture to culture, but also within a culture from one power structure to another. Political analysis must be contextual and take into account of the power practices actually manifested in the concrete political situation.[48] As Baldwin argues, although a contextual approach to power analysis would undoubtedly reduce the parsimony of theorizing about power, this disadvantage is less serious than it seems: Scope and domain, rather, can be defined more or less to suit the purpose of the analyst.[49]

Identification of scope and domain in the power relationship between the NPLs and the LPAs may show that the presence of the LPAs' power resources is context-specific. A local party organization comprised of certain LPAs may be more skillful or more advantageous in its relation with the NPL, compared to another one. Yet, possession of political skills may not be sufficient to make a LPA more powerful than the other. As discussed in "balancing operations," networking and status recognition are important initiatives that the LPA can take part in. However some local contexts may enhance the possibility of networking in a more effective way than the others. For instance, a local party organization located in a region where political conditions are more favorable to the development of alternative sources, i.e. status recognition or networking, is in a more advantageous position compared to the local organizations in other regions in terms of its potential power. In this sense, it is the scope and domain that matters. The scope and domain of a power relationship between the NPL and the LPA in the party organization varies across different (local) contexts. Therefore, intraparty authoritarianism is not a uniform phenomenon even within a party.

Another example for the significance of scope and domain, is the relationship between the NPL and the voters in general. The context of this relationship is different from the context of the relationship between the NPLs and the LPAs. These two contexts, yet, may affect one another. For instance, the utilization of *ex post* negative sanctions is an important power resource for the NPL to strengthen his/her authoritarian behavior over the LPAs within a party organization. Yet, this method undermines his/her legitimacy in the electoral arena, in other words weaken his/her power vis-à-vis the voters. Repressing the observable intraparty conflicts through negative sanctions undermines both the democratic image and the legitimacy of the party. An undermined legitimacy in electoral politics, in return, may cause a defeat in elections for the party organization as a whole. The electoral defeats are, as discussed, exogenous triggers that change the interest configuration within the party and cause the reaction of a larger number of local actors attempting to challenge the authority of the party leader.

The Time Factor

The NPLs as the principals and the LPAs as the agents form a contracted relationship based on the different interest configurations outlined in this chapter. However, the status quo in the power equilibrium (benign or clandestine authoritarianism) can be subject to change *in time*. The exogenous and endogenous triggers in the political system take place in certain times and change the interest configurations within authoritarian party structures. Therefore, the benign or the clandestine type of authoritarian party structure represents the first stage of the variance in intraparty authoritarianism. In the time of an exogenous development, such as an electoral defeat, the agents with necessary power resources can challenge the authoritarianism of the party leaders. This is the second stage of intraparty authoritarianism that can be labeled as *challenged authoritarianism*. The challenge occurs when the conflict between the principal and agent becomes observable, and the agent's resources of power create a motivational withdrawal from the goals of the party leaders.

Thus, the PA relationship in an authoritarian party organization is constituted of an equilibrium power structure at the original stage, as maintained in the benign and clandestine authoritarianism. As the sources of power change in favor of the agents, the conditions force a change in the authoritarian nature of the party. For the power equilibrium to exist at the original stage, there must be a consensus between the principals and the agents on the authoritarian nature of the party organization; and the benign and clandestine type of authoritarianism provide that consensus.

Challenged authoritarianism, following the change in the power structure constitutes an unsettled dispute between the party on the ground and the party elite, similar to the structure of the catchall party. The LPAs have the desire for autonomy. Since the conflict takes place in an authoritarian structure, the NPL as the principal may use different control mechanisms to eliminate the possibility of challenging behavior. The administrative procedures, such as the party bylaws already limit the scope of the activities of the LPAs as agents, and there are discipline mechanisms in case their activities go beyond the legal framework. Yet, when the challenge becomes obvious, principals may use negative sanctions to control the agent's shirking behavior. The "police-patrol oversight" is one of the mechanisms that the principal uses, actively monitoring the agency behavior with the aim of remedying and detecting violations.[50] Finally, the NPL may attempt to use *coercion* to repress the challenging voice of the LPAs, which is based on threats of expulsions or marginalization of their status in the party. *Coercive authoritarianism* derives from "condign

Table 4.1   Variance in intraparty authoritarianism in four stages

	Stage One	*Stage Two*	*Stage Three*	*Stage Four*
Actor(s) initiating the stage	Both principal and agent	Only agent	Only principal	Either agent or principal
Defining aspects of the stage	Benign or clandestine authoritarianism	Challenged authoritarianism	Coercive authoritarianism	Intraparty democracy or back to stage one
	Status quo in interest configurations	Change in interest configurations through the effect of exogenous or endogenous triggers		Status quo in interest configurations

power," which wins submission by inflicting or threatening appropriately adverse consequences.[51]

Table 4.1 summarizes the variance in intraparty authoritarianism as a four-staged process. The stage four shows the two possible consequences of coercive authoritarianism, based on whether the agent has become successful in shirking from and thus challenging the authority of the principal. If the agent is successful, then the consequence may be exit from authoritarianism and the emergence of intraparty democracy. If the agents are not successful in their attempts and cannot fight against the coercion, then the intraparty authoritarianism prevails. The success of the agents depends on the degree of the change in the agents' sources of power, which have been outlined as information, money, enhancement of status, and networking. If the change in the power structure is high to the extent that the agents can resist against coercion, the chances of exit from intraparty authoritarianism are higher.

Conclusion

It is possible to see variance in intraparty authoritarianism in a given political system due to the divergence of interest configurations derived from different types of interests: ideational and material. The possession of ideational interests by the LPAs such as loyalty to the ideology or concern for community issues may be used as a tool for manipulation by the NPLs in order to consolidate their power in the party. In other words, the conflicts can be made latent when the NPLs distribute collective incentives to these ideationally motivated local party actors. This situation constitutes a clandestine type of intraparty authoritarianism.

On the other hand, the materially interested LPAs may also be submissive to the authority of the NPLs if they receive sufficient material benefits or be subject to negative sanctions. In this type of *benign* authoritarianism, the conflicts are observable but repressed through positive or negative sanctions by the NPLs. The exogenous and endogenous developments, such as electoral defeats, may alter the status quo interest configurations, leading the LPAs to question the existing frame; and those with necessary power resources to challenge the intraparty authoritarianism. The NPLs, in the next stage, will have to exert coercion (coercive authoritarianism). Depending on the availability of resources, the outcome of the coercion can either be a return to the status quo intraparty authoritarianism or the emergence of intraparty democracy.

It must be underlined that the variance in intraparty authoritarianism is not static and takes place following a certain sequence of events. Furthermore, the scope and domain of the power relations between the LPAs and the NPLs are significant as it affects the availability of power resources of the LPAs. In this sense, while an exogenous or an endogenous event can create a variance in intraparty authoritarianism in one local context, it may not do so in another one. The validity of these arguments will be established in the next chapter analyzing the empirical case of Turkey.

5

Intraparty Authoritarianism in Turkey: Empirical Findings

This chapter aims to outline the empirical findings on the variance in authoritarian party structures observed within and across four political parties in Turkey. As discussed in chapter 4, these patterns show variance across space and time; and this study identifies four types of intraparty authoritarianism: clandestine, benign, challenged, and coercive.

According to Duverger, those who are most knowledgeable about the power structure and organizational dynamics of parties are the experienced party members and activists.[1] In line with this statement, in order to find out different patterns of intraparty authoritarianism in Turkey, the empirical research consisted of 91 in-depth interviews with experienced local party members and local party activists from four political parties, Justice and Development Party (AKP—*Adalet ve Kalkınma Partisi*), Republican People's Party (CHP—*Cumhuriyet Halk Partisi*), Nationalist Action Party (MHP—*Milliyetçi Hareket Partisi*), Democratic Society Party (DTP—*Demokratik Toplum Partisi*), and in four selected districts—Tarsus (Mersin), Karşıyaka (İzmir), Merkez (Diyarbakır), and Ümraniye (İstanbul)—of Turkey.[2] The interviews took place within a three-month period of time in the aftermath of the national elections in 2007.

In order to understand the nature of intraparty authoritarianism, the two measures of intraparty democracy—candidate selection and policy formulation—processes have been emphasized in the interview questions, hoping to shed light on how the local party actors evaluate the power structure of their parties (see Appendix A for a detailed list of interview questions). Do they think their party is authoritarian at all? How should an ideal candidate-selection process be like in their party? Do they think the candidate-selection process was democratic in the last election? Do their attitudes on policy issues ever conflict with their leaders' attitudes in the party? Do they ever defend their position when their attitudes conflict with their leaders' on policy issues? The answers that have been received to these questions helped to reveal the different patterns of authoritarianism across and within parties.

This chapter is organized in the following order: the section "Methodological Notes on the Field Research" depicts some important methodological notes on the conducted field research, such as the political context when the interviews were carried out, the selection criteria of the districts, and the sample of interviewees. The section "Observing the Variance in Intraparty Authoritarianism in Turkey" introduces the variance in intraparty authoritarianism analyzing the statements of LPAs and LPMs across and within the selected four parties in accordance with the answers given to the interview questions. In "Conclusion," the observed patterns of intraparty authoritarianism are reviewed in the form of a transition to the next chapter, which will explain the reasons for this variance and test the empirical plausibility of the theoretical arguments presented before.

Methodological Notes on the Field Research

The field research focused on understanding the dynamics within parties shortly *before* and *after* the 2007 parliamentary election in Turkey. The period before the election was analyzed because it included the dynamics related to decision-making processes (particularly candidate selection) within the selected parties. The period after the election, on the other hand, was a strategic time for any possibilities of change in the power structure of parties due to potential exogenous and endogenous events such as an electoral defeats or leadership crises. The interviews were conducted in a two-month time in the selected districts, following the parliamentary election held on July 22, 2007. The early timing of the interviews in the postelection period particularly helped to obtain accurate information from the refreshed memories of the local party actors based on candidate-selection processes in the preelection period.

The National Political Context in Turkey at the Time of the Field Research

In 2007, the AKP received the majority of votes and came to power as the single party in government. The CHP, the MHP, and the DTP held the second, third, and fourth positions in the vote share respectively and entered the parliament as opposition parties. These three parties were also the only ones which were able to form a party group in the parliament.[3] The representation of the four parties in the parliament after the election strengthened the claim that the Turkish party system was comprised of a two-dimensional ideological competition: (1) Secularist versus pro-Islamist cleavage, (2) Ethnic cleavage which sets the Turkish and the Kurdish identities in opposition to one another.[4] During the electoral campaigns in 2007, the first dimension was observable in the rhetoric employed by the prosecular CHP against the AKP; whereas the second dimension was observable in the electoral discourse of the MHP and the DTP.

The parliamentary election took place in a polarized atmosphere, following the failure of the parliament to elect a new president in April 2007. The roots of this political crisis lay in original tensions between secularist and Islamist influences in Turkey: In 2001, the AKP came out of the reformist wing of a political party that represented the pro-Islamic movement in Turkish politics, known as the national view (*Milli Görüş*) movement. The parties established under the "national view" tradition in Turkey have experienced a long record of being banned from politics by the secular state elite because of their strong Islamic references. The last one of these banned parties was the Virtue Party (FP—*Fazilet Partisi*), which was split into a traditionalist and a reformist faction, and out of the latter, the AKP had emerged.

Aware of the "national view" background of the party, Turkey's secular elite kept an anxiety and skepticism about the real intentions of the AKP government since the day the party first came to power in 2002. Yet, the AKP leaders declared to have no bonds with the national view movement. The "national view" traditionally emphasized the national and spiritual development of the society based on Islamic values and showed reservations for Turkey's membership in the European Union.[5] On the contrary, the AKP leaders adopted a discourse showing strong devotion to the principle of secularism and a pragmatic approach to politics, combining the effort for EU membership with neoliberal economic policies.[6]

Still, the pious personalities of Erdoğan and Gül as well as the headscarves of their wives made the secular elite skeptical of the new AKP government.[7] The skepticism over the AKP's pro-Islamic identity was prevalent in the bureaucratic center when the AKP majority in the parliament announced Abdullah Gül, who was by then the minister of foreign affairs, as the candidate for presidency. The president of the Republic of Turkey, as a constitutional rule, has to be a secular person, representing the unity of Turkey, standing at equal distance from all political parties and ideologies.[8]

The secularist camp was highly uncomfortable with the choice of Gül because he had an influential character within the AKP. Therefore, the main opposition party, the CHP boycotted the first round of voting by the parliament for presidency with a strong rhetoric on secularism. Political tensions rose markedly when the army issued a memorandum on its website in the form of a threat to the civilian AKP government. Mass demonstrations from the secular groups followed in Istanbul and other major cities. The election failed after the Constitutional Court, on May 1, on application by the CHP, stated that the first round of voting was invalid, on the grounds that a quorum of two-thirds of the membership of the parliament was necessary in the first round of voting. Therefore, the candidacy of Abdullah Gül was withdrawn and the crisis led to early parliamentary elections.

The political campaigns further polarized the electoral process. While the AKP leader, Erdoğan, underlined the party's record of economic stabilization, improvement in living standards and infrastructure development, the CHP leader, Deniz Baykal, based its campaign on the argument that the AKP had used its powers to erode the republican principle of secularism. Yet, winning 46.6 percent of the votes, up nearly 13 points on the 2002 electoral results, the AKP's electoral victory delivered a major rebuff to the CHP. While in the 2002 election, the CHP had received 19 percent of the votes, in 2007, despite its cooperation with the Democratic Left Party (DSP—*Demokratik Sol Parti*), the CHP was only able to increase its share of the vote slightly.

Regarding the ethnic dimension of the ideological spectrum of Turkey, the discourses of the DTP and the MHP were very influential on the campaigns during the 2007 elections. The DTP, whose support base is largely based on the Kurdish population from the southeastern Anatolia and the Kurdish migrants living in metropolitan cities, was established in 2005. The party acts as the successor of the People's Labor Party (HEP—*Halkın Emek Partisi*), Democratic Party (DEP—*Demokratik Parti*), People's Democracy Party (HADEP—*Halkın Demokrasi Partisi*), and Democratic People's Party (DEHAP—*Demokratik Halk Partisi*), which were closed by a court decision on the grounds that they posed a divisive threat to the national unity of Turkey.[9] The party had participated in 2002 as DEHAP but failed to pass the 10 percent threshold, but won massively in some cities in the southeastern regions of Turkey in local elections. In 2007, the DTP ran only through independent candidates in order to avoid the 10 percent threshold and entered the parliament, forming a party group of Kurdish interests. However, it had to confront a great loss of votes in the Southeast region where the pro-Kurdish votes traditionally supported the DTP. This time, many of the Kurdish citizens who voted for DEHAP in 2002, cast their votes to the AKP in this region.[10] The MHP, founded in

1969, represents the nationalist front in Turkey. It followed a rather radical line in the 1970s under the leadership of Alpaslan Türkeş. Yet, until recently, the party's current leader, Devlet Bahçeli has displayed a more moderate nationalist identity in the party.[11] Just as the DTP, the MHP had failed to pass the threshold in 2002. The 2007 election can be considered as a success for the MHP due to its appearance in the parliament with a party group; yet the level of this success is definitely not as high as the AKP's.

The interviews with the local party actors from the AKP, the CHP, the MHP, and the DTP were conducted in 2007 right after the electoral process within such a polarized political context.

The District Selection Criteria

The local party activists and members in this empirical study are selected from four district party organizations: *Karşıyaka, Diyarbakır-Merkez, Tarsus, Ümraniye.* These districts are located in four geographically distant provinces with metropolitan characteristics in Turkey. The selection of the four districts depends on *two criteria*: the degree of urbanization and the local political culture.

The Degree of Urbanization within the Districts

The urban-rural distinction has an evident impact on the structure of district party organizations in Turkey. As previous studies noted, the district party organizations located in urban areas are more organized and less shadowed by one-person rule, in other words they are least likely to be local oligarchies.[12] Therefore, in order to control this variable, the most-similar method was utilized and all the districts were selected from distinctively urban areas in Turkey. The ratio of the urban population to the total population in *Ümraniye, Karşıyaka, Tarsus,* and *Diyarbakır-Merkez* is 72.77 percent, 99.92 percent, 62.14 percent and 75.68 percent respectively.[13] Among these, *Tarsus* is the least urbanized district with the least population size. On the opposite end, *Karşıyaka* is the most, almost fully, urbanized district. Therefore, one might argue that the degree of urbanization among these districts does not meet the conditions of a most-similar method. Yet, they do constitute the best possible sample for this purpose *when* the second selection criterion, local political culture, was and had to be taken into account, which is to be explained below.

The Local Political Culture within the Districts

As outlined in chapter 3, power is a relational phenomenon and power resources of the actors may vary according to different contexts, which lead to different types of power relationships. The local political culture can be an influential factor in providing power resources to the local party actors: for instance, a party may experience a major defeat in national elections, yet gain the majority of votes in one local constituency due to the presence of a dominant ideology in the local constituency. This situation may increase the legitimacy of the local party activists in that constituency, and at the same time, decrease the legitimacy of the national party leaders, altering the equilibrium in the power relationship in favor of the agents.

Thus, in order to understand whether local political culture matters as a power resource of the local agents, the districts were selected using the most-different method, in other words, each district was selected in a way to represent one of the four main cleavages visible in Turkish political culture in 2007; which were secularism versus pro-Islamism, and Kurdish versus Turkish nationalism. In each district, a different political party representing one of these four cleavages had electoral supremacy over the others as observed in Table 5.1. However, it should also be noted that stating "local political culture" as an explanation for the variance in intraparty authoritarianism would oversimplify the theoretical framework of authoritarian party structures; reducing each power relationship between national party leaders and local party actors to be a unique case in itself due to the distinctive cultural aspects of local constituencies. In order to overcome this limitation, thus, interviews were conducted with party activists and members from all parties (AKP, CHP, MHP, DTP) in each selected district and it was observed that it was possible to see variance in intraparty authoritarianism even within the districts.

Karşıyaka, a highly urbanized district of İzmir, is also largely dominated by the populism of the CHP, which grounded its ideology on the Kemalist principle of secularism in the last decade. Yet, the gap between the AKP's and the CHP's vote shares declined from 21 percent to nearly 16 percent from 2002 to 2007. Therefore the election result shows that the AKP was slightly more successful than the CHP in the 2007 election in Karşıyaka, no matter the CHP votes still outnumber the AKP votes. The reason for the AKP success can be explained as its ability to provide an alternative vision of modernity, touching voters in social terms in İzmir rather than the rural-urban distinctions.[14]

In Ümraniye, the AKP maintained its electoral supremacy over the other parties both in 2002 and 2007, even increasing its votes by a seven

Table 5.1   National election results in four selected districts—2002 and 2007

2002 National Election Selected Results over Districts* Percentages			
	AKP	CHP	MHP	DEHAP** (DTP)
Ümraniye	44.56	21.98	4.25	7.46
Karşıyaka	15.79	36.79	6.50	5.06
Tarsus	12.57	22.35	22.58	11.23
Diyarbakır Merkez	16.14	5.08	1.16	60.98

2007 National Election Selected Results over Districts Percentages			
	AKP	CHP	MHP	DEHAP (DTP)***
Ümraniye	51.80	23.85	7.96	6.42
Karşıyaka	27.121	43.569	11.824	3.267
Tarsus	22.585	23.598	36.873	6.047
Diyarbakır Merkez	37.993	1.941	1.841	51.968

Source: Supreme Board of Elections Website.
*In 2002 elections, the MHP and the DEHAP could not overcome the 10% threshold and be represented in the parliament.
**DEHAP was closed by a court decision and replaced by the DTP in 2005.
***In order to overcome the 10% threshold, the MP candidates of the DTP declared to participate in the elections as independent candidates. The percentage of votes for the independents does not represent the whole DTP. Yet it shows the closest results for the DTP votes.

percent margin in 2007. The district is a model for a type of urbanization in which the traditional customs of the rural community life are greatly conserved. Pro-Islamic parties begin to appeal to the conservative social values in *Ümraniye* starting in 1994, reflecting the change in the whole country. With an emphasis on income distribution and the moral necessity of improving the material position of the poor, pro-Islamist parties, have developed wide societal networks both through the parties' local branches as well as the foundations and associations, reaching the demands of the citizens through vernacular politics.[15] The AKP, founded in 2001 through the reformist faction in the pro-Islamic FP, has successfully pursued the same organizational and populist appeal to the residents of *Ümraniye* and become the dominant party in the district since 2001.

In *Tarsus*, the MHP showed a great success in 2007 elections, increasing its votes approximately by 14 percent since 2002, maintaining the highest ratio in the vote share—36.9 percent, and defeating the AKP—22.6 percent, which was the most successful party at the national level. The AKP had increased its votes by 10 percent in *Tarsus* as well but it was still far behind the votes of the MHP. One of the AKP activists stated that it was very difficult in *Tarsus* to break the MHP influence over the society.[16] In fact, in 2009 local elections, the AKP received 27 percent of the votes while the MHP was still dominant with 41 percent, leading to the reelection of the same mayor for the fourth time in *Tarsus*. Since the mayor of *Tarsus* had a big popularity at the local level, even the people who did not form the MHP support base in *Tarsus* had been voting for this mayor in local elections.[17] According to some other rival party activists, though, there was obvious fraud in elections, which was the only explanation for the support of the MHP.[18] The representatives of a small-scale local newspaper in *Tarsus*, on the other hand, stated that it was possible to see several constraints on freedom and press in *Tarsus* due to the cartelization of the MHP in local politics and that their newspaper was subject to several investigations.[19] Due to the migration of many Kurdish citizens from the southeast of Turkey to *Adana* and *Mersin*, there is also a certain support base for the DTP in *Tarsus*. Yet the DTP is represented very poorly because of the financial and organizational constraints that the party is faced with in *Tarsus*.

In *Diyarbakır-Merkez* (central district of *Diyarbakır* province), the DTP is the dominant party due to the presence of a wide pro-Kurdish population. Since the pro-Kurdish parties became important players within the Turkish political system, most of the citizens with Kurdish origin have voted for these parties (DEHAP, HADEP, DTP). *Diyarbakır* is regarded as the capital province for Kurds, where the politics of the whole Kurdish population is produced. In the province of *Diyarbakır*, in the 1999 and 2004 local elections, it was the HADEP and its successor DEHAP respectively that achieved the highest number of votes and therefore conquered the municipal governments. However in 2007 national elections, the AKP, which had become an influential party in the region, challenged the DTP's dominant position. The chief editor of a local newspaper explained that the DTP made strategic mistakes in appealing to the Kurdish citizens through the top-down determination of the candidates in the party; while the AKP approached its potential voters in a very organized and professional manner.[20] Another reason for the decline in the DTP votes was, as explained by a local NGO representative, the party's use of the "old-fashioned" discourse based on the significance of ethnic identities during the electoral campaigns.[21] Another important point in *Diyarbakır-Merkez* was that the CHP votes decreased by a three percent margin whereas the MHP votes increased by a 0.7 percent margin. It was observed that this slight increase in the MHP votes was associated with the personal character of the MHP provincial party chair in *Diyarbakır*.[22] However, the CHP leader Baykal's policy approach toward the pro-Kurdish region and intolerance against the DTP organization reduced the support for the CHP in *Diyarbakır-Merkez*.[23]

Hence, each district represents one of the four main cleavages in the Turkish political context, selected according to the election results in 2002 and 2007. Yet, one might ask if other demographic and societal data could be used other than the election results. It should be noted that it is extremely hard in the Turkish context to associate local political culture with any demographic or societal data (such as education level, number of the unemployed, income level, population age) because there is no clear social or demographic pattern that goes parallel with a certain political context. According to the data provided by the KONDA research group on 2007 elections, for instance, the AKP receives votes from each demographic segment in society.[24] On the other hand, while the CHP receives a higher portion of votes from urban areas compared to rural villages; it is observed that the MHP voters are rarely university graduates.[25] However, these data are still not decisive enough in shaping major political cleavages and therefore would not be determinant in identifying local political cultures.

The Selected Sample of Local Party Activists and Interview Techniques

The number of the party activists to be interviewed in each district from each party was determined in an even and balanced manner for each of the four parties: the objective was to conduct a total of 96 interviews; which would make six interviews for each party in each district: three party officials from local executive boards (representing the LPAs) and three members, usually but not necessarily from the women or youth wings were to be selected. The number of the successful interviews was 91 in total. The profile of the interviewees (gender, education, age, income level, etc) is further illustrated in detail in Appendix B. The reason why in some districts, the goal of interviewing six activists was not achieved is twofold: first, in some places, it was not possible to find an activist at all, just like the case with the MHP in *Diyarbakır-Merkez*. Second, in some district party organizations, the activists were unwilling to speak or give information about their organizational structure to an outsider.

In some occasions, party members and activists can be reluctant to reveal the truth about their parties during the interviews. They may further find it difficult to maintain their objectivity while speaking about party affairs.[26] From time to time, the answers of the interviewees can be based on formalistic statements, either because they may have been instructed to give formalistic replies, or because the real answer is not something that they can make public.[27] Party activists, too, are bound by the party constitution and the authority of their national party leaders. In many instances, the interviewees in this research have requested to hide their identities and from time to time, even turn off the recorder in case the information they provide may simply get them in trouble. In line with the ethical obligations,[28] the interviews have been conducted ensuring that the interviewees—local party activists and members—are protected from any harm. Thus, the identities of the interviewees and their roles in the local party organization are concealed in this study.

Observing the Variance in Intraparty Authoritarianism in Turkey

As discussed in chapter 2, the political culture in Turkey has not only led to the emergence but also the consolidation of authoritarian party structures. The citizens perceive the exclusive and top-down nature of candidate selection and policy formulation processes as what is right or what is normal. The party leaders do not hold any accountability to the party members and the activists. With regards to the authoritarian manner of parties in the candidate-selection practice, the evaluation of the Organization for Security and Cooperation in Europe—Office for Democratic Institutions and Human Rights (OSCE/ODIHR) on Turkey's 2007 election states:

> The OSCE/ODIHR EAM heard numerous concerns about the top-down manner in which candidates' lists had been drawn up...parties did not hold pre-elections or primaries, but reportedly determined candidates by decision of the party leaders. This led to frequent calls for more internal party democracy...[29]

The candidate lists for the parliamentary office were controlled by the national party leaders (NPLs) during the 2007 elections. The AKP declared its methods at the central and organizational enquiry to determine the deputy candidates. Yet, it was solely based on the decision of the party leader, Erdoğan, to determine the candidates.[30] He kept the candidate list as secret until the last day of submission of the lists to the Supreme Board of Elections and the declared results were known to be surprising even for the other influential actors in the elite cadre, such as Bülent Arınç and Abdullah Gül.[31] Most interestingly, out of the existing 341 parliamentary deputies of the AKP in the 2002-2007 parliamentary term, Erdoğan removed 166 of them from the new candidate list. Later on, his decision was boycotted by these removed deputies. In a meeting with ex-deputies, he stated his justification for the removal as:

> Do not consider this issue as something personal, there was a need for renewal in the party. We were satisfied with your performance but this is a relay race. These seats are not permanent for anybody. You might consider it as a mistake but there is nothing intentional against you.[32]

During the candidate-selection process, yet, the AKP leaders conducted opinion surveys among the local party activists. The agenda of these surveys varied from candidate-selection issues to other strategic party decisions. For instance, an activist in *Ümraniye* explained the content of the surveys as follows:

> The surveys that the central party committee carried out during the candidate selection process contained questions like what a parliamentarian should be like and where he or she should be from. There were no suggestions or names of the possible MP candidates on the surveys.[33]

Thus, rather than providing an opportunity to influence the decisions, the surveys conducted within the local party organizations seemed to provide ideational incentives, a sense of belonging to the party for the rank and file.

The CHP was no different from the AKP in candidate-selection process. The lists were under the tight control of the party leader, Deniz Baykal. Only in a few cities, the CHP executive committee decided to organize primaries for the determination of candidates. But these primaries did not affect the final decision of the party leader. One local party executive in *Tarsus* explained the nature of primaries as follows:

> The candidate selection process was not democratic at all. Yes, the primaries were held but they did not determine anything. One of the candidates, who was in the 16th rank according to the primary results, was nominated in the 1st rank by the party leader. One can hardly call this "internal party democracy."[34]

The MHP introduced an electronic voting system for its members to determine the candidates, as pointed out by the party activists. However democratic this process may seem, the final decision belonged to the party leader himself. As one local leader in *Ümraniye* stated:

> I appreciate the e-voting system that our leader introduced to us in this election. Yet, this e-voting system was only a formal democratic procedure.

Just like in other parties, our party members have not influenced the final decision of the party leader in this candidate selection process.'[35]

Furthermore, in *Tarsus* too, the top-down nature of the candidate selection was clear despite the e-voting system:

The central executive committee nominated a candidate that the people in *Tarsus* did not approve. The nominated candidate was not one of us. He might be a well-educated person but since he is not one of us, I am not sure whether he will be able to appeal to our concerns. The party members voted for another candidate during the e-voting process but it is evident that the central executive ignored those results.[36]

The DTP party leadership was another example for the authoritarian behavior of the national party leaders during the candidate-selection process. However, unlike the other parties, the DTP organization strictly obeyed the party constitution, which emphasized a 40 percent gender quota in the candidate lists. A provincial executive committee member explained the process as follows:

To be honest, the candidate selection process in our party was not democratic. I believe that our party sometimes makes mistakes; unfortunately the organizational characteristics of the DTP have begun to resemble other party organizations in the political system. This is the mistake made by our leaders in the central executive committee. The candidates that were determined in this election were the ones with significant ties with the party elite.... However, I am proud of our gender quota and we as local units pressurized the national party leaders to apply the gender quota required by our by-laws. For instance, we wanted Sevahir Bayındır to be placed in the candidate list of *Şırnak*. The central committee insisted to place her in the list of Bursa. But we knew that it was not possible for her to be elected from Bursa. In the end, our demand was realized and she is now an elected parliamentarian from *Şırnak*. We are strict about the 40 percent gender quota.' [37]

As this activist clearly explains, the DTP, in many instances, had to pay special attention to the candidate lists in the southeast region (*Şırnak* is a province located in this region) since a large portion of the DTP support base resides here. In other words, for the specifically desired candidates to be elected, they needed to be placed in the lists of the pro-Kurdish provinces. Even though this activist living in *Karşıyaka* mentioned that they were successful putting organizational constraints on their leaders about their preferences, for the people of *Şırnak*, it might not be the case as the candidate appearing in the top rank of the list is an unknown, unpopular name for them. This situation, in fact, strengthens the claim that intra-party authoritarianism is a relational phenomenon.

Looking at these examples from four parties, it is possible to see that the local party activists and members were excluded from the decision-making processes during the 2007 elections, being subject to certain authoritarianism of their leaders.

Detecting Different Patterns across and within Authoritarian Party Structures

During the field research, the LPAs and LPMs from four districts were asked to respond to the following questions:

1. How do you think an ideal candidate-selection process should be like?
2. Do you think the candidate-selection process was democratic in your party?
3. Do your opinions ever conflict with the policies formulated by the central executive committee? Do you display any actions in con-flictual situations?
4. Do you see any traits of leadership domination (*liderlik sultası*) within your party?

Analyzing the responses, four patterns were observed not only *across* but also *within* the party structures: clandestine, benign, challenged, and coercive. Yet, detecting these four different patterns was not that easy, considering the complexity of the responses that the party activists pro-vided for the questions.

The research analysis started with the assumption that intraparty authoritarianism cannot be a static and uniform phenomenon. Yet, cat-egorizing the responses according to districts and party identities did not provide any harmonious pattern. Party activists from similar parties gave different reactions in different (but not in all) regions. Similarly, it was possible to observe not only a variance but also similarities in the reactions among the parties in the same district. The patterns began to emerge, rather, when the differences in the districts and the party identi-ties were discounted.

The clandestine type of authoritarianism was, then, the first emerg-ing pattern, when a contradiction was found within the response of some interviewees who actually believed that their party was internally democratic even though the candidate-selection process took place in a highly autocratic manner. Later on, it was understood that the top-down nature of the candidate-selection process was internalized by these interviewees and considered as what *should be* in the party. Yet, surely not all the interviewees had the same approach. Among the responses, it was analyzed that there were also many activists who were aware of the undemocratic nature of their party. Yet, there was one big distinction among those who were aware. Some were critical, some were not. The question then became obvious: Why aren't some activists as disturbed as the others about intraparty authoritarianism? It was then realized that these are the activists who actually benefit from the authoritarian structure, receiving material incentives from the party leadership. This type constituted the *benign authoritarianism*.

The group who was critical of the authoritarian party structure constituted the *challenged type of authoritarianism*. Yet, there was a distinction within this group, too: some were taking action against authoritarianism and challenging until their demands were met, yet there were some others who actually challenged and did not act accordingly. Then, the question became, "why would not the latter group take action like the former?" The answer was related to the power resources of the activists. Those who did not act were simply those who *could not,* due to a lack of power resources and a fear of negative sanctions. Yet, among those who took action in challenge, there were some who confronted the coercion of the authoritarian party leaders, leading to their marginalization in the party. This latter type was labeled as *coercive authoritarianism.*

Instances of Clandestine Authoritarianism

In clandestine authoritarianism, local party actors are indifferent to the authoritarian behavior of the central party. The local party actors fulfill their tasks in the way they are asked to and do not question the authority of the party leaders. The conflict is latent between the two levels of party organization. During the field research, clandestine type of authoritarianism was observed within the power structure of three party organizations: the AKP, the DTP, and the MHP. For the AKP, it was observable in *Diyarbakır-Merkez* and *Ümraniye*; for the MHP, it was observable in *Karşıyaka* and for some party activists in *Tarsus* as well; for the DTP it was observable in *Karşıyaka, Tarsus* and *Ümraniye*.

The Justice and Development Party (AKP)
Within the AKP organization in *Diyarbakır-Merkez*, the opinions of the AKP's local members rather than the local activists on the

candidate-selection process provide important insights for clandestine authoritarianism. For example, one district party member in *Diyarbakır-Merkez* stated:

> Of course, our party leader should have the weight in candidate selection process. We would not be working for the party unless we believed in our leader's decisions. Our leader and his perspectives are the reasons for why we are here today.[38]

A similar attitude from another district party member in *Diyarbakır-Merkez* on the candidate selection process is as follows:

> The central party committee asked our opinions on candidate selection before the elections. Our opinions are partly influential; we fill out surveys about the candidates and the results of these surveys are evaluated at the central level. But I believe that the central committee should give the final decision. I do not think leaders' dominance is the case for my party.[39]

The head of the youth wings, on the other hand, from *Diyarbakır-Merkez* stated:

> The candidate selection process was democratic. There were small problems in the process but they are unimportant details. I believe that the AKP is unique, the first of its kind. It will show us the way to true democratic values. We work for this party because we believe in it and we are content with the direction it leads to.[40]

On the question of whether they see any traits of leaders' dominance in their party, most AKP party activists in *Diyarbakır-Merkez* reacted that their party was the most democratic one among others. For instance, two different members from the women wings stated:

> If you asked about the other party organizations, I would say yes. In other parties, the leadership system is similar to the processes in which the authority descends from father to son. I can't say the same thing for the AKP. Because our leader Erdoğan fulfils his duties deservedly.[41]
> Absolutely not! Our leaders ask our opinions on every issue one by one.[42]

In addition to *Diyarbakır-Merkez*, many local party members as well as activists in the *Ümraniye* organization of the AKP gave similar answers, showing another instance for clandestine authoritarianism. The survey method that the AKP central party committee employed seemed to make the party activists content with the authoritarian behavior of the party leaders. One of the district executive board members stated:

> I cannot say that our party is not democratic because our opinions were evaluated on several issues through the surveys that the central executive committee conducted. For instance, the central executive committee asked our opinion on the presidency issue; whether it should be Abdullah Gül whom the party nominates for presidency in the parliament. We all supported his candidacy for presidency because we did not want our prime minister (*the party leader Erdoğan*) to leave the party. In fact, he could easily have nominated himself if he wanted; but our leader values our party so much that he did not choose to do so. He had that power but did not use it. He thought of us. There is no other example for such generosity in this world.[43]

In his statement, the activist refers to one of the highly important decision-making processes within the AKP, nomination for presidency, which occupied the political agenda of Turkey both before and after the 2007 elections. Since the AKP formed the majority of seats in the parliament; the AKP's nominee for presidency had the highest chance of being elected by the parliament. Therefore, the public opinion expected the leader Erdoğan himself to be the AKP's nominee because he had the power to decide, as this activist mentions. What affected his final choice is not known; whether the survey results or his own calculations; yet even though the final decision was made by the central executive committee, Erdoğan seemed to gain the admiration of many local party activists like this example shows for not nominating himself. This situation is a clear evidence for clandestine authoritarianism because the activists not only do not question the leaders' ultimate power in making the decisions but also intensify their commitment to authoritarianism through idolizing their leader.

Another district board member in *Ümraniye* stated that he did think his party had a democratic structure due to the surveys that they completed even though he did not hesitate to criticize the AKP's candidate-selection process. He, in fact, challenged his own statement at the end:

> I really hope to see primaries in the future in candidate selection processes. In the last election, the candidate supported by our district was placed in the 24th rank in the candidate list although the party gained 55 percent of the votes in this district. As a result of this high percentage, we think it is our right to decide on the rankings among the candidates....
> I do not think authoritarianism exists in our party. Our leader values our opinions. If we particularly compare our party with other parties, ours

is democratic, after all, we complete opinion surveys that are evaluated by our leaders.[44]

The other party members in the *Ümraniye* organization also supported the claim that their party was democratic. Another district executive member stated:

> In our party, the method used to determine the candidates was organizational enquiry. We were asked about our own choices. The other party leaders in other organizations do not even ask the opinions of their members.[45]

On the question about "leaders' dominance", an executive board member of the women wings stated:

> There is absolutely no such dominance. Consider other parties, particularly the CHP. That structure is shaped by leadership domination. Our party cannot be compared with such parties.[46]

In addition to the rejection of authoritarianism within their party structures, one of the activists on the question of whether the candidate-selection process was democratic in their party responded quite differently from his colleagues. Such response, in fact, showed an instance for awareness about the authoritarian decision-making structure. Yet, authoritarianism was what *should be* for this activist. He believed that the candidate selection should be made by the sole decision of the leaders. The response came from one of the board members of the district party organization in *Ümraniye*:

> Yes, leadership domination is a clear fact. But this is how it should be. It is the right of the leader to make the final decision. First of all, he derives his power from the people. Only if he abuses that power, there is a problem. But our leader makes several inquiries in the organization and then gives his decisions.[47]

Stating that their party leader derives his authority from the people, this party activist clearly confuses the delegation of authority that comes through general elections with the one that comes through the elections that take place within the party structure. Furthermore, stressing that "only if he abuses that power, there is a problem", the activist, in fact, admits that the party leader can abuse his power if he wants but since he does not do so, he has clear legitimacy in making the final decisions. This attitude is also far from desiring the necessary checks-and-balances in the party structure because when it is further questioned "what would happen if the party leader abused his power," the answer is similar to an expression like "but he does not abuse his power."

A similar attitude was observed in the statement of an activist from the youth wings when he was asked whether his opinions ever conflicted with the policies formulated by the central executive committee. He stated:

> My opinions are mostly in tandem with our leader's decisions. But even if it conflicts, I believe he will make the right decision. I think it is necessary to have an authoritarian structure. The leader must have the dominance in giving the decisions.[48]

In this sense, both responses show that the trust in the party leader's authority brings clandestine authoritarianism, in which the activists do not question the authority of their leader.

The Nationalist Action Party (MHP)

Within the MHP, clandestine authoritarianism was observed particularly in the district party organization in *Karşıyaka*. The loyalty to the party leader was what mattered most to the local party activists and members in this district rather than questioning the authority. Such an attitude is in fact in line with the nationalist ideology of the MHP. One local party activist from the MHP in *Karşıyaka* clearly stated:

> Any decision made by our leader is right. I am not smarter than Devlet Bahçeli. He gave us the right to vote electronically on the candidate lists prior to the elections. He provided this opportunity to us... Authoritarianism? I am irritated by this word. Any person who has the capability, wisdom and foresight becomes the leader. This is natural. We need a leader to govern us. Atatürk was a leader, he saved this country on his own. Nobody can object to this fact. Today as well, only one man can save us all.[49]

Another local MHP leader in *Karşıyaka* stated:

> I was quite satisfied with the candidate list. I did not have any preferences. I do not think there is authoritarianism in our party, it is loyalty to the leader that matters. Furthermore, our party can be considered as democratic because our leader does not make the decisions on his own, he makes them after negotiating with his advisors in the central executive committee.[50]

Another local party member in MHP-*Karşıyaka*, on the other hand, stated:

> The central party organization conducts a research in cities and districts while preparing the candidate lists. This research is something above us. We are probably unaware of several things while the decisions are made. But I was satisfied with the list and I believe in the sincerity of our leader.[51]

These examples show that even though the decision-making on the candidate-selection process was under the strict control of the party leaders—no matter electronic voting was offered to the party members—the local party actors did not believe in the authoritarianism within their party, satisfied with the decisions made, mostly because they trust their leader.

Within the MHP, clandestine authoritarianism was also observed in the LPMs rather than the activists in *Tarsus*. The degree of loyalty to the party leader was higher than the need for democratization within the party according to these members. In response to the question of whether there is leadership domination in the MHP, two party members emphasized the same statement:

> Of course there is. The leader, the doctrine and the organization...These three cannot and must not be questioned.[52]
>
> The dominance of the leader in our party is, of course, a true phenomenon. This country brings up leaders. Devlet Bahçeli has become the leader to fill the void of Türkeş. And it is us, the members, that establish the ground for leaders' dominance. We follow the policy orders of our party leader. We do not step out of his words.[53]

The latter of the two members, in fact, openly confirms that his party is structured on the notion of leaders' dominance, and therefore, it is the duty of the party members to follow the decisions of the party leaders. These members, therefore, believe that they are following the rules and norms upon which their party's ideology is constructed.

The Democratic Society Party (DTP)
The local party actors in the local DTP organization in *Karşıyaka*, *Tarsus*, and *Ümraniye* also provide three instances of clandestine intra-party authoritarianism, analyzed through the attitudes of the local party actors. Even though the candidate selection took place in a very top-down manner, the LPMs and the LPAs all gave very similar answers to the questions on the power structure of their parties, stating that no matter how

centralized the process was, their party, with all its members, accept these decisions because they are all united with the ideology and goal of their party. In addition, intraparty authoritarianism was fully rejected by the LPAs and the LPMs in any case. They have stated that, compared to other parties in the political system, the DTP was the most democratic one because they believed their opinions were valued. The following quotations from the conducted interviews in *Ümraniye*, *Karşıyaka*, and *Tarsus* indicate this common view within the party.

In *Tarsus*, in response to the questions on how candidate selection is and should be conducted within their party, the interviewed DTP activists were nearly in agreement about the democratic nature of their party structure except one. One of activists who agreed with the democratic structure of the party stated:

> There were meetings and conventions held in towns and neighborhoods during the candidate selection process. The central executive board asked whether we accepted the choice they made. There were a total of 21 candidates in *Mersin* and among them it was Orhan Miroğlu that was chosen by the central party organization. During the inquiries, most people preferred Miroğlu in line with the central party's choice and we decided our best to have him elected during the campaigns.[54]

Even though the process that this activist describes seems to have some democratic traits, in terms of Miroğlu's candidacy, another activist mentioned that it was the party center that pressured the local party organization to accept his candidacy. Therefore this activist rejected the claim that the candidate-selection process was democratic. He stated:

> I was against Miroglu's candidacy. He is neither from *Tarsus*, nor from the province of *Mersin*. I told the central executive board that Mersin had a great potential of votes and the candidate should be someone determined by the local people and organizations. The central party organization must respect this process. If the final decision is to be made by the central party executive, then why are we trying so hard here? Such a behavior disappoints the people as well.[55]

Apart from this deviational statement, it was observed that the other DTP activists in *Tarsus* tried to protect their party and did not want to describe their structure as an authoritarian one during the interviews. In fact they have found reasons above their party structure for the nondemocratic manner in the candidate-selection process. One activist explained that the authoritarian decision-making processes in their party derived from the legal and institutional framework of Turkey. He implied that if there had been no constraint like the 10 percent threshold to enter the parliament, their party would be much more democratic. He explained his point of view as follows:

> You know we took part in the elections only through independent candidates. The central executive board must list some important candidates in the lists of the provinces where there is potential for success. In short, it depends on the needs of the party. If there were no threshold, no constraint would be left for our party to enter the parliament; we would have had primaries at the local level. [56]

Another district party activist also gave a similar statement:

> Our party is democratic if you compare it with the other parties in the system. For our party to be fully democratic, this constraining process over the DTP must be over. We do not have the opportunity to be democratic. Most of our parliamentarians are under investigation. Under such circumstances, we cannot actualize democracy in the party. That is why we have witnessed so many impositions by the central executive committee over the local units on selecting candidates; not only in this election but in all previous elections as well. I can say this election process was far better than the previous ones in terms of the degree of democracy in our party. Our opinions were asked to a higher degree.[57]

Another district executive member of the DTP in *Tarsus*, yet, described the latest candidate-selection process as very democratic; stating that it was the provincial and district party chairs that determined the candidates. In response to the question on whether he finds his party democratic, he simply stated:

> If there were no democracy within the party, what would I be doing here? Why would I be trying this hard for my party? It wouldn't be worth to this time and effort I have been spending.[58]

In sum, the responses of the DTP party activists and members in *Tarsus* to the questions regarding the power structure of their parties have been largely inconsistent. Yet, the common ground of their responses was that they did not want to reveal any discontentment about their party structure (except one), and that it was the goal and the ideology of the organization that united them in that party. Parallel to the features of clandestine authoritarianism in which the party activists do not question the authoritarian behavior of the central party elite; they rather blame the external factors and effects.

The DTP party activists in *Karşıyaka* and *Ümraniye* gave very similar responses to the ones in *Tarsus*. They described a candidate-selection process in their local constituency, which was very identical with the process that some of the activists described in *Tarsus*. The decision on the selected candidates was made by the central executive committee; following such decision, the opinions of the LPAs and LPMs were asked on these choices. Yet, just like in *Tarsus*, the responses for the question on "who determines the candidates in your party" were not clear due to the nature of this candidate-selection process. Some activists thought they were influential in the decision-making process; some thought not. One of the district board members in *Karşıyaka* stated:

> It is the people that decide on the candidate lists in the DTP. After all, many public meetings and negotiations were held on this issue even though the final decision on the candidate lists was made by the election committee of the central party office...It is true to state that the party structure is centralized. However, in our party, all local leaders, members, national party leaders as well as the representatives of public office think in the same line. We are all united on these decisions.[59]

Yet another district board member in *Karşıyaka* stated:

> It was the central party office that determined the candidates in our party. Primaries could have been an alternative, but we supported the selected candidates. The central party office issues a notice about the decisions, and we fulfill our duties according to these decisions...I do not think this is an authoritarian process.[60]

Evidently, it did not matter for such activists whether the final decision should be controlled by the national party leaders or not; what mattered most was that they were all united under the party goals. Besides the activists in *Karşıyaka* gave similar responses with the activists in *Tarsus* on the question of whether their party structure was democratic or not. An active member on this topic stated:

> The parties have an authoritarian structure in Turkey; there is no alternative to authoritarian structures. But this is not the case in our party. The leaders do not have the ultimate power in our party, the decisions are made through negotiations, in a democratic manner.[61]

The activists and members in the *Ümraniye* organization of the DTP further stressed on how they were united as a party and the decisions of the party leaders bound them all, even though they were excluded from the decision-making process. The two DTP district board members in *Ümraniye* respectively stated:

> The candidate selection process was initiated collectively. We all shared our ideas on who should be on the list. Yet, there was an election committee formed by the central office and the committee gave the final decision. Some problems do arise when the decisions are not welcome. But we all agree on the list at the end. This is not authoritarianism.[62]
>
> I think that the candidate selection process should be democratic, the opinions of the local party activists must be given due recognition. DEHAP and HADEP [predecessors of the DTP] were centralized; but the DTP is organized in a horizontal way. The central election committee asked our opinions... We rarely disagree on the outcomes. In the end we all come to agree with the decisions and that's how we compete in elections, as a united front.[63]

The expression that "we rarely disagree on the outcomes" not only points to the exclusive nature of candidate-selection process as the activists in local units are asked to agree or disagree with the final decisions of the central executive committee, but also imply that the activists do not challenge the current structure and usually remain content with the decisions due to their commitment to the party, as observed in a clandestine pattern of intraparty authoritarianism.

Instances of Benign Authoritarianism

As outlined in chapter 4, benign authoritarianism is based on the material gains of the local party actors. The party leaders, by providing material incentives to the local party actors, either seek to maintain their power and/or the organizational survival of their party. Even though the conflict is observable, the local actors choose to subordinate to the authoritarian decision-making processes because the leaders simply *purchase* their subordination in the form of monetary benefits or promises for concrete positions in public offices.

During the interviews, even though the materially motivated LPMs and the LPAs usually intended to conceal their true aim in the party, their materialistic interests could be recognized when they revealed their interest in public-office job opportunities that the party organization provided or mentioned that they had close ties with influential party leaders. These actors were aware and critical of the authoritarianism that they experienced in the 2007 candidate-selection process as well as some policies of the central executive committee, yet did not challenge the structure due to the selective benefits they received from the party.

Within the AKP, benign authoritarianism was observed in the relationship between the central executive board and some local party actors in *Diyarbakır-Merkez*, as well as most local party actors in *Tarsus*. It was also observable within the CHP in *Tarsus* and the DTP in *Diyarbakır-Merkez*.

The Justice and Development Party (AKP)

In *Diyarbakır-Merkez*, the statements of the local party members showed a clandestine pattern of authoritarianism in the relationship between the AKP's central leaders and the local party members. Yet, the relationship between the central executive committee and the LPAs was constructed on a benign type of authoritarianism during the time the interviews were conducted. It was observed that the LPAs such as the district party chairs or executive board members, often preferred to have close ties with the AKP central party office because the AKP had become the single party in government after the 2007 elections and gained major access to state resources. *Diyarbakır* as a province is located in a strategic region, the southeast of Turkey, where the number of votes for the AKP started increasing, and it was in the interest of the national party leaders to make more investment in this province to win the upcoming 2009 local elections. The AKP constitution designates the allocation of 30 percent of the party budget to the local party organizations;[64] and the information received from the interviewed party activists was that, the *Diyarbakır* provincial organization was particularly one of those organizations, which received its share from this budget to a certain degree; creating a great selective incentive for the LPAs to have good relations with the central executive board of the party. It was further observed that the district party organization was receiving other types of state resources as well. An activist from the district executive board stated:

> There were funds allocated to us from the Ministry of Agriculture in the previous term. Besides, the parliamentarians and some ministers provide financial assistance to a great extent. The governorship of *Diyarbakır* also sponsors our activities on some occasions.[65]

Together with the legal monetary share received from the central party budget, many rich businessmen donated to the AKP. Another district party activist stated:

> Our central party committee distributes a certain amount of money to the district and provincial party organizations, as stated in the AKP by-laws.

But in *Diyarbakır*, there is a high density of action and movement in the political arena. The province and the district welcome many visitors such as high-level officials and delegations. So we need more than those allowances given to our organization. Fortunately, the businessmen, who are highly committed to the party, make donations as well.[66]

Apart from the rich financial resources that the AKP organization in *Diyarbakır-Merkez* had, the local leaders had close ties with the deputies in the parliament as well. A district party activist in *Diyarbakır-Merkez*, for instance, stated:

I have been an active member in this district organization since 2004. I was very affected by the hardworking spirit of our party leader when he was the mayor of Istanbul. Furthermore, the AKP deputy of *Diyarbakır*, who is as hardworking as our leader himself, offered me to work together in the AKP.[67]

Two prominent local leaders in *Diyarbakır-Merkez* also mentioned in the interviews that they were spending their entire time for the party. These statements raise skepticisms regarding the real source of their own personal income because they indeed had professions outside of the political arena in jobs related to commerce and construction. The two respectively stated:

I spend all my time on party activities. Everyday, I either work in the local office or attend outdoor party activities. Since the previous chair resigned after declaring his candidacy for the parliamentary office, I have been appointed as the new chair of this district party organization. Since then, I am very busy.[68]

I am an architect. Before I became a member of the AKP in *Diyarbakır*, I was working in the construction business. Now I spend my entire time in the party.[69]

When the local leaders were asked what their opinions were on the authoritarian nature of their party's structure, they did not hesitate to criticize the current system in candidate selection. The district party chair clearly stated:

There were 86 applications for candidacy in the *Diyarbakır* province. Surveys were conducted in a way to determine the first 10 positions in the candidate list. Our provincial party chair was a candidate himself and he maintained the highest rank in the surveys.... However, I should say the central executive board has control over the list. Our provincial party chair who was supported at the highest level by our local party organization did not appear in the first rank in the candidate list.[70]

Even though the district party activist was not content with the fact that the provincial party chair in *Diyarbakır* was not placed in the first two ranks, he did not initiate any challenge against the authoritarian candidate-selection process due to the expected material benefits he could be receiving from an important position he had in a prominent district.

The AKP organization in *Tarsus* was also based on a benign type of intraparty authoritarianism. In *Tarsus*, unemployment constitutes one of the most solemn social problems, particularly among the youth. In this respect, many young people seek jobs through the channels of the AKP local organization. Yet, just like the local party activists in *Diyarbakır-Merkez*, they do criticize the candidate-selection process in their party. An activist from the youth wings stated:

> I can't say that the candidate selection process was democratic in the last election. But these things are accepted as they are. I hope in the next elections, we will experience a democratic process.[71]

No matter how unsatisfied he was with the candidate-selection process, this young party activist did not put any effort to challenge the system and "accepted things as they are" because he was actually looking for a job position within the party organization in *Tarsus*. As an unemployed high school graduate, he mentioned that he had worked as a serviceman within the party before. In fact, his friend, another activist of the youth wings of his own age, continues to work as a party personnel in the data processing section of the AKP *Tarsus* organization. His friend also stated the same criticism on the party's candidate selection process:

> The candidates should be determined through the organization not only by the central executive committee. But unfortunately, it is not processed in this way in our party.[72]

Yet due to the benefits he gets from the party in terms of having a job, this youth activist also does not challenge the authoritarianism within the party. A similar attitude came from the executive board member of the women wings who stated:

> I think there should be primaries for selecting candidates. It should be the people that decide. Even though there was an organizational enquiry

on determining the candidates, the final list was prepared by the central executive committee, which was highly different from the list we prepared.[73]

While this activist from the women wings stated her criticism in this realm, she also did not challenge the party structure because later on she mentioned she had close ties with one of the AKP parliamentarians.

The Republican People's Party (CHP)

The CHP district party organization in *Tarsus* is another example for benign authoritarianism. In the district, a close relationship between some LPAs or LPMs and one of the CHP parliamentarians was observed. In fact, the local chair in *Tarsus* has mentioned his kinship with this parliamentarian. Being close to influential people, the district party activists and members in *Tarsus* have the motivation to work for the party, despite the accepted nature of the authoritarianism that the central party office pursues in decision-making processes. In fact they openly criticized their party's authoritarian structure. One of the members of the district executive committee openly stated:

> The district party organizations are subject to the policy program that is prepared by the central party office. We do not take part in policy formulation processes. In this sense, it would be true to say that there is authoritarianism within the CHP.[74]

Another active member stated:

> *Mersin* (where *Tarsus* is located) is one of the provinces where our party held primaries. We sent the results to the central executive committee but unfortunately the central party organization, following the orders of the party leader made changes on the candidate list. I think this was a huge mistake made by the central party organization. I do not know why they did so. Of course the central party must have some certain influence but not in this way, it should respect the primary results.[75]

The undemocratic candidate-selection process was critically described in detail by one of the district delegates of the CHP organization in *Tarsus*:

> The candidates were determined in a highly undemocratic manner in the last election. The central party organization intervened in the list, which had come out as the result of the local primaries. For instance, the candidate who was in the first rank of the list was dropped down to the second

place. The candidate in the second rank was placed in the fourth. The candidate, whose name ranked in the sixteenth place, suddenly emerged in the first place. Similarly the candidate who was ranking in the ninth place went up to the third place.[76]

During the informal conversations with the local party activists in *Tarsus*, it was later on, observed that the parliamentarian who had close ties with this district was the one who received the first rank in the primaries but then dropped down to the second place after the central party organization's intervention. Since the CHP gained three seats from *Mersin* in the parliamentary election, the candidate supported by the *Tarsus* party organization could be elected as a parliamentarian. Due to the close relationship with this parliamentarian, the activists and members in the district party organization expected to have material benefits and continue to be an active member of the CHP in *Tarsus*, without initiating any challenges to the authoritarian party structure. In fact, the activist profile in *Tarsus* was largely composed of the relatives and the close friends of this parliamentarian.

The Democratic Society Party (DTP)

The last example for benign authoritarianism is the district party organization of the DTP in *Diyarbakır-Merkez*. In fact, almost all DTP activists and members in each of the four districts underlined that their party had a very democratic structure compared to other parties in the system and that the members act as a united front, defending the rights of the Kurdish people and further democratization for their rights. Even though the candidates were determined in a very exclusive manner, the local party actors were almost of the same opinion on the internal democracy of their party (with a few exceptions). The rhetoric on internal democracy also included two more issues: 40 percent gender quota in the candidate lists and the party's coleadership system. The indifference toward the exclusion of the LPMs and LPAs from the decision-making processes, thus, moved the party toward a clandestine type of authoritarianism. The district party organization in *Diyarbakır-Merkez* also, at first glance, showed similar patterns with clandestine authoritarianism. In fact, regarding the question on "how is and should be the candidate selection process in your party organization", the DTP activists in *Diyarbakır-Merkez* again responded staying in the habitual line of answers. Two active members respectively stated:

> The candidates are determined in a decision-making process where both the central and local party organizations have voice. Several meetings are

organized at the local level, first at the provincial and then at the district level with the party members whose opinions are sought. After an in-depth evaluation, the results are announced. But, it is important to integrate the local organizations into the decision-making process and that is how it is initiated in our party.[77]

You know this is a district where the tribal ties are very strong; and it prevents the democratization of such decision-making processes. In spite of this disadvantage, we are following a very democratic line in our party. We want the candidates to be selected by the local people. We are trying so hard to this end. Sometimes we can face small problems, but most of the time we are very successful in being a democratic party.[78]

The "small problems" referred in this statement is related to the authoritarian nature of decision-making, which has in fact led to a great loss in the DTP votes in *Diyarbakır*. As the chief editor of a local newspaper explained:

In this election, the DTP failed to convince its own support-base about its honesty. At one point, the DTP states that it is a party of the people, for the people. But the people in *Diyarbakır-Merkez* have become skeptical of their attitude because the leaders made strategic mistakes in preparing candidate lists. The top ranks of the lists were filled with unpopular names in *Diyarbakır*. People showed reaction against that. Why was there no name in the list from *Diyarbakır*?[79]

Despite this fact, during the interviews, the party members and activists followed the same line of argument in evaluating the degree of democracy in their party. It was observed that, in reality, the party organization was subject to the benign authoritarianism of the national party leaders. The LPAs had close ties with the public officials in local offices. In fact, a scholar from the *Diyarbakır* region observed:

The DTP as a party organization has a material bond with the municipality in *Diyarbakır*. It is very obvious that the two institutions work very closely; in *Diyarbakır*, they do not keep such bonds secret.[80]

Because *Diyarbakır-Merkez* has a very dominant Kurdish population, the DTP, a party with a discourse based on Kurdish rights, is very powerful in that district. The local context in *Diyarbakır-Merkez*, produces materially motivated party activists expecting to be given positions in the municipal public offices as well as jobs that the municipal officers can find through their personal contacts. A similar remark was made by the representative of a local newspaper about the DTP, while explaining the degree of loss that the DTP experienced in the 2007 national elections in *Diyarbakır-Merkez*:

> The DTP is a party, which articulates its sincerity and care for the disadvantaged groups in the society. However, during the election process, the local party activists and members displayed a very antipathetic behavior, driving luxurious cars in public places, even within the poor and underprivileged neighborhoods. People want to know how the party officials in *Diyarbakır* have become so rich.[81]

In this sense, the party activists and members in *Diyarbakır-Merkez* seem to be more interested in material benefits, therefore show contentment with the candidate lists prepared under the control of the central executive committee.

Instances of Challenged Authoritarianism

In challenged authoritarianism, the national party leaders are faced with a challenge initiated from the bottom against the authoritarian party structure. The challenge in intraparty authoritarianism occurs when the local party actors, first, "frame" an identification of the new dilemmas and tensions that have internally arisen and second, through operationalize action, giving effect to this new "frame".[82] The tensions can arise following the exogenous and endogenous events such as defeats in the elections or nomination of the MP candidates who are considered as inappropriate by the local party actors.

In the cases where challenged authoritarianism was observed within the four selected parties in Turkey, the local party actors were either in the "framing" process or in the "operationalizing" process of challenging the authoritarian structure. In the latter, the local party actors utilize their alternative power resources such as information, local legitimacy, social and economic status to undermine the authority of the national party leaders in their local constituency. In the former, the local party actors attitudinally challenge the authoritarian party structure, which has the potential to lead to a behavioral challenge should the necessary power resources are generated or used. In the cases of MHP—*Diyarbakır-Merkez* and AKP—*Karşıyaka*, challenged authoritarianism was observed in the operationalization process. In the cases of CHP—*Diyarbakır-Merkez*, MHP—*Tarsus,* and MHP—*Ümraniye* challenged authoritarianism was observed in the framing process.

The Nationalist Action Party (MHP)
MHP—Diyarbakır: the power relationship between the MHP's central party organization and the MHP in the province of *Diyarbakır* is a good example for challenged authoritarianism. Since the district party organization in *Diyarbakır-Merkez* was highly under the control of the provincial party chair; it was, in fact, the words of the provincial party chair on behalf of all districts in *Diyarbakır* that posed a challenge to the central party organization's power:

> The central party organization must support my words or otherwise I would quit being the provincial party chair here. As the provincial party organization, we constantly submit reports about the region (meaning the districts within *Diyarbakır*) to the attention of the central party organization. In our reports, we state the needs and demands of the people and the central party organization recognizes the fact that we must proceed according to our own local plans.[83]

In this statement, the provincial party chair underlines the obligation of the central party organization to take into account the words of the local party organizations. In other words, he states that the party leader must follow the local agent's lead, not *vice versa*, in order to be successful in that constituency.

It was further observed in *Diyarbakır* that the candidate-selection process caused a conflict between the local party organization and the central party organization of the MHP. Even though the first place in the candidate list was assigned to the provincial chair by the central party organization as expected; the second place was, unexpectedly, assigned to an unknown person, which caused the conflict between the activists and the party leader, Bahçeli. Yet, that conflict was resolved in line with the demands of the provincial organization. Two local party activists explained the process as follows:

> The candidates were determined by the central party organization. They did not ask our opinion; however we knew that the name of the provincial party chair would be on top of the candidate list, but we were surprised to see an unexpected name in the second place.[84]
>
> The party leader, Bahçeli had previously told me to form the candidate list at the provincial level and that they (*central party*) were going to approve the exact list we prepared. However, when we saw the final list approved by the central party organization, we realized that the second place was assigned to a name we did not know. The list was changed. It was a major mistake made by the central party organization. Later on Bahçeli explained that it was his advisors who changed the list without

his permission. Anyway, this was a mistake and we hope that it will not recur…If any conflict happens, I will quit being the provincial chair here.[85]

As this example shows, the MHP provincial party organization in *Diyarbakır* reacted against the rising conflict with the central party organization, underlining that it was the decisions of the MHP—*Diyarbakır* that must be taken into consideration regarding the politics of *Diyarbakır*, otherwise the local chair repeatedly stated the phrase "otherwise I will quit". At this point, it is plausible to ask why the central party organization has to take into consideration the decision of the provincial party organization and not let the local chair resign from his position. It is because the "agency cost" would probably be much higher. *Diyarbakır* is a province where the MHP lacks a great deal of support since the nationalist ideology of the MHP creates a certain disadvantage for the party to gain votes in a place that is highly populated by the Kurdish people. Despite the lack of MHP legitimacy in this district, the party achieved a significant success in gaining a notable number of votes in 2007 national elections.[86] It was mainly because the MHP-*Diyarbakır* managed to appeal to the *Diyarbakır* people in a manner different than the MHP central party organization.

MHP—Tarsus: in *Tarsus*, the MHP is the most dominant party in electoral terms (see the results of 2002 and 2007 elections in Table 5.1). Besides, since 1994 local elections, for four consecutive terms, the MHP managed to seize power, taking hold of the municipality of *Tarsus*.[87] In this sense, both the central party office and the local party office have legitimacy in the district.

Yet, the conflict over the 2007 candidate list between the central party organization and the district party organization has led to a challenge by the district party leaders against the central party organization. The district party chair commented on this issue, yet hesitated to state his views openly during the interview:

I do not want to assert my own opinion on who should have been in the candidate list. In 1999 and 2002 it was the delegates that shaped the candidate lists, however in 2007 elections the names of the candidates were assigned by the central party organization.[88]

One of the members of the district executive board explained this process more openly as follows:

The central party office determined the candidate list without asking our opinion. One of the leading candidates was not really wanted by our constituency because he cannot appeal to the people. I do not think he can serve to the people in *Tarsus* because he is originally not from here. Since any candidate is likely to be elected from *Tarsus* because of the ascendancy of our party here, the central party office placed its own candidate on top of the list. As a result, he was elected but we were very disturbed and sent our complaints to the central party office. The central party office cannot ignore the local dynamics here.[89]

As this example shows, the conflict between the district party organization and the central party organization was not yet resolved, however, the local activists began framing the tensions and the dilemmas they were facing. Since *Tarsus* is known as a district with a strong MHP support base, the local leaders believe that they should be the ones in determining the candidates from that region. In this sense the MHP dominance in *Tarsus* provides a power resource for the local leaders.

MHP—Ümraniye: similar to the previous cases, the MHP in *Ümraniye* initiated a challenge against the central party office regarding the authoritarian nature of the candidate-selection process, yet this challenge also remains at the "framing" level and is the least likely to operationalize due to the lack of certain power resources of the local party organization (information, status, economic well-being, control of local constituency). A district party activist in *Ümraniye* stated:

> The candidate selection process was extremely undemocratic. I do not believe that the e-voting system used by our central party organization was influential at all. It was rather symbolic or even *deceiving.* The candidate names that I brought to the attention were not even considered. If we are to give accurate information on the candidate selection process, I am telling you that it was not democratic (emphasis added).[90]

As noticed in the statement by the district party activist, there is a clear and strict criticism on the MHP's candidate-selection process. The same activist further stated that he delivered his organization's discontentment regarding this process to their superiors in the party (provincial party organization), together with their opinion on how candidate selection should be pursued. However, unlike the MHP—*Tarsus*, the MHP organization in *Ümraniye* did not have the necessary power resources to operationalize the initiated the challenge.

The Justice and Development Party (AKP)

AKP—Karşıyaka: Karşıyaka has been one of the most problematic districts for the AKP organization as the district lacks a great deal of electoral support due to the influence of the CHP secularism in the constituency.

As a result, the AKP central party organization does not have much legitimacy in the district. However in 2007 elections, a 12 percent increase was observed in the AKP votes in *Karşıyaka*. It was noted by the interviewees that the reason why the AKP votes increased was to a certain extent because of the strong link of the local AKP organization with the *gecekondu* inhabitants living in *Karşıyaka*. This situation, in turn, has created power resources for the local AKP to challenge the authoritarianism within the party.

It was observed that the LPAs in Karşıyaka and the NPLs already had very tense relations in policy related issues and that the conflicts over the candidate-selection process further fueled this tension. An influential district party activist from the AKP in *Karşıyaka* stated:

> The candidate selection process was undertaken by central enquiry in this constituency. There should have been a primary because it is the local people who can determine the best candidates for office. The party leader should not interfere in the decision-making process that belongs to the locals. Regarding the national policy issues, the central party office sometimes takes our opinion but I do not think that they even pay attention to our opinions in making their decisions. We were highly disturbed by this behavior of the central party office and we sent our complaints to the central office…'[91]

The Republican People's Party (CHP)

The CHP lost a majority of votes in the southeastern region including *Diyarbakır* because prior to the elections, the CHP adopted a very exclusive approach toward the Kurdish issue. Even though it gained around 21 percent of the votes nationwide, the party had a highly inflexible support base composed of the urban middle class.[92] The CHP in *Diyarbakır-Merkez* challenged the authoritarian behavior of the central party organization both in candidate selection and policy determination processes. One of the activists stated:

> We think that it should be the local party organizations that determine candidates for public office. Primaries can be held to this end. We discuss these possibilities at our executive board meetings, and we have not really made any attempt to change things. We will prepare a report and send our demands to the central party office soon.[93]

On policy issues, another district party activist stated:

> Of course there is a major difference between our opinions and the central party organization. We are more knowledgeable about the politics of the Southeast. For instance, I do not support our leader on his view that

military operations should be undertaken in Northern Iraq in a way to solve the Kurdish problem. We do not find him convincing on these matters. But no matter we state that we are in disagreement with them on these issues, the people in *Diyarbakır* take their opinions into account. We do try to make the party leaders see what we see here but of course central party organization has the power and we cannot achieve a lot to this end.[94]

Instances of Coercive Authoritarianism

The conducted field research has found out two instances of coercive authoritarianism among the 16 cases: the CHP local activists in *Karşıyaka* and *Ümraniye* were subject to the coercive authoritarianism by the national party leaders, who posed negative sanctions on the local members and leaders, causing a threat of marginalization of their status within the party.

The district of *Karşıyaka*, together with other districts in the province of *İzmir*, is located in an overwhelmingly secularist context, close to the ideology of the CHP. The district party organizations in Izmir and the neighbor provinces have initiated a collective challenge against the party leader, after the defeat in elections. Yet, the reaction from the party leader was coercive, and the members of these district party organizations were subject to marginalization (and later on forced to leave the party). The district party organization of *Karşıyaka* was one of those district organizations subject to these *ex post* negative sanctions; the threat of marginalization from the party. The interviews conducted in *Karşıyaka* took place in a very tense, uneasy atmosphere in which the local party members and activists hesitated to provide sincere answers related to candidate selection or internal party democracy.[95] While the number of interviews conducted could not reach the target number six and remained at four, the interviewed activists were also not willing to share information during the recorded interviews. Yet, they could criticize the party leadership off-the-record. Only one of the activists in *Karşıyaka*, during the recorded interviews could openly state:

> There is no need to hide anything. Coercion does exist within our intra-party dynamics. In determining the candidates, we are pressured to select those in line with the central organization's choice. I wish it were our free will that could determine the candidates but it is not true for our party.[96]

The district party organization of the CHP in *Ümraniye* is another organization subject to the coercive authoritarianism of the party leader due to similar reasons. In fact, by the time of the interviews, the organization had a new district party chair, appointed by the party leadership. The new district chair explained that the previous local administration in *Ümraniye* was "removed as a whole due to the conflicts with the party leadership."[97] What was rather observed in *Ümraniye* was a transition from coercive authoritarianism to a clandestine authoritarianism with the new appointed local CHP administration. A newly appointed district activist stated:

> Our leader might seem antipathetic for our society nowadays but what can we change about this situation? People cannot determine their leaders in a capitalist society today, it is the system that determines the leaders. I will be an active party member within the CHP, no matter what. I have been with the CHP for long years. The principles of Atatürk are what we are here for.[98]

Conclusion

Table 5.2 summarizes the findings of the research with respect to the variance in intraparty authoritarianism across and within four parties

Table 5.2 Variance in intraparty authoritarianism among 16 PA structures

Agents in districts	Local political context	AKP principals	MHP principals	CHP principals	DTP principals
Agents in Karşıyaka	Secularism (CHP support)	Challenged	Clandestine	Coercive	Clandestine
Agents in Diyarbakır-Merkez	Pro-Kurdish stance (DTP support)	Clandestine & benign	Challenged	Challenged	Benign
Agents in Tarsus	Nationalism (MHP support)	Benign	Clandestine & challenged	Benign	Clandestine
Agents in Ümraniye	Religious conservatism (AKP support)	Clandestine	Challenged	Coercive	Clandestine

← Variance within Parties →

← Variance across Parties →

(AKP, MHP, CHP, DTP) based on the relationship between the NPLs and the local party actors. According to these findings, intraparty authoritarianism varies not only *across* but also *within* party organizations.

There are seven instances of clandestine authoritarianism in which the local party actors are unaware of or are indifferent to the authoritarian party structure. There are four instances of benign authoritarianism where the local party actors do not challenge the authoritarian party structure due to the material benefits they receive from their leaders. There are five instances of challenged authoritarianism, in which the local party actors initiate a challenge against the central party organization. There are, on the other hand, only two instances of coercive authoritarianism, both within the CHP in which the challenging actors are silenced by the central party organization through negative sanctions. In the next chapter, these findings will be analyzed and explained, testing the hypotheses set in chapter 3 and chapter 4.

6

Explaining the Variance in Intraparty Authoritarianism in Turkey

Chapter 5 has demonstrated the four patterns of intraparty authoritarianism—clandestine, benign, challenged, and coercive—observed within the 16 relationships between the national party leaders and local party actors from four districts and four party organizations of Turkey. Having observed such variance, the aim of this chapter is to investigate the empirical plausibility of the theoretical arguments outlined in Chapter 3 and 4: First it shows that the principle-agent (PA) relationship within these party organizations is constructed in a way where the national party leaders (NPLs) act as the principals and the local party activists (LPAs) and the members (LPMs) are the agents. Second, it outlines the variance in intraparty authoritarianism as the consequence of the differentiation in interest configurations between these principals and agents based on two variables: (1) the differences between the material and ideational interests of the agents; (2) the exogenous and endogenous triggers in the political system altering the *status quo* in these interest configurations. For the exogenous and endogenous triggers to be influential on the power structure within parties, the agents must further possess sufficient *power resources*—such as information, social and economic status, legitimacy—that can challenge the authoritarianism within parties. The exit from authoritarianism in party organizations also depends on the magnitude and type of these power resources.

This chapter is organized in the following order: In the first section, the nature of the PA relationship is shown in four parties—AKP, MHP, CHP, DTP—based on the statements of the interviewed LPAs. The Turkish case, in this sense, proves that the power is vested in the NPLs as the principals delegating their authority to the LPAs, who are generally appointed to their positions by their superiors rather than being elected in local conventions. The LPAs therefore represent the interests of the NPLs, rather than societal interests.

The second section of the chapter will explain the structure of the interest configurations between the agents and principals based on the two types of interests—material and ideational—as discussed in chapter 4. The distinction in the types of interests derives from the statements of the LPAs and LPMs regarding their motivations for joining the party. The interest configurations within the party structures have a *constitutive* impact on the nature of the power relationship between the principals and the agents in the party. In this chapter, the reason why in some cases the pattern of authoritarianism is clandestine and in other cases it is benign is exemplified through revealing the distinction between the types of interests that the local party actors seek.

The third section of the chapter discusses the role of exogenous and endogenous triggers as well as the power resources of the LPAs: During the interviews, the educational and economic status of the LPAs, their social prestige, relations with the party members, the voters, as well as the degree of control that they exert over their local constituencies have been questioned to reveal their power resources. As long as the party actors have the necessary power resources, the exogenous and endogenous events—such as electoral defeats or outcomes of candidate selection processes—may lead to a challenge against intraparty authoritarianism. Thus, the lack of power resources in some cases explains why challenged authoritarianism does not take place in a few expected cases at the time of the endogenous/exogenous triggers.

The Principal-Agent Relationship within Party Structures in Turkey

In authoritarian party structures, NPLs delegate their authority to the LPAs to act on behalf of their own interests, including the organizational interests such as office-seeking and vote-seeking aims. This type of delegation is even more evident when the LPAs—the district party chairs, heads of the district women and youth wings, and district executive board members—are appointed to their positions on approval by the national party leaders rather than being elected at the local level.

It is important to highlight that the Law on Political Parties (SPK—*Siyasi Partiler Kanunu No:2820*) in Turkey does not permit the appointment of the district party chairs or the executive boards by their superiors. According to the law, it is rather the local conventions where the party delegates elect these chairs and local executive boards.[1] Furthermore it is stated by the law that the district party chairs can only be elected for a three-year term.[2] However, most practices within the four selected parties have shown that the formal election process of the district party chairs takes place only after they are appointed by the NPLs. In other words, first, the appointment from above takes place in the party; second, in order to show congruence with the legal provisions, the local leaders get elected in local conventions. The structure of the local conventions, on the other hand, comprises delegates who are selected under the control of the district party organization's leadership circle.[3] One of the party activists who did not want to reveal his identity and district, explained the delegate selection process as follows:

> Basically, it is the district party leader who determines the delegates in the conventions. Prior to the conventions, the delegates are invited to dinners and feasts in a way to guarantee the vote. The elections during the conventions take place in line with the legal framework because they are supervised by district election boards. It is the process prior to the conventions that causes trouble.[4]

The following examples from the statements of the LPAs will show how the PA relationship between the local party actors and NPLs is constructed within the power structure of the selected parties.

The Justice and Development Party (AKP)

"Appointment" as a method of selecting district party chair is not indicated in the AKP constitution. On the contrary, the party constitution states that district chairs are elected in district party conventions through secret voting.[5] However, an AKP district chair explained his experience as follows:

> I became the district party chair as soon as I became a member of the AKP. Our provincial party chair suggested me to be the party chair of this district. There were a total of 5 candidates including me who considered the position of district party chair. The central executive committee of the party conducted interviews with these 5 candidates because they wanted to be acquainted with the candidates. Later on, they chose me. After I was appointed to this position, a district convention took place in March 2006. I was elected in that convention. There was no other candidate competing with me. [6]

This example shows that the local party leader is not an elected representative of the party in that constituency, but rather an appointed agent of the central party office. The appointment of the party members to the local executive boards means, in a way, the delegation of authority from above to the lower branches in the party. Other examples for similar PA relationships within the AKP is observed as follows:

> I was invited to this position by the friends who were active in the provincial executive board. I mean it was an offer. I think they thought I was an honest person who could be involved in the AKP activities in a more detailed way.[7]

According to the AKP Constitution, the district party chairs and the members of the district executive boards are elected together as their names appear in the same candidate list at the convention. For a competition to occur in such conventions, there must be more than one list of candidates running for local executive boards. In his statement, the board member of the AKP in *Diyarbakır-Merkez* explained there was only one list of candidates including his name during the convention:

> There was one list of candidates running for the local executive office in the 2006 district convention and that is why there was no competition. However, the convention took place in tandem with the rules and provisions of the AKP constitution.[8]

The rest of the interviewed AKP activists in *Diyarbakır-Merkez*, also indicated that they were appointed to their position by their superiors. A member of the district executive women board in *Diyarbakır-Merkez* indicated that she was appointed to her position by her superiors from the upper executive boards in the party. She stated:

> While I had duties in the local administration of the party, I was participating in several meetings; now I am a member of the district executive board of the women wings here. I have to spend a lot of time and effort for the party activities. I came to this position through appointment. In other words, both the head of the women wings and the provincial party chair in Diyarbakır brought me here. I am the second person leading the women wings in this district and I am very satisfied with where I am.[9]

It was possible to observe a similar type of PA structure (local party actors = agents, national party leaders = principals) in other districts of the AKP as the following examples indicate. Another party activist in *Ümraniye* stated:

> I came to this position through an offer by the central party organization. I knew people at the central and provincial party headquarters since I was previously the head of the youth wings in the provincial organization.[10]

Apart from the appointments, there is another striking example that shows the top-down nature of the PA approach in the party: A party activist who pursued her own initiative to establish a department for the disabled groups in the district party organization, had to consult this with her superiors, even with the national party leader, Erdoğan, as it was not under the will of the district party organization to establish it. She stated:

> I was brought to the executive board of the district two years ago. Before that, I was the head of the department for the disabled groups. I had been working with a parliamentarian on projects related to the disabled and disadvantaged groups. Moreover, I had attended a dinner where I had the opportunity to tell our leader Mr. Erdoğan to establish a department for the disabled in the party and he basically said if I were to be the head of this department, it should surely be established. Since I was the founder of this department in the district, they offered me to take part in the executive board as well and represent the disabled. Afterwards, I was also elected in the district convention together with the other candidates in the list.[11]

Another point mentioned in this statement is the close tie that the local activist had with a parliamentarian from the party, which she saw as her superior. In this respect, this statement further strengthens the assumption that even the party in public office sometimes acts as the principal of the local party organizations. Another example on this issue is stated below:

> I have been appointed as the head of the women wings in the district. I was first an activist in towns and villages pursuing women activities, then I got appointed to the department of economic relations where I had the chance to work closely with our parliamentarian, Alev Dedegil. We were working on several projects together, but the work did not contain fieldwork. I wanted to be a part of the fieldwork so I requested for a position change in the party and later on I was appointed to this position through her.[12]

The following two statements from *Ümraniye* and *Tarsus* are two youth-wing activists respectively, who further prove the top-down PA structure. The leader of the youth wings is appointed to his position by his superiors, and the convention takes place after the appointment is realized, leaving no room for competition in the convention:

> I was working with the local executive board previously, particularly focusing on media and human resources. I spent nearly most of my time in the party. I participated in all the programs, never missing any one of

them. Continuity is a must. If you continue to participate in these events, you have the possibility to promote. In our party, the activists receive tasks from their superiors. The youth wings are partially independent, I was brought to this position by the head of the central youth wings. But of course, your actions also have to be in conformity with the activities of the district executive board.[13]

We are waiting for our new leader of the youth wings in the district. He will be appointed soon. We will continue to work with the new leader. The district youth convention will take place in a month afterwards.[14]

Similarly, the influential district party activists in *Tarsus* were appointed to their position being subject to no election in the party convention. As one activist stated:

I was a founding member of the party and then appointed to the executive board. I have acted as a vice-chair, responsible for local administration. There were no elections in the convention.[15]

The following two statements made by the district women wings of *Tarsus* and *Karşıyaka* respectively are two further examples for the top-down PA structure:

I have been the head of the women wings for six years now in this district. I was appointed by the central women wings. I knew a parliamentarian. He told me that I could be good at this task and since I was a retired nurse, I began working in this place since he asked me to do. Afterwards, I was elected in the convention of 2004 and there was no other candidate running against me. There is another women wings convention soon and I have to register 400 delegates for this convention.[16]

I have always worked within the women wings. I am the head of the women wings now. In the district party organization, I am also a substitute member of the executive board. I worked very hard, spent a lot of time and money, initiating a local newspaper for the AKP *Karşıyaka* district. After working this hard, the district executive board appointed me to this position in the party.[17]

In cases where the local actors were *not* appointed to their positions by their superiors, the top-down character of the PA relationship was observable in the tasks given to the local party actors by the party leaders which had to be fulfilled. Within the AKP structure, the example for such a case was observed in *Karşıyaka*, as one influential activist stated:

I have been in this position for one and a half years. I was elected in the district convention, which took place under very competitive conditions.

> Before the convention, I was a member of the district executive board in *Karşıyaka*. Being in this position is a tough mission. Not only I have to fulfill the tasks assigned to me by the central executive board but also I have to meet the demands of the society, the people living in *Karşıyaka*.[18]

Even though the district party chair came to his position through competitive elections, he seemed to be aware that he had certain responsibilities to fulfill at the local level, assigned to him by the central party organization; which again resembled a PA relationship in which the LPA was acting on behalf of the NPL.

The Republican People's Party (CHP)

The top-down nature of the PA relationship through appointments was observed in some of the cases within the CHP structure as well. The district party chair in *Karşıyaka* stated:

> Since the previous chair of our district declared his candidacy for the general elections, he resigned from his position and the provincial executive committee offered me to take his position for a temporary period, since then I am still the district party chair in *Karşıyaka*.[19]

An influential youth-wing activist in *Karşıyaka* also affirmed that he was appointed to his position:

> I worked in several branches within this party both at the provincial and district level. I think I was able to prove myself during this period and that is why the main branch of our party at the district offered me this position in *Karşıyaka*.[20]

On a question regarding the nature of the relationship between the district party organization and the provincial executive committee, one of the members of the district executive board in *Karşıyaka* stated:

> We are working on behalf of the provincial party organization here, we represent the provincial organization in *Karşıyaka*. Whenever we are faced with a problem, it is the provincial leaders that we contact with. Similarly the provincial party organization represents the central party organization in *İzmir*. It is a hierarchical structure.[21]

In *Tarsus*, however, the CHP district party chair did not state that he was appointed to his position by his superiors. He mentioned that he had been the district chair in the periods between 1992–2003 and 2005–2007, and that in all the district conventions where he was a candidate, he was elected by the votes of the delegates.[22] However, it is an interesting fact that each time he was running for the position of "party chair" in *Tarsus*, he was the only candidate and did not have a rival to compete with. Such a noncompetitive process raises question marks on how the delegates are elected to the district party conventions. The head of the district women wings on the other hand stated that she was offered to come to that position:

> Our district party chair offered me to be the head of the women wings in Tarsus. One can automatically receive such offers if s/he proves that s/he is a hardworking and a social person who can easily establish dialogues with other people.[23]

In *Diyarbakır-Merkez*, the CHP activists also underlined the mechanisms of appointment while explaining how they came to their current position in the party. An executive board member of the district party organization in *Diyarbakır-Merkez* explained the process of delegate selection in the district party conventions as follows:

> The delegate selection is not based on elections. The provincial party organization does have a significant influence in determining the delegates for the conventions. I have participated both in district and provincial party conventions and the results of the elections in those conventions are already known from the beginning. I personally did not also come to my current position through elections.[24]

The same activist explained the selection of the head of the youth and the head of the women wings as follows:

> The provincial executive board gives the decision on selecting the heads of the youth wings and women wings. But it is decided collaboratively. People who work hard and get some distinction are offered these positions.[25]

In fact, an executive member of the CHP youth wings in *Diyarbakır-Merkez* stated that he had close ties with the ex-CHP parliamentarian and that it was important to have such ties and be recognized to come to such positions.[26]

The CHP organization in *Ümraniye*, however, was completely renewed by the central party organization during the time of the interviews. In other words, the district executive board of *Ümraniye* was expelled from the party due to their failure in 2007 elections. The district party chair who was newly appointed to his position stated:

> I was not elected at a convention, but rather appointed by the central party organization. I wish I came to this position through elections but the district organization needed to be restructured because the previous administration was subject to annulment.[27]

Similarly another member of the district executive board in *Ümraniye* stated:

> The colleagues who were going to build this new administration in Ümraniye offered me to join them, there were no elections.[28]

These examples provide evidence for the fact that the CHP as a party organization is strongly constructed upon a PA relationship where the local party actors act as the agents of the central party organizations at the local level.

The Nationalist Action Party (MHP)

Just like in other parties, appointment is used as a practical method to select the members of the local executive boards within the MHP structure even though the MHP constitution underlines the election method in district party conventions.[29] The elections do take place in tandem with the laws during the conventions, yet if the results of the elections do not provide results in which the district executive boards fail to act as successful agents of the principals, then they are subject to the possibility of being discharged from the party. When the district party chair in MHP-*Karşıyaka* was asked how he came to his current position, he explained the process exactly within this framework:

> I was a candidate for the position of district party chair in the 2003 district convention but I lost the elections. At that time, I was also the vice-chair of the Grey Wolves (*Ülkü Ocakları*) at the provincial level in İzmir. When the MHP district administration in *Karşıyaka* was discharged by the central party organization together with the newly elected district chair, the MHP provincial chair called me back and told me that "it is you who can put this organization back together in *Karşıyaka*" and that's how I easily became the district party chair.[30]

The executive board member in *Karşıyaka* also supported the district party chair's statement, describing how their appointment took place in the party:

> I came to this position three years ago. In 1988, I became a member of the MHP. They do not accept you in the organization so quickly, first you need to get recognized. I was recognized in 1990 and they offered me to become the second head of *Bayraklı* [another district in İzmir]. Then I met our district party chair in *Karşıyaka*; he wanted to work with me here. But we together lost in the elections in the 2003 district party convention. Later on both of us were appointed by the provincial party organization. Since then I am a member of the executive committee in *Karşıyaka*.[31]

The district party organization in *Diyarbakır-Merkez* was another example for the top-down PA model within the MHP. In fact, even though this research is focused on local party organizations at the district level and not at the provincial level, the MHP in the province of *Diyarbakır* was a special case to study as it was the interview with the provincial party chair, Mr. Abdullah Arzakçı, that showed the type of power structure between the central and local leaders within the MHP. It was observed that all districts including *Diyarbakır-Merkez* in the province of *Diyarbakır* were under the control of Mr. Arzakçı, who himself stated that there was no need for the researcher to interview the district party chair and other members in *Diyarbakır-Merkez* as he was sure they would provide the same information as he did.[32] Mr. Arzakçı stated that he was also appointed to his position by the MHP central party organization.

> I came to this position through appointment. Right after the national elections in 2002, they appointed me to Diyarbakır and afterwards I was elected at the provincial party convention. Since then I have been the provincial party chair here.[33]

Mr. Arzakçı, while acting as the agent of the central party organization in Diyarbakır, is himself the principal of the LPAs and LPMs of the executive board members in *Diyarbakır-Merkez*. One of the executive board members in the district stated:

> I was a candidate running for the office of mayor in *Çınar* [another district in Diyarbakır] in the previous 2004 municipal elections. We gave the decision on my candidacy together with the provincial chair, Mr. Arzakçı. For future positions, I do not know, our principle in this party is that 'a position is not demanded, it is supplied'. If I do not receive any offers from my superiors, I cannot demand any positions. I mean my superiors are my

provincial party chair and his assistants. There is hierarchy in our organization, it is not the central party organization but the provincial chair who is to supply me that offer.[34]

Through this statement, the activist in *Diyarbakır-Merkez* clarifies the chain of commands in the party organization of the MHP. As a district activist, he sees the provincial party organization, particularly the chair as his principal who is the agent of the central party organization.

The MHP party organization in *Tarsus* also showed similar patterns with the previous local organizations in terms of its relationship with the central party organization. As distinct from the previous cases, the district party chair in *Tarsus* stated that he was elected as the chair through competitive elections that took place in the district party convention rather than being appointed by the central party organization. However he did mention that it was the central party organization that backed his candidacy for being the chair of MHP-*Tarsus* whereas his rival did not have such support from the central party organization.[35]

The members of the district executive board in MHP-*Tarsus*, on the other hand, have stated that it was through the offer of the district party chair that they were able to become board members. One of them stated:

I was previously a member of the MHP-*Tarsus*. But I was an active member attending all kinds of party events; that's why I was well recognized. It has been only one year since I became the executive board member. The district party chair offered me as a result of my active engagement with the party.[36]

Moreover, the activist from the women's wing in MHP-*Tarsus* also stated that she came to her current position through the offer of the district party chair:

After our district party chair was appointed to his position, the district women wings had to change its administration as well. I was a close friend of the district party chair before. He directly stated that I should be in the women wings and I accepted his offer without the need for elections.[37]

In *Ümraniye*, the district party chair was similarly appointed by the provincial party organization to his position. Yet, he clearly asserted that he was not content with this position in the party:

I came to this position through appointment by the provincial party organization. In fact, I accepted the offer due to a lot of pressures and insistence among the provincial organization. I think the chair should be selected from the young well-educated activists; I do not want to be permanent in this position.[38]

One of the members of the district executive board further stated that he was offered to become the executive member by the district party chair. He also described the process of appointment as follows:

I came to this position as a result of the demand by the district party chair. Our structure is similar to the military organizations; it requires a strict chain of commands. The superiors assign you certain tasks and you have to fulfill such tasks. I did not want to take part in the executive board; but since the district party chair asked me to do so, I had to accept it. But these positions are allocated to the hardworking activists who deserve to be there.[39]

An influential activist from the women wings in Ümraniye stated that she came to her current position through the elections that took place in the district convention of the women wings. However she described how the convention delegates were selected as follows:

The convention delegates are determined through the district executive boards. The list of delegates approved by the district board then is submitted to the provincial board and the provincial board provides a final approval on the list of delegates.[40]

In this respect since the delegates at the district convention represent the interest of the superiors in the party, any candidate elected in such conventions automatically becomes the agent acting on behalf of the interest of the superiors.

The Democratic Society Party (DTP)

The interviews have shown that the only party that deviated from the recurrent usage of the "appointment method" in determining the local party chairs and executive board members is the DTP. Most of the interviewed DTP members have employed the "democracy" discourse for their party in describing processes such as determining the candidates, selecting the convention delegates as well as the party chairs. Only in Karşıyaka and Ümraniye, some party activists mentioned that appointments actually took place in their district; but following the appointments, there were elections in district conventions, which, *in their view*, had a democratic structure. A LPA explained the process in *Karşıyaka* as follows:

> The district party chair was appointed to his position by the provincial party organization. Then at the district party convention he was elected. But he was the only candidate running for that position.[41]

Another executive board member from *Karşıyaka* explained the same process in a general framework:

> In order to come to a position within the executive board, it is important how well you are known among the people, among the members of this party. This is how the delegates elect the board members in the conventions.

Even though the above statement does not seem to be undemocratic, the representative of the youth wings in *Karşıyaka*, in a very general perspective, stated:

> For sure, the district conventions sometimes have weaknesses in their democratic structure. But it is natural for each kind of organization. I have not experienced in person but it is very possible that the elections in the conventions are not held in a democratic manner.[42]

Most party members in other districts gave round answers of this kind to the questions on whether the district party conventions were democratic or not. In *Diyarbakır-Merkez*, one executive board member of the district women wings stated:

> Yes, sometimes it is possible to see undemocratic manners during conventions but it is observed in every organization. And we are trying to overcome these problems. For instance, in terms of women's participation in the conventions, we are trying very hard, encouraging women to be delegates. We did have success to some degree.[43]

As a response to the question on how he came to his current position in the party, the district party chair in *Diyarbakır-Merkez* stated:

> First, the central party organization and the provincial party organization, negotiating with the party delegates appointed me to the executive board of the party. When the previous district party chair left his position, I declared my candidacy to be the new chair and got elected in the district convention.[44]

One member in the executive board of the district youth wings in *Diyarbakır-Merkez* further stated on this issue that

> if you by any chance come to a position through appointment, you cannot be successful in the party because one has to be aware of the political and social structure of the constituency s/he is responsible for. It requires lots of experience.[45]

Similarly in *Ümraniye*, the party members described the delegate selection process as a very democratic process, continually emphasizing the importance of grassroots. One of the executive members of the district youth wings stated that:

> The DTP is a different kind of party. The delegates and the executive board members are elected by the people. It is the effort and the endeavor of the person that brings him to any important position in the party. The DTP derives its power from the grassroots politics.[46]

Two executive board members in *Ümraniye* also stated that they came to their current positions through being appointed by the provincial party organization but then were elected in the convention.[47]

In *Tarsus* too, the local party leaders and members mentioned that the district party conventions took place in a very democratic atmosphere. One of the activists stated:

> The delegates are selected through the grassroots members. In every neighborhood and town we organize meetings with our members and they select their delegates in these meetings.[48]

The other activists in *Tarsus* also supported the above claim except one district party activist who added a small hesitating comment:

> I have been a delegate both at the provincial and national party conventions. The intra-party elections do not always take place in a perfectly democratic manner. There can sometimes be mistakes.[49]

Even though this local activist did not explain the content of such mistakes in the interview, he implied some undemocratic features during the intraelections at conventions.

The statements of the DTP district party activists and members, therefore did not really provide examples for the method of "appointment" in determining local executive boards. In fact, the leadership change in the aftermath of the 2007 general elections within the DTP seems to strengthen the claim that the leaders are not the principals in this party organization.[50] However, there are two problems with this claim. First, the leadership change within the DTP in 2007 reflected the long-lasting division on the values of the party in the elite cadre of the party.[51] Many of the leaders from the pro-Kurdish parties have been subject to investigation, arrest, or ban from politics by court decisions. This situation has often led to several leadership changes in the party (including the predecessors of the DTP) throughout in time; without maintaining a stable leadership. In this respect, the means of "candidate selection", in fact, remains as the most effective measurement of authoritarianism; which took place in a highly top-down manner.

Second, even though the LPAs may be elected through democratic ways in local conventions, they do *perceive* themselves as the agents of their superiors at the local level. For instance, the district leaders of the DTP explained that the party activities they were mostly dealing with were indeed composed of tasks to fulfill, prearranged by the central party organization. For instance a district party activist in *Karşıyaka* even stated that he had other responsibilities in other districts, given by the central party organization.

> I have to fulfil the duties assigned to me by the central party organization. The district of *Torbalı* has some organizational problems and the central leaders gave me the mission to solve these problems.[52]

Another district board member explained his tasks during the election times as follows:

> The central party organization sends election mission memorandums to district organizations. We determine our tasks according to that memorandum, organizing public meetings, visiting fellow townsman associations (*hemşehri dernekleri*).[53]

A district party activist in *Tarsus* also mentioned the mission memorandums sent to their party organization prior to the elections. He stated:

> According to the campaign methods determined by the central party organization, we visited several villages for campaigning.[54]

Another activist in *Tarsus* explained the content of the campaign methods as follows:

> Because of the 10 percent threshold [in national elections], we knew that our party was not able to enter the parliament if we participated in the

elections as the DTP. That's why our candidates declared themselves as independent candidates. When a candidate was determined by the central party organization, we took him to several towns and villages for him/her to meet the local people in *Tarsus*.[55]

In this respect, these party activists perceived that they had tasks to fulfill as a result of the mission memorandums sent to their districts by the NPLs and considered themselves as the *agents* of the party in central office rather than as *principals*.

Interest Configurations within Parties

Why do some agents in authoritarian party structures have no incentive to challenge the intraparty authoritarianism if acting on behalf of their principals is against the principle of self-interest? In chapter 5, the clandestine and benign patterns of intraparty authoritarianism have shown that some agents in Turkey are either indifferent to authoritarianism or simply accept the fact that they are subject to subordination.

The explanation lies in grasping the significance of interest configurations in authoritarian party structures. Interest configuration has a *constitutive* impact on the nature of the power relationship between the principal and the agent in the party. Since there are multiple agents (local party actors and organizations), different types of power relationships are like to emerge depending on the interest type of the agents because they might have either ideational or material interests. As outlined in chapter 4, if the agents have ideational interests, then the conflicts within the party structure become latent; in other words the agents remain indifferent to the potential and actual conflicts. Strong ideational interests such as ideological attachment, leadership loyalty, service to the "cause" constitute this type of behavior, leading to a clandestine pattern in intraparty authoritarianism.

Yet, if the agents have material interests, they simply accept to subordinate to their principals because they receive certain benefits from the authoritarian structure of the party. That is why they do not initiate a challenge against it. This type of behavior is observed in benign authoritarianism.

Similarly, within an interest configuration, the principals' (party leaders') interests may also be either ideational or material. However, as argued in chapter 4, the different patterns of authoritarianism do not depend on the principals' interests. Since the framework is based on a party system where all party leaders tend to behave in an authoritarian manner, whether such behavior is based on ideational or material interests does not affect the outcome. In this respect, it is important to emphasize once again that what matters is the agents' interests in understanding different patterns of authoritarianism and not the principals'.

The differences between the interests of local party actors in the selected district party organizations in Turkey can be outlined as follows:

- *Local party actors with material interests*: CHP-*Tarsus*, AKP-*Tarsus*, AKP-*DiyarbakırMerkez* (LPAs), DTP-*DiyarbakırMerkez*.
- *Local party actors with ideational interests*: AKP-*Ümraniye*, AKP-*DiyarbakırMerkez* (LPMs), MHP-*Tarsus* (LPMs), DTP-*DiyarbakırMerkez*, DTP-*Karşıyaka*, DTP-*Tarsus*, DTP-*Ümraniye*.

It is important to note that the LPAs and the LPMs may not always have the same type of interests as observed in the case of the AKP-*DiyarbakırMerkez* and MHP-*Tarsus*. While the LPMs (ordinary members with a more passive role) in AKP-*DiyarbakırMerkez* were indifferent to the authoritarian party structure, the LPAs (i.e., executive board members) were aware, yet did not initiate a challenge due to the certain benefits they expected to receive. Similarly, while the LPMs in MHP-*Tarsus* were attached to the leader and ideology of the party and thus unconcerned about authoritarianism, the LPAs were initiating a challenge against the central party organization.

In this section of the study, some statements from the LPMs and LPAs in the district party organizations are provided in order to illustrate the type of interests they possess. The local members and activists were asked to identify their motivations for being a party activist or a member as well as the reasons why they specifically chose the party that they were working for. Among these 11 cases outlined above, the existence of strong ideational and material interests did not let the exogenous or endogenous triggers to change the power relationship within the party. That was why these 11 cases pursued their status quo structures either in benign or clandestine authoritarianism after the 2007 elections while the seven of them had experienced the stage of challenged authoritarianism.

Interest Configuration in Clandestine Authoritarianism

In cases where clandestine authoritarianism is the major power structure in a party organization, the local party actors have *ideational interests* so that they do not question the authoritarian behavior of their principals in the party. The ideational interests of the local party actors refer to the interests shaped in the *sociocultural context* of the party organization;

such as ideological commitment, admiration for the leader, service to the country, sense of community, and enhancement of the social status.

Justice and Development Party: The AKP's local party members in Diyarbakır-Merkez have such motivations in this respect. Two of the members stated their admiration for the party leader, Erdoğan as follows:

> I have been an active member for four years. And for three years I have been an executive board member of the women wings. I am not working for the AKP because it is a government party. My reason for being in the AKP is more related to the personality and hardworking spirit of our party leader, who was a very successful mayor in Istanbul. His speeches, style, vision, and everything related to his leadership motivated me to become a member of this party.[56]

> I did not have any relations with a party before the AKP. One day, I witnessed the speech of our prime minister, Erdoğan, on television; he made a call to us stating that we should all come together, working for one end. I asked myself, 'Why should I not be with the AKP?' Since then, I work as a party member within the AKP. It has been three years. Besides, it is a party of service and I want to be a part of this service for the country.[57]

Besides, two of the party activists in *Diyarbakır-Merkez* emphasized that only through the AKP, they believed they could serve the country successfully:

> Since 1993, I have been actively involved in politics. Previously, I was the head of the women wings in the Felicity Party (*Saadet Partisi* – SP). In 2004, I decided to be a member of the AKP because I wanted to be a part of success. That's why I began working actively for the AKP during the 2004 local elections.[58]

> The AKP is a party that fights against corruption, invests in development and has brought a new perspective to politics. That's why I chose to be in the AKP.[59]

The local activists and the members of the AKP in *Ümraniye* also had strong ideational interests in working as an activist for the AKP. Four of them stressed that the party leader Erdoğan, was an important reason for why they worked for the AKP:

> The AKP is the only party through which I can express myself. I am wearing a headscarf and have been the subject of discrimination; therefore I wanted to be an activist and fight for my rights. I will work for this party as long as I can but it is very important for me that our party leader continues to be in this party. If he, by any means, has to leave the party, I will carry on voting for the AKP but definitely cease to be an

activist. His leadership is the most important reason for my presence here.[60]

I was not working for any political party before. I do not have a family with a background in politics, either. The reason why I began to work for the AKP was mainly the party leader. I knew that Erdoğan was a hardworking, successful leader while he was the mayor of İstanbul. It's the love and admiration for him that keeps me here. In fact, this is true for most people working for the AKP.[61]

I work for the AKP because of the sympathy for the leader. Erdoğan was very well recognized during his mayoralty in İstanbul. I was affected and motivated by the fact that he was building a new party.[62]

The personality of the leader, Erdoğan. That's why I am with the AKP today. [63]

Apart from the admiration for the leader, one local activist in *Ümraniye* stated his reason for working for the AKP as:

I have been a member of the AKP since its establishment. The goal of the party is to achieve justice and development. Besides, the party administration is decent. Only through the AKP, our country can have better prospects.[64]

The activists in the district party organization of the MHP in *Karşıyaka* also had ideational interests; but unlike the AKP activists, their ideational interests were more in the form of an attachment to the nationalist ideology of the party rather than to the leader. Some examples from the statements of the activists/members are as follows:

The unity of the homeland, my love for this country and the honest administration in the party are the main reasons why I work as an MHP activist.[65]

The love for the country is the main reason why I am here today. Besides, the MHP is a party that is line with the principles of Atatürk. If Atatürk was alive, he would be supporting the MHP too.[66]

I grew up in very difficult, fearful conditions in 1970s (referring to the forceful period of polarization between the right-wing and the left-wing politics in Turkey). While I was a child, they were teaching us how Atatürk founded the Republic in much more difficult conditions at school. Together with my family's guidance, I sweared to follow the direction led by the MHP.[67]

If you look at other parties, whenever they fail to come to power, they wither away from politics. The MHP is different, it is not a party that only aims to come to power. Even if the party doesn't succeed in elections, the people do not stop embracing this idealistic (*ülkücü*) trail. That is why we are a permanent party. Alpaslan Türkeş founded this organization and it is as strong as it used to be. That is why I spiritually feel myself as a part of the MHP.[68]

I have examined the programs of several other parties but it was only the MHP where I found the love for the country. The people and the state…There are so few parties that embrace these two together. I am 66 years old and if I lived another 66 years, I would continue to be with the MHP. I have nine children and they are all following the track of the MHP.[69]

In addition to these statements, an influential district party activist in *Karşıyaka* explained his reason to be an MHP activist, through combining his ideological attachment to the MHP with his loyalty to the founding leader of the party, Alpaslan Türkeş:

The reason why I work for the MHP today is Alpaslan Türkeş. He brought this belief to our country: The faith in Islam and Turkishness. I see the love of God, the Prophet, and the nation in the MHP. I see enlightenment, wisdom, justice, Atatürk, history, the roots of our nation…This is the kind of nationalism that can take us forward.[70]

The views of the local MHP activists and members in *Tarsus* were not so different from the ones in *Karşıyaka* in explaining why they were motivated to work for the MHP:

It is a party whose ideology supports the indivisibility of the nation and the state. It is a party that embraces the people. It is a party that takes into account the demands of the people. It is a party that doesn't differentiate the citizens from one another.[71]

The love for the country and its people…This is the most important idea behind the MHP. It does not distinguish people as Kurds and Turks; it unites everybody with the love for the country. That is why I am here.[72]

I wanted to articulate my opinions for the love of my country and that's how I decided to be an activist. I was already an MHP sympathizer since the age of 17 so I joined the MHP.[73]

Democratic Society Party (DTP): The interests of the party activists and members within the DTP organization showed many similarities with the ideational interests of the MHP activists and members in terms of strong ideological attachment to the party. This explains, why none of the DTP activists initiated a challenge against the authority of the leaders even though their party lost a great deal of votes in 2007 elections particularly in the southeast region. In chapter 5, it was also illustrated through the interviews conducted with external observers that the DTP made many strategic mistakes during the campaigning process in appealing to the voters: The selected candidates were not publicly well-known, and the party leaders exposed an upper-class image to their potential voters. Then, it is interesting to note that the party activists did not initiate a challenge against the national party leaders at all. On the contrary, most of the DTP activists underlined how democratic their party structure was. The conducted interviews showed that in *Ümraniye*, *Tarsus* and *Karşıyaka*, there was great degree of loyalty to the party principles.

Furthermore, most of the DTP party activists underlined the degree of struggle and harsh conditions that they went through in explaining their motivations of becoming a party member. They underlined the importance of the Kurdish identity as the reason for becoming a DTP activist. The DTP party activists in *Tarsus* all emphasized that their party was different from the other parties in the current party system of Turkey in terms of ideology and party goals. They believed that the DTP in fact constituted their own identity as a party of the oppressed, subject to several closures in time:

> We have been the subject of unjust treatment for long years. My uncle's house was demolished by the state forces. We have lived under arrest, in prison for long years…Then we moved to metropolitan cities. We were sympathizers of HADEP in that period. It was a party responsive to the needs of our people. That's why I joined this party.[74]
>
> The denial of our identity has led to the establishment of this party. After all, political morale is what a decent person should have. That is why I work for the DTP today. Besides, this party is a means for us to pursue politics on legal grounds. Without using weapons, we are trying to be responsive to the people's need.[75]
>
> This party is established based on the realities of Turkey. It is a party against the current political system; against the present administration in the system. Since it offers a new alternative, it has been the subject of oppression; its predecessors have all been closed down by the state. Even though the party has experienced a total of eight closures since 1991, we stand still. The name of the party may be different but we are the same. Our hopes are the same.[76]
>
> It is impossible for me to leave this party. My identity is shaped through this organization, this movement. I am a father, having struggled and paid a price to this end. I lost two of my children. I had devoted all my opportunities for them previously; they were both well-educated and lost their lives in this struggle.[77]
>
> Before the HEP and the DEP were established (*the predecessors of the DTP*), I did have sympathy for the left-wing parties like the CHP. However, the pro-Kurdish parties have been closed down several times, you see, they have been the parties of the oppressed. The DTP is a party of the

people, survives only through the resources of the people, not the state. It is different.[78]

The DTP party activists in *Karşıyaka*, similar to the ones in *Tarsus* mentioned that they were working for this party because it was the only one among other parties that appealed to their own interests: such as respect for human rights and equality. In this sense, the DTP activists in *Karşıyaka*, too, had ideational interests in becoming a party member within the DTP:

> The DTP sees all the people as equal: the Kurds, the Lazs, the Circassians. It does not distinguish different classes as well. It is a democratic party. That is why I am here; I respect the human rights.[79]
>
> I work for this party because its main goal is democracy and human rights. This perspective suits my political attitude most.[80]
>
> I suppose I have to work for an organization that I believe in. If I am a citizen of this country and if I see some problems that this country is facing, then I need to be a part of an organization, whether it is a trade union or an association or a party. I see it as a duty. Previously I worked for trade unions. Now I work for the DTP because it is the best organization that fits my interest. Through the DTP, I serve to the people.[81]

As the examples in *Karşıyaka* illustrates, not all the DTP activists outlined their reasons for becoming a party activist because of their attachment to the Kurdish identity or struggle for "Kurdishness". They underlined principles such as human rights, equality, democracy, and socialism in addition to the significance of the Kurdish issue. Such values seemed to shape the ideational interests of these party activists. Three of the DTP party activists in *Ümraniye* emphasized similar interests in this regard:

> I am personally a social democrat; a socialist and I believe I have a moral duty to work for the party I believe in. I am Kurdish in origin, but it is not the main reason why I am involved within the DTP today. The DTP is the only party that can respond to the major problems of Turkey. I try to look at things through a universalistic perspective. It is the duty of a socialist to keep the brotherhood of men.[82]
>
> There are several political parties in Turkey but none of them is successful as the DTP in fighting for women rights. I can express myself only in this party. I got to know my own identity through the DTP.[83]
>
> I work for this party because today only the DTP sees the Kurdish issue as the major problem of Turkey. It is a left-wing party caring for human rights and the brotherhood of the people. The other so-called 'left-wing' parties cannot be considered as the real left-wing. The CHP is not left-wing either, it is a party of the state, of the current system.[84]

Moreover, the personal background of the local activists and members has a great influence on the nature and extent of interests. For instance, the education and income level of the DTP local party actors is much lower than the actors from other parties. Besides, the degree of their activism in Pro-Kurdish parties is very high. Sixteen of the 24 interviewed DTP local actors stated that they spent more than ten years working for the party while six of them stated they spent five to ten years (see Appendix B).

Therefore, compared to the local actors from other parties, the DTP activists and members came from lower classes and are more attached to the values of their party. In this respect, it is harder to expect a high degree of challenge against the authoritarianism within their party.

Interest Configuration in Benign Authoritarianism

The AKP local activists in *Diyarbakır-Merkez*, the AKP members/activists in *Tarsus*, the CHP members/activists in *Tarsus* as well as the DTP members/activists in *Diyarbakır-Merkez* were the districts where benign type of authoritarianism was observed. In other words, the reason why the local party actors chose to subordinate to the decisions of party leaders, even under the conditions of conflict, was the material benefits they received from the authoritarian party structure. One of the AKP district party activists in *Diyarbakır-Merkez* was, for instance, a close friend of the ex-provincial chair of *Diyarbakır*, who was later on, elected as a parliamentarian in 2007. He explained his membership process in the AKP as follows:

> I have been a member and activist within the AKP since 2004. The AKP deputy of Diyarbakır, who is as hardworking as our party leader Erdoğan, offered me to work together in the AKP. I also believed that the activities of the AKP could really help in the development of *Diyarbakır* so I accepted the offer and became the district party chair.[85]

During the interviews, it was hard to receive a forthright answer from the party activists on their material expectations from their party. Rather, they continuously reemphasized their commitment to the AKP's principals, as the example of the district party activist in *Diyarbakır-Merkez* shows. However, while he was brought to his position in *Diyarbakır-Merkez*, being close to influential people such as the AKP deputy played an important role in accepting the offer because the deputy was known as a well recognized political figure in *Diyarbakır-Merkez*, serving previously as the provincial chair of the AKP.

In terms of other types of material interests, for instance, another activist from the AKP *Diyarbakır-Merkez* stated that he had expectations for running for public office in the near future:

> I have not been a candidate before; but yes I consider running for the position for municipal council member in the upcoming local elections.[86]

In *Tarsus*, it was already outlined in chapter 5 that the most important benefits provided to the AKP activists and members were the possibilities for job opportunities. The party activist from the youth wings stated that he had started working for the AKP as an official employee of the party. Another unemployed youth activist stated that he became a member of the AKP for possible job opportunities in the future. Besides the opportunities were not only found within the party organization; but the AKP-*Tarsus* organization provided a networking opportunity for its members to find jobs. For instance, during the interviews taking place in the AKP-*Tarsus* office, the district party chair accepted several visitors and phonecalls stating their demands for future job opportunities.

The CHP-*Tarsus* and the DTP-*Diyarbakır-Merkez* were two other examples for such kind of networking among the local party actors. The district party chair remained in his seat at CHP-*Tarsus* for nearly 15 years, having a very well recognized status at the local level and maintaining his close ties with the CHP deputy. On the other hand, *Diyarbakır* is considered to have a strategic importance for the DTP and many influential people from the party visit *Diyarbakır* quite often. As explained in chapter 5, even though the party activists both in DTP-*DiyarbakırMerkez* and CHP-*Tarsus* did not reveal their real intentions, most of them were working for the party either for job possibilities or future investment in their personal relations with influential people.

The Role of Exogenous/Endogenous Events and Power Resources

In chapter 4, it was argued that the exogenous and endogenous events arising in the political system such as loss in an election, entrance of a new party into the political system, or disappearance of an old one[87] might bring a change on the power structure of political parties. These events may *cause* intraparty conflicts between the agents and the principals. Under such conditions, the agent might attempt to challenge the authoritarian party structure, which falls short in meeting his/her expectations.

In chapter 5, among the 16 power relationships between district and central party organizations, five cases have been illustrated as instances of challenged authoritarianism: AKP-*Karşıyaka*, CHP-*DiyarbakırMerkez*, MHP-*DiyarbakırMerkez*, MHP-*Ümraniye*, and MHP local leaders in *Tarsus*. On the other hand, in two of the cases, CHP-*Karşıyaka* and CHP-*Ümraniye*, coercive authoritarianism is observed; which is the following stage of challenged authoritarianism. Therefore in seven power relationships in total, the exogenous or endogenous developments have created a change.

Since the CHP experienced a major defeat in 2007 elections, there were two occasions of challenge followed by coercion within its structure: CHP-*Ümraniye* and CHP-*Karşıyaka*. The CHP-*Diyarbakır-Merkez* could not go further than creating an identification of the weakening legitimacy of the party leadership; due to a lack of power resources, the challenge against intraparty authoritarianism remained only at the passive level—"framing." The three district organizations of the MHP in *Diyarbakır-Merkez*, *Ümraniye* and *Tarsus* challenged the central party organization due to the dissatisfaction over the candidate lists. Yet out of these three MHP cases, the MHP in *Ümraniye* was not likely to pose an active challenge against the upper echelons—"operationalizing" and thus, the challenge also remained at the passive level. Even though the AKP was the most successful party of all in 2007 elections at the national level, the AKP district party organization in *Karşıyaka* was not satisfied with the central party authority and challenged the authoritarian nature of candidate selection with the potential to take concrete steps against this structure, in other words "operationalize" the challenge. These differences across and within party power structures are explained through the effects of (1) endogenous and exogenous triggers on the interest configurations as well as (2) the power resources of the agents.

Causes of Challenge: The Nationalist Action Party (MHP)

At the national level, the MHP increased its votes by nearly six percent and emerged in the parliament with 71 seats. However, as discussed in chapter 5, the district party organizations in *Diyarbakır-merkez*, *Tarsus* and *Ümraniye* have challenged the authoritarian nature of the candidate selection process within the MHP. On the other hand it was clandestine authoritarianism that was observed in *Karşıyaka* district. In this respect, the reasons for the challenge occurring in three cases organizations were the endogenous triggers based on the authoritarian nature of the candidate selection process itself. The district organizations were highly disappointed with the names appearing in the lists. Yet, only MHP-*Karşıyaka* remained within the status quo. The reason for this difference is based on the effect of endogenous triggers and the power resources of the agents.

In *Diyarbakır-Merkez*, the MHP is in a highly disadvantaged position with its nationalist discourse because the majority of the population in the district is constituted by the Kurdish people. Despite the lack of MHP legitimacy in this district, the party, for the first time, achieved a significant number of votes in 2007 national elections. The MHP completed the race as the third party, following the DTP and the AKP and leaving the CHP behind. As one local member stated, this could be regarded as a victory for the MHP organization, which was not present in the province of *Diyabakır*, prior to 2003.[88] The success was, to a great extent, a result of the local MHP organization's effort, and particularly the provincial party chair's discourse and behavior in appealing to the local people. Rather than using the MHP's general discourse of Turkish nationalism, the MHP-*Diyarbakır* approached the people through responding to their concerns such as unemployment or economic welfare. The MHP provincial chair was, at the same time, a candidate running for office in 2007 elections, and he clearly stated that if his own personal position was not supported by the central party office, he would not work for the party in the region at all. His recognized social status in *Diyarbakır* created an extra source of power for the MHP local party organization, challenging the MHP central office's decisions on candidate selection. The MHP chair in *Diyarbakır* stated that:

> Politics is about serving people. I do not know and care about what other parties do but my party's major aim is to serve to this country. I promised to undertake six grand projects for the development of *Diyarbakır* if I were to be elected an MP. That's what I explained to the people here: Construction of highways, a railway system, carrying out a dam project over the Dicle river...These were concrete promises, my commitments to the people in *Diyarbakır*.[89]

Thus, the MHP's policy discourse at the local level managed to overshadow its nationalist discourse in *Diyarbakır-Merkez*, leading the party to acquire the third place in elections. Besides the MHP provincial chair in *Diyarbakır* is economically very well off as he owns certain lands in that region. He finances all district organizations in Diyarbakır through his own sources. He stated:

> The central party organization never supported us financially. We do not collect membership dues either. I provide all the funding, I pay the rents of all district organization of *Diyarbakır*. That was how we ran our campaign during the elections.[90]

The other LPAs in *Diyarbakır* showed a great deal of loyalty to the local party chair in *Diyarbakır*. Two exemplary statements are as follows:

> Our provincial chair has devoted himself to the activities of this party in Diyarbakır. We are very thankful to him. He revived the MHP spirit here thanks to his own efforts, sources and everything.[91]
>
> Our provincial chair meets all the needs of the district party organizations in Diyarbakır. No other provincial leader had sacrificed to this extent. He bought the provincial party building with his own sources and gave it to the party. The central party organization was going to send some funds for the election period but our provincial party chair did not accept it.[92]

Therefore, the MHP organization in *Diyarbakır-Merkez* is attached to the provincial leader rather than the central party organization. The social status and economic well-being of the MHP local leader provided important sources for the local organization to pose a challenge to the central party organization. Since the provincial chair provides all sorts of funding and effort for the MHP activities in Diyarbakır, it would cause a considerable cost for the national party leaders to remove this agent in *Diyarbakır*.

The MHP in *Tarsus* was another organization dissatisfied with the central party organization's decision on the candidate lists and revealed this discontentment through *framing* their own opinions. The MHP in *Tarsus* had further potential to pose a greater challenge moving from *framing* toward *operationalization* because of the power resources that the local party organization held in the district. The major resource derived from the split between the party in central office and the party in local public office (municipality of *Tarsus*). The interviewed district party leaders in *Tarsus* stated that the interests of the MHP in the municipal office contradicted the interests of the central party office on certain issues.[93] Yet, the district party organization in *Tarsus* represented the central party office and had a very conflictual relationship with the MHP municipality of *Tarsus*. Since the MHP-*Tarsus* had a great informational advantage over the local politics and behaviors of the MHP municipality unlike the national party leaders, the district party leaders in *Tarsus* are aware of their power resources. The potential of a future alliance with the MHP municipality against the national party leaders provides the district party organization in *Tarsus* the opportunity to actively challenge ("operationalize") intraparty authoritarianism in a concrete way.

In *Ümraniye*, on the other hand, the MHP district party organization was also dissatisfied with the candidate lists prepared by the central party organization and thus sent a notification to the central party organization regarding the district organization's discontent with this process. In this case, unlike the other district organizations of the MHP, the *Ümraniye* organization did not have the adequate power resources to operationalize its challenge. The local leaders neither had strong social status nor economic well-being. Yet how did the candidate lists lead to such a challenge in the central organization's relation with MHP-*Ümraniye* but not with MHP-*Karşıyaka*? After all, the candidate lists were prepared in the same top-down manner in both districts. In this respect, interest configurations are the determining factors. It was observed that the local leaders in MHP-*Ümraniye* were not as committed as the *Karşıyaka* local leaders to the party ideology or the party leader. The district party chair in *Ümraniye* stated that:

> It was not my intention to lead this party in *Ümraniye*. I do not think I will be permanent in this position. It is the responsibility of the young activists to deal with the party problems in the future. They urged me to be the district party chair and I could not refuse it. But I will not stay long.[94]

Thus, in particular, the district party chair in *Ümraniye* did not have any interest in initiating any kind of change within the power structure, because he revealed that he did not want to stay in his party position for a long time.

Causes of Challenge: The Justice and Development Party (AKP)

Unlike the other three district party organizations of the AKP, the AKP in *Karşıyaka* challenged the central party organization as a reaction against the authoritarian nature of the candidate selection process. The reasons for this deviation can be explained by the AKP agents' interests and power resources in *Karşıyaka*. Just like the MHP-*Diyarbakır* case, the AKP-*Karşıyaka* has a disadvantaged position in its own local constituency. *Karşıyaka* is largely influenced by the secularism discourse of the CHP, which is the major party supported in that region. Yet, it was observed that the AKP local party organization in *Karşıyaka* had developed a close association with the low classes and the poverty-stricken migrants living in suburban areas known as the *gecekondu* inhabitants, raising its votes by a 12 percent margin in *Karşıyaka*. An influential district party leader stated that:

> 'Whenever they [meaning the *gecekondu* inhabitants] are in trouble, they call me. They have made me a legend here. For instance, even a woman delivering a baby calls me to take her to the hospital. Then the rumor

spreads, and they treat me as a hero. It is sometimes hard to deal with these because people begin calling you when they demand any kind of help...'[95]

The AKP LPAs, thus, were aware of the fact that the majority of support for the AKP in *Karşıyaka* came as a result of the local recognition of their status. In this respect, they generated their own power vis-à-vis the central party office. Since the AKP-*Karşıyaka* was aware of its potential to acquire societal support in its actions, the district organization, particularly its leaders, had the necessary power resources to challenge the authoritarian behavior of the central party office.

Another point that must be raised is the fact that the AKP's chances of gaining the majority of votes in *Karşıyaka* still seems unlikely for future perspectives.[96] Thus the low chances of the AKP to control the public office in *Karşıyaka* reduced the level of loyalty to the central party organization among the LPAs. The district party chair stated his motivations as follows:

> I am not so eager to work here. But if I leave this organization today, it will be a rude action for the team I am working with. I became a member of the AKP through some friends and relatives.[97]

Contrary to the AKP-*Karşıyaka*, within the district party organizations in *Ümraniye* and *Diyarbakır*, a great ideational interest was observed among the party activists in terms of loyalty to the party leader and the commitment to the party program. In this sense, such a challenge was not initiated in these cases. As distinct from these two, yet, *Tarsus* had the similar framework with *Karşıyaka*, where the AKP did not have a future possibility to control the municipal public office. In this district, yet, the material interests of the party activists such as job opportunities kept them silent against authoritarianism.

Causes of Challenge and Coercion: The Republican People's Party (CHP)

The electoral defeat in 2007 elections was the major exogenous trigger altering the power structure within the CHP. In many regions of the country, the conflicts between the national and local levels of party organization appeared on the surface. The CHP leader, Deniz Baykal's legitimacy declined within the party as a result of failing to have achieved the collective goals of the party. Furthermore, one of the most representative public opinion surveys on the parliamentary elections demonstrated that among the CHP voters, the percentage of the people who recognized the need for a new party and the need for a new leader in solving Turkey's problems was 34.8 percent and 59.6 percent respectively.[98] The distrust for the Baykal administration was therefore evident among the voters. Following the outbreak of this distrust, a new faction within the party emerged under the leadership of the Şişli (İstanbul) mayor, Mustafa Sarıgül who, after the parliamentary elections, began making statements in the media about his intentions to be the next CHP party leader and sharply condemning the Baykal administration for the CHP's failure in elections.[99] He attempted to gather up all the CHP opposition members under his leadership and organized backdoor meetings with the provincial and district party chairs.[100] However, Sarıgül was soon expelled from the party based upon the decision of the party disciplinary committee.

The interviews with the CHP LPAs took place during these conditions in October 2007. The major conflict between the CHP in *DiyarbakırMerkez* and the central party organization was not only about the top-down selection of candidates but also the policy issues regarding the Kurdish issue in the region. However as the activists made it clear, they could not go further than sending their views to the provincial or central party organization. It was because the CHP-*DiyarbakırMerkez* lacked the necessary power resources. In fact, one of the well-known ex-local activists in CHP-*DiyarbakırMerkez* gave essential information off the record; stating that he joined the meetings that Sarıgül organized, in order to see the chances whether the Sarıgül network was going to be successful. Yet, he said that he neither found any chance for success nor trusted the personalist character of the faction; and that was why he did not continue to take part in that network.[101] Sarıgül, through his statements and actions, right after the 2007 elections, seemed to enhance this network with his clientelistic ties rather than facilitate its development through grassroots activism.

On the other hand, the administrative boards of the CHP-*Ümraniye* and CHP-*Karşıyaka*, which objected to the decisions of the central party administration through rebellious acts, suffered for their opposing stance by being marginalized within the party. The CHP in *Ümraniye* had joined the Sarıgül network, and yet during the time of the interviews, the local CHP administration had already been abolished and replaced by a new local executive board through appointment, including a new district party chair. A representative of the new party administration explained the process as follows:

> The previous CHP administration in *Ümraniye* was removed due to its
> rebellious acts against the central and provincial party organization. After

the failure we experienced in the elections, these things happen and our leader Baykal wants to move on with a new party structure.[102]

On the other hand, the local administration in CHP-*Karşıyaka* revolted together with the other district CHP organizations in İzmir against the party leader, Baykal. The resistance of the provincial organization CHP-*İzmir* against the central administration, after the 2007 parliamentary elections, brought about its own dissolution by being replaced with a new provincial administration in favor of Baykal and his leadership circle. The newly appointed provincial chair restructured not only the provincial administration cadre but also many of the cadres in district party administrations. The district leaders subject to marginalization protested against this change by gathering and unfurling banners titled "Our only fault has been to be with the CHP," which received great attention from the local media.[103] This, later on, exerted *ex post* negative sanctions on the *Karşıyaka* organization to obey the rules set by the national party leader, Deniz Baykal. In this respect, the coercion on *Karşıyaka* organization has resulted in regression to the first stage of intraparty authoritarianism (clandestine and benign authoritarianism), just like the case in *Ümraniye*. Therefore, during the interviews in *Karşıyaka*, the CHP activists were mostly hesitant to talk or give information on this issue when the tape recorder was on.

Conclusion

This chapter has shown that the party leaders act as the principals in authoritarian party structures of Turkey, delegating their authority to the local party actors either through appointing them to the local party positions or subjugating the elected LPAs to the rules and regulations set by the central party organizations. The interest configurations within the party power structures, particularly the interest type of the agents—ideational or material—has a *constitutive* effect on the nature of the power relationship. It was observed that in 11 power relationships analyzed in authoritarian party structures of Turkey, the agents with strong ideational or material interests did not attempt to challenge the intraparty authoritarianism. Among these 11 cases, the CHP in *Tarsus* as well as the four DTP district organizations in *Karşıyaka, Ümraniye, Tarsus,* and *DiyarbakırMerkez* can particularly be considered as puzzling cases where no challenge had taken place in spite of the electoral failure that both the DTP and the CHP faced in 2007 elections. These cases have shown that strong ideological attachment to the party or acknowledgment of material benefits from the party structure prevent the potential rise of conflicts between local and central party organizations. In this respect, these power relationships cannot move toward the second phase "challenged authoritarianism" at the time of exogenous triggers.

Figure 6.1 illustrates the position of these cases in the three-staged authoritarianism within parties. The MHP in *Ümraniye, Diyarbakır-Merkez,* and *Tarsus* as well as the AKP in *Karşıyaka* were four other puzzling cases where challenged authoritarianism against the central party organization took place. For two reasons these cases can be considered as puzzling: First, the ideological attachment or leadership loyalty was expected to be high among the rank-and-file as observed in other district organizations; second, both parties had achieved a certain degree of success at the national level, increasing their vote shares compared to the 2002 elections. Therefore one might not expect a challenge to occur in these district party organizations. Yet, as a result of the causal effect of endogenous triggers on the interest configurations and power resources of these actors, they were able to enter the second phase, "challenged" intraparty authoritarianism. The major endogenous trigger for this change was the dissatisfaction among the local party actors on the candidate lists. Besides, the power resources of the local leaders in MHP-*DiyarbakırMerkez*, MHP-*Tarsus,* and AKP-*Karşıyaka* were considerably strong enough to challenge the authoritarian party structure, which was not the case in MHP-*Ümraniye*. These power resources were the well

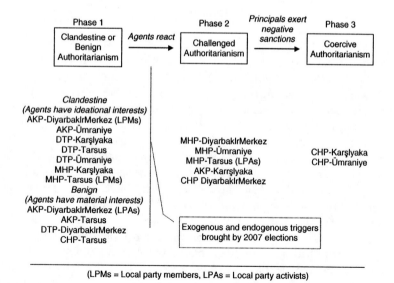

(LPMs = Local party members, LPAs = Local party activists)

Figure 6.1 The stages of intraparty authoritarianism in Turkey.

recognized social status and economic well-being of the local party actors, informational advantage and control over their local constituencies.

Among the 16 cases, the CHP in *Karşıyaka* and the CHP in *Ümraniye*, having entered the stage of "coercive" authoritarianism were the closest to reach internal party democratization had their power resources—particularly the Sarıgül power network within the CHP—been strong enough to remove the party leader Deniz Baykal. Yet, the Sarıgül network was also based on a personalist, clientelistic character with no possible success to seize the authority in the party. The district party organizations that allied with this network, thus, were abolished by the central party organization such as the one in *Ümraniye*. The *Karşıyaka* organization also had to quit the challenge as a result of the negative sanctions, that is the threat of abolition. In this respect, the internal party democratization was not successful in any of these cases.

Conclusions, Implications, Future Studies

The most noticeable feature of authoritarian party structures is that the local party actors are subordinate to the decisions of their party leaders. In this respect, the starting point of this study has been to understand why the local party actors choose to accept such domination by their leaders or whether they ever attempt to change it. Solving this puzzle required a closer analysis of the internal party dynamics in authoritarian party structures, and thus this study, first, attempted to theorize *authoritarian party governance*.

This study contributes to the *party politics* literature where intraparty authoritarianism has been a highly undertheorized political phenomenon.[1] In terms of accounting for intraparty authoritarianism, the main attention in party politics literature has been on the question of how the macro-level factors—such as political culture, institutional framework, and changing social structures—affect the internal strategies of the party leaders.[2] In other words, the independent variables of party power structures have largely remained at the macro level while the variables at the micro level did not receive much attention. Second, even at the micro level, party ideology and leadership styles on the power structure of parties are not sufficient to explain the dynamism and heterogeneity of intraparty authoritarianism. As a result, the questions such as "what constitutes an authoritarian party structure" and "why cannot some authoritarian parties become democratic" have remained unanswered. This lack of attention is surprising when the examples are numerous in developing democracies where intraparty authoritarianism has been visible as an outcome of the historical legacies of authoritarian and totalitarian regimes.[3] Therefore, understanding authoritarian party governance is expected to shed light on the future chances of internal democracy in such party structures to a larger extent in developing democracies.

This study argued that intraparty authoritarianism is neither a *static* nor a *uniform* phenomenon. Rather, it is the outcome of an internal dynamic process in which actors with divergent interests come together and enter into different types of power relationships. In this respect, even though some parties cannot be democratic, it is possible to see a significant degree of variance in their authoritarian structures in a given political system. In this study, such variance is explained through (1) the different types of interest configurations that *constitute* the power relationship between the major party actors and (2) the significant effect that the exogenous and endogenous triggers *cause* on the party structures in a political system.

Through analyzing the 2007 candidate selection process of four political parties in four districts in Turkey, the empirical chapters of this study (chapters 5 and 6) have found out four different patterns of intraparty authoritarianism in Turkey: *clandestine, benign, challenged,* and *coercive.* These patterns reflect the variance in intraparty authoritarianism across *space* and *time.* In other words, since intraparty authoritarianism is structured by various power relationships between the principals and agents, it is possible to see different patterns across and within party structures at the same time. On the other hand, each pattern represents a stage of intraparty authoritarianism, which emerges as a reaction to the preceding stage. In the first stage, authoritarianism can be either clandestine or benign: The local party activists (LPAs) do not initiate a change either because they are unaware of or indifferent to the authoritarian power structure (clandestine authoritarianism) or due to the material benefits that they receive from the national party leaders (benign authoritarianism). In the second stage, due to the emergence of the exogenous and endogenous triggers in the system such as the outcomes of candidate selection processes or electoral defeats, some activists mobilize to change the existing power structures (challenged authoritarianism). *In the third stage,* the activists who challenge the current pattern are subject to negative incentives allocated by the party leaders (coercive authoritarianism). The extent and the essence of the power resources that the activists possess to resist the coercion determine whether the fourth stage brings exit from authoritarianism (through the acquiescence of the party leaders) or regresses toward clandestine or benign authoritarianism.

This study further has argued that the interest configurations between the major internal party actors constitute the nature of the power relationship in parties (chapter 4). Two types of interests were observed among the party actors: *(1) Ideational interests* such as loyalty to the leader, service to the country, or ideological attachment to the party and *(2) material interests* such as power-seeking aims, being close to the influential people, opportunities to be in the public-office or job positions within a party.[4] When the LPAs have *ideational interests,* it is easier for the leaders to maintain their authoritarian behavior in the party. For instance, it was observed that during the 2007 candidate selection process, the AKP leaders surveyed the rank and file, and the MHP leaders used an e-voting system for their members. These methods made the local actors with ideational interests feel influential in determining the candidate lists, leading them to consider their party as democratic (as observed in AKP-*Ümraniye*, MHP-*Karşıyaka* and to some degree in AKP-*DiyarbakırMerkez* and MHP-*Tarsus*). Yet, in reality neither the surveys nor the e-voting procedure affected the final decision of the party leaders. This study has defined this pattern as *clandestine authoritarianism*.

On the other hand, for the LPAs who have material interests, the party leaders usually distribute selective incentives in order to subordinate them to their decisions. Since the local party actors receive certain benefits from the organization (job opportunities, expectations for public office, etc); they keep silent to intraparty authoritarianism. The AKP-*Tarsus*, DTP-*Diyarbakır-Merkez*, the CHP-*Tarsus* are depicted as some examples for this pattern; which this study defined as *benign authoritarianism*.

Both clandestine and benign authoritarianism represent the status quo time in authoritarian party structures. The type of interest configuration (material versus ideational interests) constitutes the major pattern of intraparty authoritarianism in the status quo time. Yet, the *change* in the power relationship between the party leaders and the local party actors cannot be explained only through the *constitutive* effect of interest configurations. The explanation of a dynamic process requires *causal* theorizing (see chapter 4). This study illustrated that certain exogenous and endogenous triggers are likely to *cause* a change within authoritarian party structures.

The 2007 election brought about a number of exogenous and endogenous triggers for political parties in Turkey: Some examples for exogenous triggers are the electoral defeat of the opposition CHP vis-à-vis the government party AKP; the rise of the AKP votes up nearly 13 points on the 2002 electoral results; the emergence of the MHP and the DTP as two new parties in the parliament. On the other hand, the candidate-selection process within some parties can itself be considered as an endogenous trigger because the unexpected appearance of some names in the candidate lists has led some party activists to start questioning the existing institutional structure based on intraparty authoritarianism. An example for the change that endogenous triggers initiated was the MHP organizations in *Diyarbakır-Merkez*, *Ümraniye*, and *Tarsus*; as well as the AKP in *Karşıyaka*. These organizations attempted to challenge the authoritarian behavior of their party leaders that took place during the candidate-selection process.

Another change in the authoritarian party structure was observed in the relationship between three local CHP organizations and the central party office of the CHP. The electoral failure of the CHP, which had previously been the only opposition party in the parliament, brought so many intraparty conflicts to the surface. The local party actors in *Diyarbakır-Merkez, Karşıyaka,* and *Ümraniye* challenged the authority of the party leader. The challenge to the authoritarian structure can be maintained first when the local actors identify and displace dilemmas arising from tensions within their parties, such as *framing* and then start building new institutions to give effect to the newly arising ideas, such as *operationalizing*.[5] Operationalizing is achieved through *balancing operations* or cultivating new power resources such as forming coalitions with other agents.[6] While the CHP in *Diyarbakır-Merkez* did not go further than framing the new dilemmas, in *Ümraniye* and *Karşıyaka,* the local party actors attempted to go to the stage of balancing operations through taking part in a *power network,* the faction created by the CHP Şişli mayor, Mustafa Sarıgül. Yet, later on they became subject to coercive authoritarianism when the central party office employed negative incentives over the local actors through a threat of marginalization in the party as observed in the *Karşıyaka* and *Ümraniye* cases of the CHP party organization.

The reason why the CHP district organization in *Tarsus* did not initiate such a challenge against the CHP central committee was based on the material interests that the local party actors were receiving from such a structure. They were obviously aware of the conflicts and even bothered with authoritarianism; however due to the close relationship that they had with a CHP parliamentarian from *Tarsus* as well as the potential material benefits that such a relationship can provide kept the local party actors silent and submissive.

The DTP local actors in *DiyarbakırMerkez, Karşıyaka, Ümraniye,* and *Tarsus* did not seem to be affected by their failure in 2007 elections, either. Even though the DTP lost a great deal of its support base in the southeast region, this failure did not change the attitude of the local party actors in their loyalty to the party. The candidates were determined in a highly top-down manner, but the local party actors repeatedly emphasized that their party was the most democratic of all the other parties in the system. The presence of strong ideational interests among the local party actors prevented this exogenous development from causing a change between the local and national levels of the party structure. Even though the national convention, which took place in *Diyarbakır* four months after the general elections, led to a leadership change in the party, this change was the result of a division between the party elites rather than a conflict arising between the national and local levels of the party organization. In fact, the statements of the DTP local party actors in *Tarsus, Karşıyaka,* and *Ümraniye* on the authoritarian nature of the candidate selection process during the interviews that took place prior to the national convention proved their indifference to the exclusively made decisions by the party leaders.

Therefore, observing a significant degree of variance both across and within party organizations in Turkey after the 2007 elections, this study has shown that intraparty authoritarianism is a relational phenomenon and subject to change in time, depending on the nature of interest configurations, exogenous and endogenous triggers as well as the extent of the power resources that the local party actors cultivate.

Implications

The implications of this study have two dimensions. The first dimension is the theoretical implications derived from theorizing authoritarian party governance. Second dimension is the policy implications regarding the potential for internal party democratization in Turkey.

Theoretical Implications

Principal-Agent (PA) Theory in Party Politics: In this study, the first significant step to understand the mechanisms of authoritarian party governance was to analyze how the PA relationship was constructed in these party structures (chapter 3). It is because an authoritarian party structure is an example for *governance as hierarchies* in which the actors, their interests, and their interacting behaviors shape the patterns of power relationships.[7] The study contributed to the usage of the PA theory in two ways: First, it has shown that the application of the PA relationship on authoritarian party structures differs from the conventional understanding of the PA relationship in party organizations. *Conventionally, the party leaders act as the agents of the party members and party members act as the principals of the party leaders.*[8] Yet, this view originates from the studies on the power structures of internally democratic party organization. *In parties where it is authoritarianism that dominates the power structures, the party leaders act as the principals and the party members act as the agents.* In fact, chapter 6 has shown evidence from the Turkish case where the local party actors are the appointed agents of the party leaders rather than the elected representatives of their local constituencies. In this sense, this study has emphasized the need to study the PA relationship in a reversed form in authoritarian party structures. Second, the study has underlined that the PA theory suffers from a materialistic bias[9] and thus needs to incorporate ideas, beliefs, and norms. In other words, the interests of the party actors are shaped not only through a purely cost-benefit calculus, but also through ideas, norms, values, and beliefs. This study, in this sense, has distinguished two types of interests between the party actors: *material* and *ideational* interests. Showing that these two types of interests lead to different patterns of *interest configurations* between the principals and agents (chapter 4), the study has argued that interest configurations *constitute* the nature of the power relationship within parties.

Power in Authoritarian Party Structures: This study has shown that intraparty authoritarianism should be understood as a form of power, which is a relational phenomenon.[10] In other words, the potential effectiveness of the leaders' power depends on the interests and power resources of the local party actors. In intraparty authoritarianism, the party leader has power over the LPAs, only because it is their interests and power resources that allow the party leader to exert his/her influence. In this respect, Michels' *iron law of oligarchy* thesis is valid only under a distinctive scope and domain. For instance, even though a party organization is constituted of an asymmetrical power structure, under the influence of exogenous and endogenous triggers, the local party activists as the weak actors can initiate "balancing operations"[11] through cultivating new power resources, such as enhancing their legitimacy or social status in the local constituency, and most importantly through creating a *power network*. This will result with a challenge against the authoritarian party structure and the degree of the exogenous and endogenous events as well as the extent of the power resources having the chance for a transition from intraparty authoritarianism to internal party democracy in time.

However, the party leaders must take into account the type of interests that the agents possess in order to get rid of intraparty conflicts and form a successful authoritarianism. Depending on the type of interests, the power can be exerted in two ways over the subordinate local party actors as observed in clandestine and benign authoritarianism: The conflictual interests can be (1) *made latent* or (2) *purchased* by the national party leaders. In the first case, the subordinate group has *ideational interests* and thus is unaware of the potential conflicts in the party organization. This is where a "three-dimensional power,"[12] or "conditioned power"[13] is exerted over the local party actors, which is power exertion through *manipulation*. In the second case, the party leaders *purchase* the submission of the local party actors through the concrete offer of rewards and benefits. This case is observed when the agents have *material interests* such as being close to influential people, an interest for a seat in public office or a job position that party organization offers.

Implications on the Internal Democratization of Parties in Turkey

Intraparty authoritarianism has long been taken for granted in Turkish politics without putting much emphasis on investigating the future possibilities of internal democracy within party organizations in Turkey. This is possibly because intraparty authoritarianism is an institutionalized phenomenon shaped by the macrolevel factors such as political culture and the institutional framework in Turkey. As chapter 2 has revealed, the parties in Turkey have been born with authoritarian characteristics at their inception and these characteristics have become embedded in their structures in time, particularly after the adoption of the Law on Political Parties (SPK—*Siyasi Partiler Kanunu* No.: 2820). Unlimited nature of leadership tenures and the top-down execution of candidate selection processes have been regarded as "what is right" or "what is normal" for many local party organizations. Taking these facts into consideration, it would then be right to state that intraparty authoritarianism is an institutionalized phenomenon and a potential process of internal party democratization in the future means "institutional change" for party organizations in Turkey.

So far, most of the attention in generating such an institutional change has been directed to reforming the law on political parties in Turkey. There have been so many pressures by the major think tanks on the governments to reform the legal framework on party organizations in Turkey.[14] However, these external pressures could never convey such an agenda of reform to the Turkish parliament.

The major implication of this study on Turkish party organizations is that external pressure for public reform is not the only way for the generation of internal party democracy. Rather, there are internal factors for democratizing party structures as well, which depend on the local party actors' investment in building and strengthening alternative power resources and power networks. Therefore, an internal pressure coming from the grassroots party organizations for reforming the current institutional framework is likely to be more effective than the external pressures. The reforms that come through internal pressures can further bring the adequate checks-and-balances on the leaders' power. As explained in chapter 4, there is a power-dependence relationship between the principals (leaders) and agents (activists) in authoritarian party structures. The greater the agents *shirk* from the authority of their principals based on their power resources, the greater the chance for internal party democratization.

The empirical cases of challenged and coercive authoritarianism observed in this study, pointed to a *change* within power structures; but the factors leading to that change obviously did not provide a sufficient degree of influence in causing an *institutional change*; such as the removal of the party leader, or an inclusive process of candidate selection for public office. Among all parties, the CHP was the closest one approaching internal democracy as a result of entering the third stage of "coercive authoritarianism". The failure that the CHP faced in 2007 elections did create some dynamic challenges within the party organization leading to a new faction, a power network created under the leadership of *Şişli* mayor, Mustafa Sarıgül.[15] However, at the end, the newly created power network was not strong enough to remove the party leader, Baykal since he was reelected at the 2008 national party convention. One can argue that even if Baykal had been removed from the party, the changing leadership may not have brought internal democratization as the newly elected party leader may have installed his own authoritarianism in the party. Yet, a party having gone through a leadership removal through effective agent mobilization has higher chances for creating its internal checks-and-balances in time. In other words, through the leadership removal experience, the agents can learn how to reproduce the similar effect in the future for other authoritarian-leaning leaders.

Yet, why were the power resources of the CHP agents not strong enough to remove the party leader in 2007? First of all, as an alternative leader, Sarıgül did not have a promising background. He built a network of a clientelistic character, formed by his own personal supporters. The network was not based on a vivid grassroots movement. Secondly, the electoral defeat of the CHP in 2007 was not perceived as the flaw of the party by Deniz Baykal. Even though the public opinion blamed him on the grounds that the CHP discourse and electoral strategy as an opposition party was flawed and led to the increase in the votes of the AKP, the Baykal administration explained the reasons for the party failure only through external factors such as the "biased role of the media," "religious communities," "EU support for the AKP."[16] In this respect, the electoral defeat of the CHP, which was the main trigger for the challenges arising within the party, could be placed on "legitimate reasons" by the party leadership. Thus, the *nature* of the exogenous trigger and the *weak* power resources of the agents did not allow the internal democratization of the CHP.

One might further question whether the removal of the CHP party leader, Deniz Baykal and his central executive team in 2010 was a transition from intraparty authoritarianism toward internal party democracy. The change took place, following the corruption scandal that Baykal was personally involved. The event was followed by his resignation from the party on May 10, 2010 and the debate on who should be the next leader. In fact, the process showed a great example of how the top-down PA structure was embedded in the CHP: Even though the leader's legitimacy was highly damaged in public media, many provincial and district party activists expressed their longing for Baykal to retake the party leadership.[17] After all, most of them were appointed to their positions through his choice (*benign authoritarianism*). Therefore, it was rather a conflict between the party elite, particularly between the Secretary General and the central executive committee, that led to the announcement of a new candidate, Kemal Kılıçdaroğlu who became the single nominee of the party, ultimately led to his unanimous election at the party convention, May 22, 2010.[18] Prior to the national elections in 2011, Kılıçdaroğlu utilized a leadership style that aimed to transform the party structure, including internal democratization, introducing primaries in some selected provinces.[19] However, it is still up to the central executive committee of the CHP and its leader, to decide whether and to what extent the primary results should influence the list of MP candidates. Therefore, the party still lacks the necessary checks-and-balances over the power of the party leadership and they can only be brought by the agents.

Future Studies

The hypotheses of this study derived from the case of Turkey can be tested in other political contexts where authoritarian party structures are embedded in political culture and institutional frameworks. Particularly the cases from developing democracies where authoritarian party structures originate in democratic transitions can provide adequate frameworks to test the causal validity of interest configurations, exogenous and endogenous triggers as well as power resources for the *variance in* and *exit from* intraparty authoritarianism. In fact, the study can also be extended within Turkey, including research on power relationships from different parties, districts, and provincial organizations.

Yet, in order for a political system to be selected as a case to test the hypotheses of this study, the presence of authoritarian party structures in that system is not the only criterion. The selected political systems must also have certain patterns of *party system institutionalization* such as "party rootedness in society" and "regularity in patterns of party competition."[20] These two conditions provide a stable structure of parties competing in the political system where the internal decision-making processes such as candidate selection and policy formulation can be analyzed in order to find out the main patterns of authoritarianism across and within party organizations. According to the Freedom House definition, the selected democracies, then, must at least be "partly free" or fall into the category of "electoral democracies."[21] In such democracies, there are substantial limitations on political rights, yet they are composed of competitive systems. On the contrary, in political systems that are "not free" or that do no fall into the "electoral democracy" category, there is no political competition and no party rootedness in society. This situation does not make it possible to study authoritarian party governance since it is not possible to find dynamism between the local-national levels of the parties. The countries in the Middle East such as Syria, Egypt, Iran, and some of the former Soviet Union states such as Turkmenistan, Uzbekistan, Kazakhistan are not adequate cases which belong to the "not free" category according to the 2009 Freedom House Report.

However, it would be interesting to study authoritarian party governance in some of the developing democracies of Latin America. For instance Chile has a long tradition of democratic party system where elections run mostly around large party coalitions rather than among single parties. The Pinochet dictatorial interval (1973–1989) has led to two main political alliances: (1) *Concertation for Democracy*, (2) *Democracy and Progress*.[22] As Scully explains:

> Intense negotiations among alliance partners prior to the elections determined which candidate would be slated for what office. For example, though the Christian Democratic Party [*of Concertation*] as the largest party in Chile could have claimed the right to nominate candidates from its ranks for each congressional district, for pact-keeping considerations it sometimes yielded to smaller centrist parties in areas where Christian Democrats were not the preference. Marathon sessions of delicate and complex negotiations between party leaders characterized the weeks and months before the December 1989 elections.[23]

In this respect, it is the negotiations among the party leaders that determine the candidate lists prior to the elections in Chile. The questions like how the party leaders deal with the rank-and-file pressures, in which parties it is possible to see such pressures, whether it shows variance in different parties within the same alliance would be relevant in testing the following hypotheses of this study: (1) In an authoritarian party structure, the interest configurations between principals and agents constitute the nature of the power relationship between them. (2) Exogenous triggers and endogenous triggers in the system cause the shirk of the agents (local actors) from the principals' authority (party leaders). (3) Only the agents with sufficient power resources can create a change in power relationships and thus in the power structure of the party.

Similar to Chile, Brazil is another case where party alliances structure the political system. The party system has transited from multiparty fragmentation to a broad bi-partyism, that is, a system structured by two-party alliances: one, led by the Workers Party (PT) alongside allied satellite parties including the Socialist Party, Communist Party, Republican Party, and the Liberal Party; the other alliance led by the Brazilian Social-Democratic party (PSDB) flanked by its main ally, the Liberal Front.[24] In this respect, the future studies in such Latin American examples can reshape the hypotheses of this study considering the effect of party alliances on party power structures.

Furthermore, some studies in party politics have shown that the party leaders are constrained by electoral imperatives.[25] In other words, party leaders, even while safeguarding their power within the party must monitor the desires of important constituencies. On the other hand, this study has shown that one of the most important power resources of the local party actors is their ability to control the local constituencies that they are responsible for. In this respect while such control can create a challenge in the power relationship between the agent and the principal; alliance among the agents with such power resources can create a challenge to the whole authoritarian party structure, paving the way for internal democratization. This can be a final hypothesis to be tested in future studies, which include cases analyzing transitions to internal party democratization from intraparty authoritarianism.

Appendix A

List of Open-Ended Interview Questions

Personal Information

1. Date and Place of Birth
2. Father's Date and Place of Birth
3. What is your job?
4. What is your education status?
5. What is the monthly salary that you get? Does anyone in your family work?
6. Are you a member of another organization (NGO, trade union, business association, etc)?
7. How long have you been a member of this party?
8. Did you have any ties with other parties before?
9. What are the three most important reasons that motivated you to be a party member? And why specifically this party?
10. What is your role in the party?
11. How did you come up to this position (chair, activity coordinator, etc) in the party? Can you please share your story with me?
12. What was your previous position in the party?
13. How much time do you spend on party activities in one week?
14. Have you ever considered running for the office? Is so for which position?

Party Organization Questions

Local level

1. What is the most important three responsibilities that you fulfill during election times?

2. What is the most important three responsibilities that you fulfill during nonelection times?

3. What methods do you use to reach voters during election times?

4. What is your major source of funding for your party activities? Do you collect membership fees?

5. Is your party in any connection with other parties at the local level? What kind of connections?

6. Do you work with any community-based organizations, or non-governmental organizations at the local level? Which organizations are they?

7. How many members do you have at the district level? How many of them are active?

8. Has there been any district or provincial party conventions in the last two years? Have you taken part in any of these conventions? How many delegates participate in the conventions? Who determines the delegates?

9. What kind of alternative strategies or policies do you offer in solving local problems (traffic, environment, etc.)

Relations with the national party leaders / Perceptions about decision-making and leadership domination

10. If you observe a problem (i.e., complaints, member issues) at the local level within your party organization, what do you do? With whom do you first contact in the party?

11. Do the parliamentary members / central party members often visit your district party organization? How often do you see them?

12. Who do you think should determine the parliamentary candidates within the organization?

13. Who determines the parliamentary candidates in your organization? Are you satisfied with this situation?

14. How important is the party discipline for your party?

15. We see in many papers, in the news that the parties in Turkey are generally subject to a phenomenon of *leadership domination*. What do you think about this statement?

16. Do you think that there is *leadership domination* in your party?

17. Do you believe that the candidate selection process is democratic in your party?

18. What criteria should determine the candidates?
19. What is the most important concept / idea that best defines your party?
20. What should be done to make your party more successful (in elections or as an organization)?

Appendix B

Outline of the Interviews

(Each cell shows the number of interviewees)

	Gender		Education Level				
	Male	Female	No education	Elementary School	Middle School	High School	University
AKP-Diyarbakır	4	3	–	–	–	3	4
AKP-Ümraniye	4	2	–	–	–	1	5
AKP-Tarsus	3	2	–	–	–	2	3
AKP-Karşıyaka	4	2	–	–	–	1	5
AKP-TOTAL	15	9	–	–	–	7	17
CHP-Diyarbakır	3	3	–	–	–	4	2
CHP-Ümraniye	2	4	–	1	1	3	1
CHP-Tarsus	4	2	–	2	1	3	–
CHP-Karşıyaka	3	1	–	–	–	1	3
CHP-TOTAL	12	10	–	3	2	11	6
MHP-Diyarrbakır	4	–	–	–	1	2	1
MHP-Ümraniye	3	2	–	–	1	1	3
MHP-Tarsus	4	2	–	1	–	2	3
MHP-Karşıyaka	5	1	–	–	1	3	2
MHP-TOTAL	16	5	–	1	3	8	9
DTP-Diyarbakır	5	1	2	–	–	2	2
DTP-Ümraniye	5	2	–	2	3	–	2
DTP-Tarsus	4	1	–	4	1	–	–
DTP-Karşıyaka	3	3	–	3	–	1	2
DTP-TOTAL	17	7	2	9	4	3	6

| | Income Level | | | | | Age | | |
	Less than 1000 TL	1001–3000 TL	3001–5000 TL	More than 5000 TL	Unknown	Less than 30	31–55	56–70
AKP-Diyarbakır	–	4	1	–	2	1	6	–
AKP-Ümraniye	–	3	1	1	1	–	6	–
AKP-Tarsus	2	1	–	1	1	2	3	–
AKP-Karşıyaka	–	3	3	–	–	2	3	1
AKP-TOTAL	2	11	5	2	4	5	18	1
CHP-Diyarbakır	1	4	–	–	1	1	4	1
CHP-Ümraniye	–	6	–	–	–	1	3	2
CHP-Tarsus	2	3	–	–	1	–	4	2
CHP-Karşıyaka	–	3	–	1	–	1	3	–
CHP-TOTAL	3	16	–	1	2	3	14	5
MHP-Diyarrbakır	1	2	–	1	–	–	2	2
MHP-Ümraniye	–	3	1	1	–	1	4	–
MHP-Tarsus	3	1	1	–	1	–	6	–
MHP-Karşıyaka	–	3	1	–	2	1	4	1
MHP-TOTAL	4	9	3	2	3	2	16	3
DTP-Diyarbakır	2	1	2	–	1	1	5	–
DTP-Ümraniye	2	2	–	–	3	1	5	1
DTP-Tarsus	5	–	–	–	–	–	2	3
DTP-Karşıyaka	5	1	–	–	–	2	2	2
DTP-TOTAL	14	4	2	–	4	4	14	6

	Activism Period in the Party (Years)					Party Working Hours (Per Week)			
	Less than 1	1–3	4–5	6–10	More than 10	Less than 5	5–10	11–20	More than 20
AKP-Diyarbakır	–	–	–	6	1	–	2	2	3
AKP-Ümraniye	–	–	–	–	6	–	2	2	2
AKP-Tarsus	–	–	–	1	4	–	–	3	2
AKP-Karşıyaka	–	–	2	2	2	–	2	2	2
AKP-TOTAL	–	–	2	9	13	–	6	9	9
CHP-Diyarbakır	–	–	1	2	3	–	–	3	3
CHP-Ümraniye	–	–	2	–	4	1	1	3	1
CHP-Tarsus	–	–	–	1	6	–	1	1	4
CHP-Karşıyaka	–	–	1	1	2	–	1	2	1
CHP-TOTAL	–	–	4	3	15	1	3	9	9
MHP-Diyarrbakır	–	–	–	–	4	–	1	–	3
MHP-Ümraniye	–	2	2	–	1	–	1	3	1
MHP-Tarsus	–	–	2	1	3	–	–	3	3
MHP-Karşıyaka	–	2	2	1	4	1	1	1	3
MHP-TOTAL	–	2	6	1	12	1	3	7	10
DTP-Diyarbakır	–	–	–	2	4	–	1	1	4
DTP-Ümraniye	–	–	–	3	4	–	1	3	3
DTP-Tarsus	–	–	–	1	4	–	–	2	3
DTP-Karşıyaka	–	–	2	–	4	–	1	1	4
DTP-TOTAL	–	–	2	6	16	–	3	7	14

Notes

Introduction

1. Robert Michels, *Political Parties: A Sociological Study of the Oligarchical Tendencies of Modern Democracies* (New York: Dover Publications, 1959).
2. Richard S. Katz and Peter Mair, "The Evolution of Party Organizations in Europe: The Three Faces of Party Organization," *American Review of Politics* 14 (1993): 593–617.
3. For the inclusiveness dimension, see Gideon Rahat and Reuven Y. Hazan, "Candidate Selection Methods: An Analytical Framework," *Party Politics* 7 (2001): 297–322; Paul Pennings and Reuven Y. Hazan, "Democratizing Candidate Selection: Causes and Consequences," *Party Politics* 7 (2001): 273. For decentralization within parties, see Carole Pateman, *Participation and Democratic Theory* (Cambridge: Cambridge University Press, 1970); and Vaclav Havel, "Anti-political Parties," in *Democracy and Civil Society*, ed. John Keane (London: Verso, 1988), 391–398. For a brief overview of all three dimensions, see Susan Scarrow, *Implementing Intra-party Democracy*. New York: NDI, 2005), 6.
4. Michels, *Political Parties*, 377–392.
5. Ibid., 49–59.
6 Maurice Duverger, *Political Parties* (London: Methuen, 1963).
7. Some examples for these studies are Richard S. Katz and Peter Mair, "Changing Models of Party Organization and Party Democracy," *Party Politics* 1 (1995): 5–28; Ruud Koole, "Cadre, Catch-all or Cartel? A Comment on the Notion of the Cartel Party," *Party Politics* 2 (1996): 507–524; Richard S. Katz and Peter Mair, "The Ascendancy of the Party in Public Office: Party Organizational Change in Twentieth-Century Democracies," in *Political Parties: Old Concepts and New Challenges*, ed. Richard Gunther et al. (Oxford: Oxford University Press, 2002), 113–135; Peter Mair and Ingrid van Biezen, "Party Membership in Twenty European Democracies, 1980–2000," *Party Politics* 7 (2001): 5–21; Philippe Schmitter, "Parties Are Not What They Once Were," in *Political Parties and Democracy*, ed. Larry Diamond et al. (Baltimore: Johns Hopkins University Press, 2001), 67–89.
8. Peter Mair, "Party Organizations: From Civil Society to the State," in *How Parties Organize: Change and Adaptation in Party Organizations in*

Western Democracies, ed. Richard Katz et al. (London: Sage Publications, 1994), 1–23.

9. Peter Mair, "Continuity, Change and the Vulnerability of Party," *West European Politics* 12 (1989): 169–187; Hermann Schmitt and Soren Holmberg, "Political Parties in Decline?" in *Citizens and the State*, ed. Hans-Dieter Klingemann et al. (Oxford: Oxford University Press, 1995), 95–133.

10. Examples for such counterarguments can be found in Herbert Kitschelt, "Citizens, Politicians, and Party Cartelization: Political Representation and State Failure in Post-Industrial Democracies," *European Journal of Political Research* 37 (2000): 149–79; Susan Scarrow, "Parties and the Expansion of Direct Democracy. Who Benefits?" *Party Politics* 5, no. 3 (1999): 341–362; Susan Scarrow, "Parties without Members? Party Organization in a Changing Electoral Environment," in *Parties Without Partisans: Political Change in Advanced Industrial Democracies*, ed. Russell Dalton et al. (Oxford: Oxford University Press, 2000), 79–101; Patrick Seyd, "New Parties / New Politics: A Case Study of the British Labour Party," *Party Politics* 5 (1999): 383–407.

11. Ingrid van Biezen, *Political Parties in New Democracies: Party Organization in Southern and East-Central Europe* (London: Palgrave Macmillan, 2003); Zsolt Enyedi, "Party Politics in Post-Communist Transition," in *Handbook of Political Parties*, ed. Richard Katz et al. (London: Sage Publications, 2006), 228–238; Petr Kopecky, "Developing Party Organizations in East-Central Europe: What Type of Party is Likely to Emerge?" *Party Politics* 1 (1995): 515–534; Paul G. Lewis, "Party Funding in Post-communist East-Central Europe," in *Funding Democratization*, ed. Peter Burnell et al. (Manchester: Manchester University Press, 1998), 137–157; Gabor Toka, "Political Parties and Democratic Consolidation in East Central Europe," in *Consolidating the Third Wave Democracies: Themes and Perspectives*, ed. by Larry Diamond et al. (Baltimore, MD: John Hopkins University Press, 1997), 93–134; Aleks Szczerbiak, *Poles Together? The Emergence and Development of Political Parties in Post-Communist Poland* (Budapest: Central European University, 2001).

12. Alan Ware, *Political Parties and Party Systems* (Oxford: Oxford University Press, 1996), 139; Richard Gunther and Larry Diamond, "Species of Political Parties: A New Typology." *Party Politics* 9 (2003): 173.

13. Dankwart Rustow, "The Development of Parties in Turkey," in *Political Parties and Political Development*, ed. Joseph La Palombara et al. (New Jersey: Princeton University Press, 1966), 107–136.

14. Teorell, Jan, "A Deliberative Defence," Ergun Özbudun, *Siyasal Partiler* (Ankara: Sosyal Bilimler Derneği, 1974).

15. Kay Lawson, "When Linkage Fails," in *When Parties Fail: Emerging Alternative Organizations*, ed. Kay Lawson et al. (Princeton, NJ: Princeton University Press, 1988), 16.

16. APSA (American Political Science Association) Committee on Political Parties, *Toward a More Responsible Two-Party System* (New York: Rinehart, 1950); C.B. Macpherson, *The Life and Times of Liberal Democracy* (Oxford: Oxford University Press, 1977); Teorell, "A Deliberative Defence."

17. Alan Ware, *The Logic of Party Democracy* (London: Macmillan, 1979).

18. Elmer E. Schattschneider, *Party Government* (New York: Farrar and Rinehart, 1942); Anthony Downs, *An Economic Theory of Democracy* (New York: Harper, 1957); Duverger, *Political Parties*.

19. Scarrow, *Implementing Intra-party Democracy*, 3–5.

20. Adoption of the direct primary method in the United States was a means to give the power of selection to large number of voters and prevent the rise of oligarchy or authoritarianism, but it rather facilitated the growth of personal attachments rather than party loyalty. See Leon D. Epstein, *Political Parties in Western Democracies* (New Brunswick, NJ: Transaction Books, 1982) and V.O. Jr. Key, *Politics, Parties, and Pressure Groups* (New York: Crowell, 1964).

21. Rahat and Hazan, "Candidate Selection Methods," 317.

22. For power as a relational phenomenon, see David Baldwin, "Power Analysis and World Politics: New Trends versus Old Tendencies," *World Politics* 31 (1979): 176; Peter M. Blau, *Exchange and Power in Social Life* (New York: John Wiley and Sons, 1964), 118–125; and Richard M. Emerson, "Power–Dependence Relations," *American Sociological Review* 27 (1962): 31–40.

23. Therefore, this study should be distinguished from case-oriented comparative studies, which introduce evidence for a comprehensive examination of historical phenomena. For a comparison of case-oriented and variable-oriented studies, see Charles Ragin, *The Comparative Method: Moving Beyond Qualitative and Quantitative Strategies* (Berkeley: University of California Press, 1987), Chapters 3–4.

24. "Controlled comparison method" is a term used by Alexander L. George and Andrew Bennett, *Case Studies and Theory Development in the Social Sciences* (Cambridge, MA: MIT Press, 2005), 153. Lijphart calls the same term as "comparable-cases method." See Arend Lijphart, "The Comparable–Cases Strategy in Comparative Research," *Comparative Political Studies* 8 (1975): 158–177.

25. Alexander L. George and Andrew Bennett, *Case Studies and Theory Development*, 153.

26. Ibid., 179.

27. Harry Eckstein, "Case Study and Theory in Political Science," in *Handbook of Political Science*, ed. Fred I. Greenstein et al. (Reading: Addison-Wesley, 1975).

28. Ibid., 110.

29. Ergun Özbudun, "From Political Islam to Conservative Democracy: The Case of the Justice and Development Party in Turkey," *South European Society and Politics* 11 (2006): 550.

30. Sabri Sayarı, "Aspects of Party Organization in Turkey," *The Middle East Journal* 30 (1976): 199.

31. Examples include Mustafa Albayrak, *Türk Siyasi Tarihinde Demokrat Parti* (Ankara: Phoenix Yayınları, 2004); Ayşe Güneş Ayata, *CHP Örgüt ve İdeoloji* (Ankara: Gündoğan Yayınları, 1992); Cem Eroğul, *Demokrat Parti* (Ankara: SBF Yayınları, 1970); Suna Kili, *1960-1975 Dönemi CHP'de Gelişmeler*,

Siyasal Bilimler Açısından Bir İnceleme (İstanbul: Boğaziçi Üniversitesi Yayınevi, 1976).

32. These exceptions are Mehmet Kabasakal, *Türkiye'de Siyasal Parti Örgütlenmesi 1908-1960* (İstanbul: Tekin Yayınevi, 1991); Arsev Bektaş, *Demokratikleşme Sürecinde Liderler Oligarşisi: CHP ve AP (1961-1981)* (İstanbul: Bağlam Yayıncılık, 1993).

33. The DTP was closed by a court decision on December 11, 2009 and succeeded by the Peace and Democracy Party (BDP—*Barış ve Demokrasi Partisi*). Yet, the research within this study was conducted right after the national elections in 2007; and therefore addresses the party with its previous label, DTP.

34. For instance, the top leadership of the ANAP has experienced six resignations between 2002 and 2009; it has also attempted to unite with the True Path Party (*Doğru Yol Partisi*—DYP) before the 2007 general elections, but the attempt failed. The DSP, on the other hand, was led by one leader since the party founder's resignation in 2004, and its candidates achieved to enter the parliament in 2007 only through being represented under the CHP. As the party was not successful in the local elections 2009, the party leader resigned in April 2009.

1   Existing Explanations on Intraparty Authoritarianism

1. Katz and Mair, "The Three Faces of Party Organization."
2. Ibid., 594.
3. Ingrid van Biezen, "On the Internal Balance of Party Power: Party Organizations in New Democracies," *Party Politics* 6 (2000): 395–418.
4. See Mair, "Party Organizations: From Civil Society to the State," and Richard S. Katz, "The Problem of Candidate Selection and Models of Party Democracy," *Party Politics* 7 (2001): 277–96.
5. Some classical studies that follow this argument are Michels, *Political Paries*; Duverger, *Political Parties*; Mosei Ostrogorski, *Democracy and the Organization of Political Parties* (New York: Macmillan, 1902); Vilfredo Pareto, *The Rise and Fall of the Elites: An Application of Theoretical Sociology* (New York: Arno Press, 1979); Max Weber, *Economy and Society*, trans. Guenther Roth et al. (New York: Bedminster Press, 1968).
6. Scarrow, *Implementing Intra-party Democracy*, 7–11.
7. James Jupp, *Political Parties* (London: Routledge & Kegan Paul, 1968), 58; Katz, "The Problem of Candidate Selection," 277. See also Schattschneider, *Party Government* and Otto Kirchheimer, "The Transformation of the Western European Party Systems," in *Political Parties and Political Development*, ed. Myron Weiner et al. (Princeton: Princeton University Press, 1966).
8. See Lawrence LeDuc, "Democratizing Party Leadership Selection," *Party Politics* 7 (2001): 323 andWilliam Cross and Andre Blais, "Who Selects the Party Leader," *Party Politics* (2011). Accessed February 10, 2011. doi:10.1177/1354068810382935.

9. Scarrow, *Implementing Intra-party Democracy*, 10.

10. Meg Russell, *Building New Labour: The Politics of Party Organisation* (Basingstoke: Palgrave Macmillan, 2005).

11. Anika Gauja, "The Pitfalls of Participatory Democracy: A Study of the Australian Democrats" GST," *Australian Journal of Political Science* 40 (2005): 71–85.

12. Rahat and Hazan, "Candidate Selection Methods."

13. Ibid., 301.

14. Pennings and Hazan, "Democratizing Candidate Selection," 273.

15. Katz, "The Problem of Candidate Selection," 290; Mair, "Party Organizations: From Civil Society to the State."

16. Katz, "The Problem of Candidate Selection," 290.

17. Rahat and Hazan, "Candidate Selection Methods," 304.

18. Scarrow, *Implementing Intra-party Democracy*, 6.

19. Ibid.

20. Ibid.

21. Vicky Randall and Lars Svasand, "Party Institutionalization in New Democracies," *Party Politics* 8 (2002): 10.

22. Scarrow, *Implementing Intra-party Democracy*, 6.

23. Mair, "Party Organizations: From Civil Society to the State," 16.

24. See Katz and Mair, "Changing Models of Party Organization"; Koole, "Cadre, Catch-All or Cartel?"; Kitschelt, "Citizens, Politicians, and Party Cartelization"; Katz, "The Problem of Candidate Selection;;"; Mark Blyth and Richard S. Katz, "From Catch-All Politics to Cartelization: The Political Economy of the Cartel Party," *West European Politics* 28 (2005): 33–60; Lars Bille, "Democratizing a Democratic Procedure: Myth or Reality?: Candidate Selection in Western European Parties, 1960–1990, " *Party Politics* 7 (2001): 363–380.

25. Katz and Mair, "Changing Models of Party Organization;;"; Katz, "The Problem of Candidate Selection;;"; Blyth and Katz, "From Catch-All Politics to Cartelization."

26. Kitschelt, "Citizens, Politicians, and Party Cartelization"; Scarrow, "Parties and the Expansion of Direct Democracy;" Scarrow, "Parties without Members?"; and Seyd, "New Parties / New Politics."

27. Russell J. Dalton, and Martin P. Wattenberg, eds., *Parties Without Partisans: Political Change in Advanced Industrial Democracies* (Oxford: Oxford University Press, 2000); Gunther and Diamond, "Species of Political Parties: A New Typology;" Richard Gunther, et al. eds., *Political parties: Old Concepts and New Challenges* (Oxford: Oxford University Press, 2002); Tomas Kostelecky, *Political Parties After Communism: Developments in East-Central Europe* (Baltimore, MD: Johns Hopkins University Press, 2002); and Aleks Szczerbiak, *Poles Together? The Emergence and Development of Political Parties in Post-Communist Poland* (Budapest: Central European University, 2001).

28. Yet, as mentioned, some scholars do question the validity of the hypothesis that parties are actually losing their democratic features in liberal democracies.

29. Richard S. Katz and Peter Mair, "Party Organization, Party Democracy and the Emergence of the Cartel Party," in *Party System Change: Approaches and Interpretations*, ed. by Peter Mair (Oxford University Press, 1997), 93–119.
30. Duverger, *Political Parties*; Kirchheimer, "The Transformation of the Western European Party Systems"; Angelo Panebianco, *Political Parties: Organization and Power* (Cambridge: Cambridge University Press, 1988); Katz and Mair, "Changing Models of Party Organization"; and Koole, "Cadre, Catch-All or Cartel?"
31. Andre Krouwell, "Party Models," in *Handbook of Political Parties*, ed. by Richard S. Katz et Al. (London: Sage Publications, 2006), 253.
32. Katz and Mair, "The Ascendancy of the Party in Public Office," 115.
33. Sigmund Neumann, "Towards a Comparative Study of Political Parties," in *Modern Political Parties: Approaches to Comparative Politics*, ed. by Sigmund Neumann (Chicago, IL: University of Chicago Press, 1956), 395–421; Galen A. Irwin, "The Netherlands," in *Western European Party Systems: Trends and Prospects*, ed. By Peter H. Merkl (New York: Free Press, 1980), 170; and Alexander De Grand, "Giolitti and the Socialists," in *Italian Socialism*, ed. by Spencer M. Di Scala (Amherst: University of Massachusetts Press, 1996), 28.
34. Katz, "The Problem of Candidate Selection," 284.
35. Krouwell, "Party Models," 255.
36. Darcy K. Leach, "The Iron Law of What Again? Conceptualizing Oligarchy Across Organizational Forms," *Sociological Theory* 23 (2005): 326.
37. R. Kenneth Carty and William Cross, "Can Stratarchically Organized Parties be Democratic? The Canadian Case," *Journal of Elections, Public Opinion and Parties* 16 (2006): 94.
38. Kirchheimer, "The Transformation of the Western European Party Systems."
39. This evidence of change over time was probably more meaningful in the cases of the long-established Western democracies, and, to a lesser extent, in the southern cases such as Greece, Portugal, and Spain. See Mair and Biezen, "Party Membership in Twenty European Democracies, 1980–2000," 11.
40. Alan Ware, *Political Parties: Electoral Change and Structural Response* (New York: Basil Blackwell, 1987); and Richard Gunther and Anthony Mughan, eds. *Democracy and the Media: A Comparative Perspective* (Cambridge and New York: Cambridge University Press), 2000.
41. Carty and Cross, "Can Stratarchically Organized Parties be Democratic?" 94.
42. Katz, "The Problem of Candidate Selection," 285.
43. Katz and Mair, "Changing Models of Party Organization."
44. Katz, "The Problem of Candidate Selection," 288.
45. Katz and Mair, "The Ascendancy of the Party in Public Office," 129.
46. Mair, "Party Organizations: From Civil Society to the State," 17.
47. Exceptions do exists. For instance, some recent examples from Canada, Ireland, New Zealand, and Australia have shown that stratarchically organized parties can be internally democratic. See, Carty and Cross, "Can Stratarchically Organized Parties be Democratic?"

48. This is contrary to the argument of Seymour Martin Lipset and Stein Rokkan, "Cleavage Structure, Party Systems, and Voter Alignments: An Introduction," in *Party Systems and Voter Alignments*, ed. by Seymour Martin Lipset et al. (New York: Free Press, 1967), 1–64.

49. According to Dahl, there are two dimensions of democratization: Inclusiveness and public contestation: When both dimensions are low in degree, then the political system is considered to be a "closed domination"; vice versa is considered as "polyarchy." When inclusiveness is high and public contestation is low, the system is an "inclusive domination" and vice versa is "competitive oligarchy." For an evaluation of Dahl's arguments, see Ingrid van Biezen, *Political Parties in New Democracies: Party Organization in Southern and East-Central Europe* (London: Palgrave Macmillan, 2003).

50. Biezen, *Political Parties in New Democracies*, 24–26.

51. Ibid., 30.

52. See Enyedi, "Party Politics in Post-Communist Transition"; and Toka, "Political Parties and Democratic Consolidation in East Central Europe."

53. Kopecky, "Developing Party Organizations in East-Central Europe"; and Szczerbiak, *Poles Together? The emergence and Development of Political Parties in Post-Communist Poland*; Biezen, *Political Parties in New Democracies*.

54. Richard Gunther and Larry Diamond, "Species of Political Parties: A New Typology," *Party Politics* 9 (2003): 168.

55. Alan Ware, *Political Parties and Party Systems* (Oxford: Oxford University Press, 1996), 139; Gunther and Diamond, "Species of Political Parties: A New Typology," 173.

56. Rustow, "The Development of Parties in Turkey," 108.

57. Martin Shefter, *Political Parties and the State: The American Historical Experience* (Princeton: Princeton University Press, 1994), 26–27.

58. Daniel Verdier, "The Politics of Public Aid to Private Industry: The Role of Policy Networks," *Comparative Political Studies* 28 (1995): 2–42.

59. Simona Piattoni ed., *Clientelism, Interests, and Democratic Representation: The European Experience in Historical and Comparative Perspective* (Cambridge: Cambridge University Press, 2001).

60. Ingrid van Biezen, "On the Theory and Practice of Party Formation and Adaptation in New Democracies," *European Journal of Political Research* 44 (2005): 165.

61. Ibid., 164.

62. Biezen, "On the Internal Balance of Party Power."

63. Nicole Bolleyer, "Inside the Cartel Party: Party Organization in Government and Opposition," *Political Studies* 57 (2009): 559–579.

64. Zsolt Enyedi and Lukas Linek, "Searching for the Right Organization: Ideology and Party Structure in East-Central Europe," *Party Politics* 14 (2008): 457–458.

65. Duverger, *Political Parties*, xxxiv–xxxvi. This argument is empirically validated by Kenneth Janda and Desmond S. King, "Formalizing and Testing Duverger's Theories on Political Parties," *Comparative Political Studies* 18 (1985): 139–69.

66. Herbert Kitschelt and Anthony J. McGann, *The Radical Right in Western Europe: A Comparative Analysis* (Ann Arbour: University of Michigan Press, 1997); Herbert Kitschelt, *The Logics of Party Formation: Ecological Politics in Belgium and West Germany* (Ithaca, NY and London: Cornell University Press, 1989).

67. Frank L. Wilson, "The Center-Right at the End of the Century," in *The European Center-Right at the End of the Twentieth Century*, ed. Frank L. Wilson (Basingstoke: Macmillan, 1998), 251.

68. For the analysis of the role of motivations and personality on power relations, see, for instance, Arnold A. Rogow and Harold D. Laswell, "The Definition of Corruption," in *Political Corruption: Readings in Comparative Analysis*, ed. A.J. Heidenheimer (New York: Holt, Rinehart and Winstan, 1970); and Dean K. Simonton, *Psychology, Science, and History: An Introduction to Historiometry* (New Haven, CT: Yale University Press, 1991).

69. See Robert F. Bales, *Interaction Process Analysis: A Method for the Study of Small Groups* (Cambridge, MA: Addison-Wesley, 1950); John K. Hemphill and Alvin E. Coons, "Development of the Leader Behavior Description Questionnaire," in *Leader Behavior: Its Description and Measurement*, ed. Ralph M. Stogdill et al. (Columbus: Bureau of Business Research, Ohio State University, 1957); and Rensis Likert, *New Patterns of Management* (New York: McGraw-Hill, 1961).

70. James M. Burns, *Leadership* (New York: Harper & Row, 1978).

71. Bernard M. Bass, *Leadership and Performance Beyond Expectations* (New York: Free Press, 1985).

72. Jane M. Howell and Bruce J. Avolio, "Transformational Leadership, Transactional Leadership, Loss of Control, and Support for Innovation," *Journal of Applied Psychology* 78 (1993): 891–902; Boas Shamir, Robert J. House, and Michael B. Arthur, "The Motivational Effects of Charismatic: A Self-Concept Based Theory," *Organizational Science* 4 (1993): 577–594.

73. Kurt Lewin and Robert Lippitt, "An Experimental Approach to the Study of Autocracy and Democracy: A Preliminary Note," *Sociometry* 1 (1938): 292–300.

74. Victor H. Vroom and Philip W. Yetton, *Leadership and Decision-Making* (Pittsburgh: University of Pittsburgh Press, 1973).

75. Bolleyer, "Inside the Cartel Party."

76. This situation is an example for what Parsons calls "the combinatorial decision-making process" in which the structure of restricted resources matches the structure of the system of interest-demands. See Talcott Parsons, "Power and the Social System," in *Power*, ed. Steven Lukes (New York University Press: New York, 1986), 101.

77. Bolleyer, "Inside the Cartel Party."

78. Katz, "The Problem of Candidate Selection," 287.

79. LeDuc, "Democratizing Party Leadership Selection," 327.

80. Ibid., 330.

81. Ibid., 334.

82. Panebianco, *Political Parties*, 22.

2 Intraparty Authoritarianism in Turkey

1. Examples are Guillermo O'Donnell and Philippe Schmitter, *Transitions from Authoritarian Rule: Tentative Conclusions about Uncertain Democracies* (Baltimore: Johns Hopkins University, 1986); John Higley and Richard Gunther, *Elites and Democratic Consolidation in Latin America and Southern Europe* (New York: Cambridge University Press, 1991); Juan Linz, *The Breakdown of Democratic Regimes: Crisis, Breakdown, and Reequilibrium* (Baltimore, MD: John Hopkins University Press, 1978).

2. For example, Lord Kinross, *Atatürk: A Biography of Mustafa Kemal, Father of Modern Turkey* (New York: William Morrow and Company, 1965); Andrew Mango, *Atatürk: The Biography of the Founder of Modern Turkey* (New York: Overlook, 2000); Al Macfie, *Atatürk* (Longman: London, 1994); Metin Heper, *İsmet İnönü: The Making of a Turkish Statesman* (Leiden: Brill Publications, 1998).

3. Metin Heper and Sabri Sayarı, eds., *Political Leaders and Democracy in Turkey* (Lanham MD: Lexington Books, 2002); Barry Rubin and Metin Heper, eds. *Political Parties in Turkey* (London: Cass, 2002); Sabri Sayarı, "Towards A New Turkish Party System?" *Turkish Studies* 8 (2007): 197–210.

4. Sabri Sayarı, "Introduction" in *Political Leaders and Democracy in Turkey*, eds. Metin Heper et al. (Lanham MD: Lexington Books, 2002), 3.

5. Sabri Sayarı, "Aspects of Party Organization in Turkey," *The Middle East Journal* 30 (1976): 187–199; İlter Turan, "Political Parties and the Party System in Post-1983 Turkey," in *State, Democracy and the Military: Turkey in the 1980s*, eds. Metin Heper et al. (Berlin: W. de Gruyter, 1988), 65; Ergun Özbudun, "Parties and the Party System," in *Contemporary Turkish Politics: Challenges to Democratic Consolidation*, ed. Ergun Özbudun (Boulder, London: Lynne Rienner Publishers, 2000), 83; Ergun Özbudun, "The Institutional Decline of Parties in Turkey," in *Political Parties and Democracy*, eds. Larry Diamond Baltimore (London: The Johns Hopkins University Press, 2001), 246.

6. Özbudun, "From Political Islam to Conservative Democracy," 550.

7. Yet, some exceptional changes do occur within the power structures of parties in the time of corruption scandals. One example is the removal of the AKP vice-chair Dengir Mir Mehmet Fırat in 2008; after he was accused of fictitious export and drug trafficking by the opposition party during the campaigns for local elections.

8. Barry Rubin, "Introduction—Turkey's Political Parties: A Remarkably Important Issue," in *Political Parties in Turkey*, eds. Barry Rubin et al. (London: Cass, 2002), 3.

9. There are a few exceptions in this regard. Dorronsoro and Massicard, in their study, analyze the MPs' relationship with the central party office, local party organizations as well as the bureaucratic state elite in Turkey. See Gilles Dorronsoro and Elise Massicard. "Being a Member of Parliament in contemporary Turkey," *European Journal of Turkish Studies* 3 (2005), accessed February 28, 2010, http://ejts.revues.org/index502.html. Kabasakal and

Bektaş are the two other exceptions: Kabasakal, *Türkiye'de Siyasal Parti Örgütlenmesi* and Bektaş, *Demokratikleşme Sürecinde Liderler Oligarşisi.*

10. İlter Turan, "Old Soldiers Never Die: The Republican People's Party of Turkey." *South European Society and Politics* 11 (2006): 570–571.

11. Sayarı, "Aspects of Party Organization in Turkey," 190.

12. Bektaş, *Demokratikleşme Sürecinde Liderler Oligarşisi*, 94.

13. Frank Tachau, "Bülent Ecevit: From Idealist to Pragmatist," in *Political Leaders and Democracy in Turkey*, ed. Metin Heper et al. (Lexington Books, 2002), 114.

14. Suna Kili, *1960–1975 Dönemi CHP'de Gelişmeler, Siyasal Bilimler Açısından Bir İnceleme* (İstanbul: Boğaziçi Üniversitesi Yayınevi, 1976), 268–269; Hikmet Bila, *CHP 1919–1999* (İstanbul: Doğan Kitapçılık, 1999), 247; Bektaş, *Demokratikleşme Sürecinde Liderler Oligarşisi*, 83.

15. Bektaş, *Demokratikleşme Sürecinde Liderler Oligarşisi*, 93.

16. Alev Çınar and Ergun Özbudun, "Mesut Yılmaz: From Özal's Shadow to Mediator," in *Political Leaders and Democracy in Turkey*, eds. Metin Heper et al. (Lexington Books, 2002), 183.

17. Metin Heper, "Turgut Özal's Presidency: Crisis and the Glimmerings of Consensus," in *Politics in the Third Turkish Republic*, eds. Metin Heper et al. (Boulder, CO: Westview Press, 1994), 196.

18. Murat Somer, "Turkey's Kurdish Conflict: Changing Context, and Domestic and Regional Implications," *Middle East Journal* 58 (2004): 235–253; Nicole F. Watts, "Allies and Enemies: Pro-Kurdish Parties in Turkish Politics, 1990–1994," *International Journal of Middle East Studies* 31 (1999): 631–656; Aylin Güney, "The People's Democracy Party," *Turkish Studies* 3 (2002): 122–137; Eyyüp Demir, *Yasal Kürtler* (Istanbul: Tevn Yayınları, 2005).

19. Demokratik Toplum Partisi, *DTP Program ve Tüzüğü* [The DTP Program and Constitution] (Ankara, 2005), Article No: 3/m.

20. Namık Durukan, "DTP 'şahinler'in kanatları altında," *Milliyet*, November 10, 2007, accessed April 15, 2008, http://www.milliyet.com.tr/2007/11/10 /siyaset/siy08.html

21. According to the Turkish election law, only parties gaining more than ten percent of the national vote are allowed to gain parliamentary seats. Until 2007, the pro-Kurdish parties were not represented in the parliament since they could not overcome this electoral threshold. Therefore, in 2007, the DTP did not enter the elections as a party, but rather ran "independent" candidates. The aim of this tactic was to bypass the ten percent national election threshold. That is how the party managed to gain 20 seats in the parliament.

22. These issues were elaborated in the 2007 national convention such as demand for 'autonomy' and 'separate flag' in the region. See the news, "DTP 'Öcalan halk önderi dedi, özerklik ve ayrı bayrak talep etti," *Radikal*, October 31, 2007, accessed April 15, 2007, http://www.radikal.com.tr/sayfa .php?sayfa=4&tarih=31/10/2007

23. Şerif Mardin, "Center-Periphery Relations: A Key To Turkish Politics?" *Daedalus* 102 (1973): 169–190; Metin Heper, *The State Tradition in Turkey* (Walkington: Eothen, 1985), İlkay Sunar and Sabri Sayarı, "Democracy

in Turkey: Problems and Prospects," in *Transitions From Authoritarian Rule: Experiences in Southern Europe and Latin America*, eds. Guillermo O'Donnell et al. (Baltimore: The Johns Hopkins University Press, 1986), 165–187.

24. Ersin Kalaycıoğlu, "Elections and Party Preferences in Turkey: Changes and Continuities in the 1990s," *Comparative Political Studies* 27 (1994): 403.
25. Rustow, "The Development of Parties in Turkey," 111.
26. Ibid., 120.
27. Even though both Atatürk and Inönü as the most important political leaders in the early Republican era acted in an authoritarian manner, they did so only to protect the national unity and territorial integrity of the country. The authoritarianism did not reflect an arbitrary fashion, promoting personal interests. See Metin Heper, "İsmet İnönü: A Rationalistic Democrat," in *Political Leaders and Democracy in Turkey*, eds. Metin Heper et al. (Lexington Books, 2002), 31 and Mango, *Atatürk*, 19.
28. Bektaş, *Demokratikleşme Sürecinde Liderler Oligarşisi*, 24.
29. Metin Toker, *İsmet Paşayla 10 Yıl 1954–1964* (İstanbul: Akis Yayınları, 1969), 117.
30. C. H. Dodd, "Ataturk and Political Parties," in *Political Parties and Democracy in Turkey*, eds. Metin Heper et al. (London: Tauris, 1991), 24–42.
31. Rustow, "The Development of Parties in Turkey," 127.
32. Kemal H. Karpat, "The Republican People's Party 1923–1945," in *Political Parties and Democracy in Turkey*, eds. Metin Heper et al. (London: Tauris, 1991), 42–64.
33. Kemal H. Karpat, "Society, Economics and Politics in Contemporary Turkey," *World Politics* 17 (1964): 51–54; Frederick W. Frey, *The Turkish Political Elite* (Cambridge: The M.I.T. Press), 1965.
34. Mardin, "Center-Periphery Relations."
35. The maim principles of the Republic were *republicanism*, meaning the removal of personal rule; *nationalism*, meaning a nation to generate its goals and means to realize them; *populism*, meaning that the general interest of the society should not be given short shrift; *secularism*, meaning that the goals and norms of the new State should not be derived from religious precepts; *reformism*, meaning that the state norms should be modified according to changing conditions and *etatism*, meaning an interventionist economic program. See Heper, *The State Tradition in Turkey*, 64.
36. Ayşe Güneş Ayata, "Class and Clientelism in the Republican People's Party," in *Turkish State, Turkish Society*, eds. Nükhet Sirman et al. (London: Routledge, 1990), 160.
37. Özbudun, "The Institutional Decline of Parties in Turkey," 245.
38. Cem Eroğul, *Demokrat Parti (Tarihi ve İdeolojisi)* (Ankara: SBF Yayınları, 1970); Kemal H. Karpat, *Turkey's Politics. The Transition to a Multi-Party System* (Princeton: Princeton University Press, 1959), 419.
39. Sabri Sayarı, "Adnan Menderes: Between Democratic and Authoritarian Populism," in *Political Leaders and Democracy in Turkey*, eds. Metin Heper et al. (Lanham MD: Lexington Books, 2002), 76.

40. W.B. Sherwood, "The Rise of the Justice Party in Turkey," *World Politics* 20 (1967): 57.
41. Sencer Ayata, "Patronage, Party and State: the Politicization of Islam in Turkey," *Middle East Journal* 50 (1996): 44.
42. Ibid., 52.
43. Heper, *The State Tradition in Turkey*, 100.
44. According to Heper, the state elite perceived democracy as an end for Turkey rather than a means. See Metin Heper ed., *The State and Public Bureaucracies: A Comparative Perspective* (New York: Greenwood Press), 1987. For Ismet Inönü, the second leader of the CHP, it was necessary that the nation learnt how to govern themselves before he died. Therefore, when the CHP was first defeated against the DP in 1950 national elections, he stated that 'My defeat is my greatest victory.' See Heper, *İsmet İnönü*.
45. Ömer F. Gençkaya, "The Turkish Constitutional Court and Dissolution of Political Parties: Comparative Perspectives," in *Suna Kili'ye Armağan: Cumhuriyet'e Adanan Bir Yasam* (Istanbul: Bogaziçi University Publications, 1998), 165–84. Ali Çarkoğlu, et al. *Siyasi Partilerde Reform*, (İstanbul: TESEV Yayınları, 2000). Yusuf Ş. Hakyemez and Birol Akgün, "Limitations On The Freedom Of Political Parties In Turkey And The Jurisdiction Of The European Court Of Human Rights," *Mediterranean Politics* 7 (2002): 54–78.
46. The additional Article No.1 of the SPK regulates the state subventions allocated to parties. This allocation is paid to political parties in proportion to valid votes they received in the last general elections. Political parties, which fail to pass the countrywide 10 percent threshold but received more than seven percent of the valid votes cast, are also eligible to receive state aid.
47. Ömer F. Gençkaya, "Siyasetin Finansmanı ve Siyasi Partiler," *ASOMEDYA*, October 2002.
48. Article No.37 of the SPK leaves the candidate selection method to the constitutions of the political parties.
49. Section Two of the SPK describes a detailed organizational party structure that all parties must be composed of.
50. Bektaş, *Demokratikleşme Sürecinde Liderler Oligarşisi*, 112.
51. Even though this is the general pattern observed across local party organizations in Turkey, exceptions do occur when the local party leaders are challenged at local conventions as a result of the local dynamics that change the status quo in local party structures.
52. Ömer F. Gençkaya, "Turkey," *KAS Democracy Report: Parties and Democracy* (Bonn: Bouvier Verlag, 2007).
53. The evidence largely resides on the analysis of the national conventions of the DP and the CHP from 1946 to 1960 in Kabasakal, *Türkiye'de Siyasal Parti Örgütlenmesi* and of the AP and the CHP from 1961 to 1980 in Bektaş, *Demokratikleşme Sürecinde Liderler Oligarşisi*. One noteworthy exception is the CHP organization under Ecevit's leadership, where the party structure largely gained democratic features from 1972 until the 1980 military intervention.

54. The removal of İnönü and the election of Ecevit as the new party leader of the CHP organization in 1972 is an exception.

55. The exceptions are, of course, Bülent Ecevit as the leader of the CHP (1972–1980); Mesut Yılmaz of the ANAP (1991–2002), Tansu Çiller of the DYP (1993–2002) and Devlet Bahçeli of the MHP (1997–present).

56. See Burak E. Arıkan, "The Programme of the Nationalist Action Party: An Iron Hand in a Velvet Glove?" *Middle Eastern Studies* 34 (1998): 120–134; Ümit Arklan, "Siyasal Liderlikte Karizma Olgusu: Recep Tayyip Erdoğan Örneğinde Teorik ve Uygulamalı Bir Çalışma." *Selçuk Üniversitesi Sosyal Bilimler Enstitüsü Dergisi* 16 (2006): 45–65; Metin Heper and Şule Toktaş, "Islam, Democracy, and Modernity in Contemporary Turkey: The Case of Recep Tayyip Erdoğan," *Muslim World* 93 (2003): 159.

57. Harald Schüler, *Türkiye'de Sosyal Demokrasi: Particilik, Hemşehrilik, Alevilik*, trans. Yılmaz Tonbul (İstanbul, İletişim Yayınları, 1998), 41–48.

58. The numbers are obtained from Schüler's table on the CHP's provincial membership allocation. Schüler, *Türkiye'de Sosyal Demokrasi*, 49.

59. Karpat, "The Republican People's Party 1923–1945."

60. Heper, "İsmet İnönü: A Rationalistic Democrat."

61. Ibid., 31.

62. Bektaş, *Demokratikleşme Sürecinde Liderler Oligarşisi*, 117.

63. Heper, "İsmet İnönü: A Rationalistic Democrat," 32.

64. Tachau, "Bülent Ecevit: From Idealist to Pragmatist," 114.

65. Sayarı, "Adnan Menderes," 76.

66. Feride Acar, "Turgut Özal: Pious Agent of Liberal Transformation." In *Political Leaders and Democracy in Turkey*, eds Metin Heper et al. (Lexington Books, 2002), 163–180.

67. Tachau, "Bülent Ecevit: From Idealist to Pragmatist," 115.

68. Ayşe Güneş Ayata, "The Republican People's Party," *Turkish Studies* 3 (2002): 117.

69. Tachau, "Bülent Ecevit: From Idealist to Pragmatist," 115; Bektaş, *Demokratikleşme Sürecinde Liderler Oligarşisi*, 94–99.

70. Yeşim Arat, "Süleyman Demirel: National Will and Beyond," in *Political Leaders and Democracy in Turkey*, eds. Metin Heper et al. (Lexington Books, 2002), 87–106.

71. Sencer Ayata and Ayşe Güneş Ayata, "The Center-Left Parties in Turkey," *Turkish Studies* 8 (2007): 227; Pelin Ayan, "Authoritarian Party Structures in Turkey: A Comparison of the Republican People's Party and the Justice and Development Party," *Turkish Studies* 11 (2010): 197–215.

72. The party leadership elections in the 2008 national party convention showed in fact the repressive rule of the party leader; the delegates at the party convention were not elected but rather appointed by the party leadership. See Altan Öymen, "Gizli Oylamanın Temelindeki "Apaçık Oylama'" *Radikal*, 29 April 2008, accessed April 21 2009, http://www.radikal.com.tr/haber.php?haberno=254294.

73. Ayata and Ayata, "The Center-Left Parties in Turkey."

74. Turan, "Old Soldiers Never Die," 563–564.

75. Tanıl Bora, "Nationalist Discourses in Turkey," *South Atlantic Quarterly* 102 (2003): 445.
76. Arıkan, "The Programme of the Nationalist Action Party," 123.
77. Metin Heper and Başak İnce, "Devlet Bahçeli and 'Far Right' Politics in Turkey, 1999–2002," *Middle Eastern Studies* 42 (2006): 873.
78. Bora, "Nationalist Discourses in Turkey," 447.
79. Yet, following the MHP's entrance in the parliament in 2007, Bahçeli began to act as a hardliner nationalist against the AKP policies.
80. Arklan, "Siyasal Liderlikte Karizma Olgusu."
81. Heper and Toktaş, "Islam, Democracy, and Modernity in Contemporary Turkey," 159.
82. The chapters in the edited volume by Ümit Cizre ed. *Secular and Islamic Politics in Turkey: The Making of Justice and Development Party* (London: Routledge, 2008) are the most adequate examples for this trend.
83. See İhsan D. Dağı, "The Justice and Development Party: Identity, Politics, and Human Rights Discourse in the Search for Security and Legitimacy," in *The Emergence of a New Turkey: Democracy and the AK Parti*, ed. M. Hakan Yavuz (Salt Lake City: University of Utah Press, 2006), 90; Ahmet İnsel, "AKP and Normalizing Democracy in Turkey," *South Atlantic Quarterly* 102 (2003): 293–308; Metin Heper, "The Justice and Development Party Government and the Military in Turkey," *Turkish Studies* 6 (2005): 215–231.
84. Simten Coşar and Aylin Özman. "Centre-right Politics in Turkey After the November 2002 General Election: Neoliberalism with a Muslim Face," *Contemporary Politics* 10 (2004): 68.
85. Ersin Kalaycıoğlu, "Attitudinal Orientation to Party Organizations in Turkey in the 2000s," *Turkish Studies* 9 (2008): 308.
86. Duverger, *Political Parties*, 70; Gunther and Diamond, "Species of Political Parties: A New Typology," 180.
87. Ji-Hyang Jang, "Taming Political Islamists by Islamic Capital: The Passions and Interests in Turkish Islamic Society," (PhD diss., University of Austin at Texas, 2005), 117.
88. Ayan, "Authoritarian Party Structures in Turkey."
89. Güney, "The People's Democracy Party," 124.
90. Nicole F. Watts, "Activists in Office: Pro-Kurdish Contentions Politics in Turkey," *Ethnopolitics* 5 (2006): 131.
91. Ibid., 127.

3   A Principal-Agent Approach to Intraparty Authoritarianism

1. For the matter of simplicity and clarification, the party on the ground is defined as local party actors comprised of both local party activists and members.
2. Baldwin, "Power Analysis and World Politics"; and Blau, *Exchange and Power in Social Life*; Emerson, "Power-Dependence Relations."

3. See for instance, Terry M. Moe, "The New Economics of Organization," *American Journal of Political Science* 28 (1984.): 739–777.

4. Emerson, "Power-Dependence Relations," 32.

5. Robert Dahl, "The Concept of Power," *Behavioral Science* 2 (1957): 202.

6. Baldwin, "Power Analysis and World Politics," 171.

7. Ibid.

8. Robert Dahl, *Modern Political Analysis* (NJ: Prentice Hall, 1976), 37 emphasis added.

9. Baldwin, "Power Analysis and World Politics," 171.

10. Ibid., 165.

11. Ibid., 166.

12. See Bertrand Jouvenel, *On Power: The Natural History of its Growth*, (London: Batchworth Press 1952); Robert Dahl, *Who Governs? Democracy and Power in an American City* (New Haven: Yale University Press, 1961), 229; and Harold D. Laswell and Abraham Kaplan, *Power and Society: A Framework for Political Enquiry* (New Haven: Yale University Press), 1950.

13. Katz, "The Problem of Candidate Selection"; Bolleyer, "Inside the Cartel Party."

14. Kaare Strom, "A Behavioral Theory of Competitive Political Parties," *American Journal of Political Science* 34 (1990): 565–598; and Wolfgang C. Müller and Kaare Strom, *Policy, Office or Votes? How Political Parties in Western Europe Make Hard Decisions?* (Cambridge: Cambridge University Press, 1999).

15. Talcott Parsons, "Power and the Social System," in *Power*, ed. Steven Lukes (New York University Press: New York, 1986), 101.

16. Emerson, "Power-Dependence Relations," 36.

17. Robert Dahl, "Power as the Control of Behavior," in *Power*, ed. Steven Lukes (New York: New York University Press, 1986), 45.

18. Baldwin, "Power Analysis and World Politics," 170.

19. Moe, "The New Economics of Organization," 745.

20. Jon Pierre and B. Guy Peters, *Governance, Politics, and the State* (New York: St. Martin's Press 2000), 15–18.

21. Gerry Stoker, "Governance as Theory: Five Propositions," *International Social Science Journal* 50 (1998): 22.

22. Matthew D. McCubbins and Thomas Schwartz, "Congressional Oversight Overlooked: Police Patrols versus Fire Alarms," *American Journal of Political Science* 28 (1984): 16–79; Matthew D. McCubbins, Roger Noll and Barry R. Weingast, "Administrative Procedures as Instruments of Political Control," *Journal of Law, Economics, and Organization* 3 (1987): 243–277; Roderick D. Kiewiet and Matthew D. McCubbins, *The Logic of Delegation: Congressional Parties and the Appropriations Process* (Chicago: University of Chicago Press, 1991); and Mark Pollack, "Delegation, Agency, and Agenda Setting in the European Community," *International Organization* 50 (1997): 99–134.

23. Jean-Jacques Laffont and David Martimort, *The Theory of Incentives: The Principal-Agent Model* (Princeton, NJ: Princeton University Press, 2002).

24. Robert O. Keohane, *After Hegemony: Cooperation and Discord in the World Political Economy* (Princeton: Princeton University Press, 1984).

25. Pollack, "Delegation, Agency, and Agenda Setting," 104.

26. Donald R. Songer, Jeffrey A. Segal, and Charles M. Cameron, "The Hierarchy of Justice: Testing a Principal-Agent Model of Supreme Court-Circuit Court Interactions," *American Journal of Political Science* 38 (1994): 674.

27. For an evaluation of these control mechanisms see McCubbins and Schwartz, "Congressional Oversight Overlooked," 427.

28. For this view, see William A. Niskanen, *Bureaucracy and Representative Government* (Chicago: Aldine, 1972) and James Q. Wilson, ed. *The Politics of Regulation* (New York: Basic Books, 1980).

29. Barry R. Weingast and Mark J. Moran "Bureaucratic Discretion or Congressional Control? Regulatory Policymaking by the Federal Trade Commission," *The Journal of Political Economy* 91 (1983): 765–800; and Barry R. Weingast, "The Congressional Bureaucratic System: A Principal-Agent Perspective," *Public Choice* 44 (1984): 147–88.

30. For a review on the role of institutions, see Weingast, "The Congressional Bureaucratic System," 153.

31. Strom, "A Behavioral Theory of Competitive Political Parties"; Müller and Strom, *Policy, Office or Votes?*

32. Wolfgang C. Müller, "Political Parties in Parliamentary Democracies: Making Delegation and Accountability Work," *European Journal of Political Research* 37 (2000): 319.

33. Gary W. Cox and Matthew D. McCubbins, *Legislative Leviathan: Party Government in the House*(Berkeley: University of California Press, 1993), 91.

34. Müller, "Political Parties in Parliamentary Democracies," 316.

35. Richard S. Katz, "Party in Democratic Theory," in *Handbook of Political Parties*, ed. Richard Katz et al. (London: Sage Publications, 2006), 36.

36. Galen A. Irwin, "The Netherlands," 170; M. Donald. Hancock, "Sweden," in *Western European Party Systems: Trends and Prospects*, ed. Peter H. Merkl (New York: Free Press, 1980), 187.

37. Katz, "The Problem of Candidate Selection," 283.

38. Kenneth A. Shepsle and Mark S. Bonchek, *Analyzing Politics: Rationality, Behavior, and Institutions* (New York: W. W. Norton, 1997), 383.

39. Carty and Cross, "Can Stratarchically Organized Parties be Democratic?" 94.

40. Panebianco, *Political Parties*; Katz and Mair, "Changing Models of Party Organization"; Bolleyer, "Inside the Cartel Party."

41. Thomas Quinn, "Electing the Leader: The British Labour Party's Electoral College," *The Journal of Politics and International Relations* 6, no. 3 (2004): 345.

42. Ibid., 347.

43. For instance, Kitschelt, "Citizens, Politicians, and Party Cartelization" and Klaus Detterbeck, "Cartel Parties in Western Europe?" *Party Politics* 11 (2005): 173–191.

44. Detterbeck, "Cartel Parties in Western Europe?"

45. Kitschelt, "Citizens, Politicians, and Party Cartelization," 158.
46. Scarrow, "Parties without Members?"
47. Biezen, *Political Parties in New Democracies.*
48. Biezen, "On the Theory and Practice of Party Formation and Adaptation," 165.
49. Biezen, *Political Parties in New Democracies.*
50. Mair, "Party Organizations: From Civil Society to the State," 16; and Katz, "The Problem of Candidate Selection," 290.
51. Strom, "A Behavioral Theory of Competitive Political Parties"; and Müller and Strom, *Policy, Office or Votes?*
52. Anthony Downs, *An Economic Theory of Democracy* (New York: Harper, 1957).
53. Strom, "A Behavioral Theory of Competitive Political Parties," 567.
54. Samuel J. Eldersveld, *Political Parties: A Behavioral Analysis* (Chicago: MacNally, 1964); and M. Margaret Conway and Frank B. Feigert, "Incentives and Task Performance Among Party Precinct Workers," *Western Political Quarterly* 27 (1974): 693–709.
55. Kiewiet and McCubbins, *The Logic of Delegation.*
56. Norman Frohlich et al., *Political Leadership and Collective Goods* (Princeton: Princeton University Press, 1971); Robert H. Salisbury, "An Exchange Theory of Interest Groups," *Midwest Journal of Political Science* 13 (1969): 1–32; and Michael J. Laver, *The Politics of Private Desires* (Harmondsworth, Eng.: Penguin, 1981).
57. Strom, "A Behavioral Theory of Competitive Political Parties," 575.
58. Weingast, "The Congressional Bureaucratic System," 153.
59. The third-way approach was also adopted by Pollack in his discussion on the European Commission, which acts as the agent of the member states, wherein he argues that "the autonomy and influence of the Commission vary considerably across issue-areas and over time as a function of the varying administrative procedures and oversight mechanisms and the possibility of sanctioning available to member governments." See Pollack, "Delegation, Agency, and Agenda Setting," 119.
60. Bryan D. Jones, "Bounded Rationality and Political Science: Lessons from Public Administration and Public Policy," *Journal of Public Administration Research and Theory* 13, no. 4 (2003): 395–412.
61. Ibid., 407.
62. John Brehm and Scott Gates, "Donut hops and Speed Traps: Evaluating Models of Supervision on Police Behavior," *American Journal of Political Science* 37 (1993): 555–581.
63. James G. March and Johan P. Olsen, *Rediscovering Institutions* (New York: Free Press, 1989).
64. Audie Klotz, *Norms in International Relations: The Struggle Against Apartheid* (Ithaca and London: Cornell University Press, 1995); Peter J. Katzenstein, *The Culture of National Security: Norms and Identity in World Politics* (New York: Columbia University Press, 1996); and Alexander Wendt, *Social Theory of International Politics* (Cambridge: Cambridge University Press, 1999).

65. For instance, Donald A. Wittman, "Parties as Utility Maximizers," *American Political Science Review* 67 (1973): 490–498; and Michael Laver, *Private Desires, Political action* (London: Sage, 1997).
66. Peter Clark and James Q. Wilson, "Incentive Systems: A Theory of Organization," *Administrative Science Quarterly* 6 (1961): 129–166.
67. Eldersveld, *Political Parties: A Behavioral Analysis.*

4 Understanding the Variance in Intraparty Authoritarianism

1. Alexander Wendt, "On Constitution and Causation in International Relations," *Review of International Studies* 24 (1998): 101–118.
2. Ibid., 105.
3. Ibid.
4. Ibid., 104.
5. Strom, "A Behavioral Theory of Competitive Political Parties"; Müller and Strom, *Policy, Office or Votes?*
6. Panebianco, *Political Parties*, 7, emphasis added.
7. Michels, *Political Parties*; Panebianco, *Political Parties*, 7.
8. Strom, "A Behavioral Theory of Competitive Political Parties"; Panebianco, *Political Parties*, 14; Howard E. Aldrich, "Organizational Boundaries and Interorganizational Conflict," in *Organizational Systems*, ed. Frank Baker (Homewood: Irving-Dorsey, 1973), 379–393.
9. Clark and Wilson, "Incentive Systems."
10. Edmond Costantini and Joel King, "The Motives of Political Party Activists: A Factor-Analytic Exploration," *Political Behavior* 6 (1984): 81.
11. See examples such as Richard C. Hoftstetter, "Organizational Activists: The Bases of Participation in Amateur and Professional Groups," *American Politics Quarterly* 1 (1973): 244–276 and Thomas H. Roback, "Motivation for Activism Among Republican National. Convention Delegates: Continuity and Change, 1972–1976," *Journal of Politics* 42 (1980): 181–201.
12. M. Margaret Conway and Frank B. Feigert, "Incentives and Task Performance Among Party Precinct Workers," *Western Political Quarterly* 27 (1974): 693–709.
13. Panebianco, *Political Parties*, 9.
14. Mancur Olson, *The Logic of Collective Action* (Cambridge, MA: Harvard University Press, 1965).
15. See John May, "Opinion Structure of Political Parties: The Special Law of Curvilinear Disparity," *Political Studies* 21 (1973): 135–151 and Müller and Strom, *Policy, Office or Votes?*
16. See Robert A. Hitlin and John S. Jackson, "Amateur and Professional Politicians," *Journal of Politics* 39 (1977): 786–793; Thomas H. Roback, "Amateurs and Professionals: Delegates to the 1972 Republican National Convention," *Journal of Politics* 37 (1975): 436–468; John W. Soule and

James W. Clarke, "Amateurs and Professionals: A Study of Delegates to the 1968 Democratic National Convention," *American Political Science Review* 64 (1970): 888–898; Aaron Wildavsky, "The Goldwater Phenomenon: Purists, Politicians, and the Two-Party System," *Review of Politics* 27 (1965): 386–413.

17. Conway and Frank Feigert, "Incentives and Task Performance Among Party Precinct Workers."

18. Peter M. Blau and M. W. Meyer, *Bureaucracy in Modern Society* (New York: Random House, 1956).

19. Steven Lukes, *Power: A Radical View* (London: Macmillan Press, 1974).

20. This argument originally belongs to Peter Bachrach and Morton S. Baratz, "Two faces of Power," *The American Political Science Review* 56 (1962): 947–952 and is discussed in Lukes, *Power*, 18.

21. Lukes, *Power*, 20.

22. Ibid., 24–25.

23. Ibid., 50.

24. John Kenneth Galbraith, "Power and Organization," in *Power*, ed. Steven Lukes (New York: New York University Press, 1986), 215.

25. Ibid., 214.

26. Katz and Mair, "Changing Models of Party Organization."

27. Galbraith, "Power and Organization," 213.

28. See Stephen Krasner, "Approaches to the State: Alternative Conceptions and Historical Dynamics," *Comparative Politics* 16 (1984.): 223–246; Peter A. Hall and Rosemary C.R. Taylor, "Political Science and the Three New Institutionalisms," *Political Studies* 44 (1996): 936–957.

29. Ruth B. Collier and David Collier, *Shaping the Political Arena: Critical Junctures, the Labor Movement and Regime Dynamics in Latin America* (Princeton: Princeton University Press, 1991).

30. Michael Howlett and M. Ramesh, "The Policy Effects of Internationationalization: A Subsystem Adjustment Analysis of Policy Change," *Journal of Comparative Policy Analysis* 4 (2002): 31–55.

31. Wolfgang Streeck and Kathleen Thelen, "Introduction: Institutional Change in Advanced Political Economies," in *Beyond Continuity: Institutional Change in Advanced Political Economies*, eds. Wolfgang Streeck et al. (Oxford: Oxford University Press, 2005), 1–39.

32. Caitriona A. Carter, "Identifying Causality in Public Institutional Change: The Adaptation of the National Assembly for Wales to the European Union," *Public Administration* 86 (2008): 348.

33. Daniel Nohrstedt, "The Politics of Crisis Policymaking: Chernobyl and Swedish Nuclear Energy Policy," *Policy Studies Journal* 36 (2008): 257–278.

34. Zeki Sarigil, "Paths are What Actors Make of Them," *Critical Policy Studies* 3 (2009): 121–140.

35. Russell Alan Williams, "Exogenous Shocks in Subsystem Adjustment and Policy Change: The Credit Crunch and Canadian Banking Regulation," *Journal of Public Policy* 29 (2009): 48.

36. Carter, "Identifying Causality," 348.
37. Ibid.
38. See Robert Harmel and Kenneth Janda, "An Integrated Theory of Party Goals and Party Change," *Journal of Theoretical Politics* 6 (1994): 259–287; Kenneth Janda and Tyler Colman, "Effects of Party Organization on Performance during the 'Golden Age' of Parties," *Political Studies* 46 (1998): 611–632; Thomas Koelble, "Economic Theories of Organization and the Politics of Institutional Design," *Party Politics* 2 (1996): 251–263.
39. Bolleyer, "Inside the Cartel Party."
40. Emerson "Power-Dependence Relations."
41. Ibid., 34.
42. Ibid., 34–38.
43. Jouvenel, *On Power*; Robert Dahl, *Who Governs?*, 229; Laswell and Kaplan, *Power and Society*.
44. Laffont and Martimort, *The Theory of Incentives*.
45. Emerson "Power-Dependence Relations," 36.
46. Ibid., 37.
47. Baldwin, "Power Analysis and World Politics"; Laswell and Kaplan, *Power and Society*, 76; Dahl, "The Concept of Power."
48. Laswell and Kaplan, *Power and Society*, 85.
49. Baldwin, "Power Analysis and World Politics," 167.
50. McCubbins and Schwartz, "Congressional Oversight Overlooked," 427.
51. Galbraith, "Power and Organization," 213.

5   Intraparty Authoritarianism in Turkey: Empirical Findings

1. Duverger, *Political Parties*, xvi.
2. A total of 66 of the interviewed party activists have worked more than 5 years for the party that they are affiliated with and 74 of them spend more than 10 hours for party activities every week. See activism periods and levels in Appendix B.
3. According to Article 22 of the Law on Political Parties (SPK—*Siyasi Partiler Kanunu* No: 2820), parties with at least 20 parliamentarians are allowed to form party groups in the parliament.
4. See Ali Çarkoğlu and Melvin J. Hinich, "A Spatial Analysis of Turkish Party Preferences," *Electoral Studies* 25 (2006): 369–392; and Ali Çarkoğlu, "The Nature of the Left-Right Ideological Self-Placement in the Turkish context," *Turkish Studies* 8 (2007): 253–271.
5. Erhan Doğan, "The Historical and Discursive Roots of the Justice and Development Party's EU Stance," *Turkish Studies* 6 (2005): 421–437.
6. Heper, "The Justice and Development Party Government and the Military in Turkey."
7. For the first time in the Republic's history, the prime minister's wife was wearing a headscarf, which was, according to the secular elite, against the

modernist Kemalist principles. The headscarf is banned in the universities in Turkey because it is considered as a symbol of political Islam.

8. Constitution of the Republic of Turkey, Article No.: 103.
9. Güney, "People's Democracy Party."
10. Namık Durukan, "DTP, kalelerinde oy kaybına uğradı," *Milliyet*, July 31, 2007, accessed February 5, 2009, http://www.milliyet.com.tr/2007/07/31 /siyaset/siy14.html
11. Bora, "Nationalist Discourses in Turkey," 447.
12. Bektaş, *Demokratikleşme Sürecinde Liderler Oligarşisi*, 113.
13. Turkish Statistical Institute, data from 2000, accessed July 15, 2008, http:// www.tuik.gov.tr.
14. Tanju Tosun and Gülgün E. Tosun, "Voter Preferences in Izmir from the November 3, 2002 to the July 22, 2007 Elections: Has the Election Map Altered?" *Turkish Studies* 9 (2008): 278.
15. Jenny B. White, *Islamist Mobilization in Turkey: A Study of Vernacular Politics* (Seattle: University of Washington Press, 2003).
16. Interview, *Tarsus*, October 10, 2007.
17. Interview, *Tarsus*, October 8, 2007.
18. Interview, *Tarsus*, October 9, 2007.
19. Interview, *Tarsus*, October 7, 2007.
20. Interview, *Diyarbakır*, September 25, 2007.
21. Interview, *Diyarbakır-Merkez*, September 25, 2007.
22. Interviews with a local NGO member and a local media representative (identification concealed), September 25–26, 2007, *Diyarbakır-Merkez*.
23. The interviewed representatives of the CHP all agreed on this fact regarding the failure of the CHP in *Diyarbakır-Merkez*. Interviews, September 27–28, 2007, *Diyarbakır-Merkez*.
24. KONDA Research Company, "Sandığın İcindekini Ne Belirledi?" *Research Report* (2007), accessed April 10, 2008, http://www.konda.com.tr/tr/raporlar .php.
25. Ibid.
26. Duverger, *Political Parties*, xvi.
27. Herbert J. Rubin and Irene S. Rubin, *Qualitative Interviewing: The Art of Hearing Data* (California: Sage Publications, 1995), 221.
28. Herbert J. Rubin, *Applied Social Research* (Columbus, OH: Charles E. Merrill, 1983); and William L. Neuman, *Social Research Methods: Qualitative and Quantitative Approaches* (Boston: Allyn and Bacon, 1994).
29. Organization for Security and Cooperation in Europe / Office for Democratic Institutions and Human Rights (OSCE/ODIHR), *Election Assessment Mission Report: Republic of Turkey Early Parliamentary Elections 22 July 2007* (Warsaw, November 27, 2007), 13–14.
30. Ergun Aksoy, "Erdoğan parti içinde 'balans ayarı' yaptı," Sabah, June 6, 2007, accessed August 2, 2008, http://arsiv.sabah.com.tr/2007/06/06/haber,9C1530 5F27D347BD9B008E683B543B3E.html
31. Abdullah Karakuş, "Ilımlılar listede," *Milliyet*, June 7, 2007, accessed August 2, 2008, http://www.milliyet.com.tr/2007/06/07/siyaset/axsiy03.html.

32. Nazif İflazoğlu, "Çizilen vekiller sordu: Gerekçeniz ne?" *Radikal*, June 15, 2007, accessed August 2, 2008, http://www.radikal.com.tr/haber.php?haberno =224192.
33. Interview, *Ümraniye*, October 17, 2007.
34. Interview, *Tarsus*, October 10, 2007.
35. Interview, *Ümraniye*, October 18, 2007.
36. Interview, *Tarsus*, October 10, 2007.
37. Interview, *İzmir*, October 7, 2007.
38. Interview, *Diyarbakır*, September 28, 2007.
39. Ibid.
40. Ibid.
41. Interview, *Diyarbakır*, September 30, 2007.
42. Ibid.
43. Interview, *Ümraniye*, October 17, 2007.
44. Ibid.
45. Interview, *Ümraniye*, October 18, 2007.
46. Ibid.
47. Interview, *Ümraniye*, October 17, 2007.
48. Interview, *Ümraniye*, October 18, 2007.
49. Interview, *Karşıyaka*, October 6, 2007.
50. Ibid.
51. Ibid.
52. Interview, *Tarsus*, October 10, 2007.
53. Ibid.
54. Ibid.
55. Ibid.
56. Ibid.
57. Ibid.
58. Ibid.
59. Interview, *Karşıyaka*, October 5, 2007.
60. Interview, *Karşıyaka*, October 6, 2007.
61. Interview, *Karşıyaka*, October 5, 2007.
62. Interview, *Ümraniye*, October 17, 2007.
63. Ibid.
64. Adalet Kalkınma Partisi, *Ak Parti Tüzüğü* [The AKP Constitution], Article 134/8, accessed March 31, 2009, *http://www.akparti.org.tr/tuzuk .asp?dizin=193&hangisi=2*.
65. Interview, *Diyarbakır-Merkez*, September 29, 2007
66. Interview, *Diyarbakır-Merkez*, September 28, 2007.
67. Ibid.
68. Ibid.
69. Ibid.
70. Ibid.
71. Interview, *Tarsus*, October 10, 2007.
72. Ibid.

73. Interview, *Tarsus*, October 9, 2007.
74. Ibid.
75. Interview, *Tarsus*, October 10, 2007.
76. Interview, *Tarsus*, October 9, 2007.
77. Interview, *Diyarbakır-Merkez*, September 28, 2007.
78. Ibid.
79. Interview, *Diyarbakır*, September 25, 2007.
80. Interview, *Diyarbakır*, September 27, 2007.
81. Interview, *Diyarbakır*, September 25, 2007.
82. Carter, "Identifying Causality in Public Institutional Change."
83. Interview, *Diyarbakır*, September 26, 2007.
84. Interview, *Diyarbakır-Merkez*, September 29, 2007.
85. Interview, *Diyarbakır*, September 26, 2007.
86. Note the 0.7 percent rise in the vote shares of the MHP in *Diyarbakır-Merkez* between 2002 and 2007 on Table 5.1. At the provincial level, on the other hand, the vote percentage rose from 1.52 percent to 2.45 percent; which meant that the MHP was able to gain 5000 more voters from 2002 to 2007 in such a strategic province.
87. İhlas Haber Ajansı, *Seçim 2009*, accessed August 15, 2009, http://secim.iha.com.tr.
88. Interview, *Tarsus*, October 10, 2007.
89. Ibid.
90. Interview, *Ümraniye*, October 18, 2007.
91. Interview, *Karşıyaka*, October 6, 2007.
92. On this issue, see Vincent Boland, "AKP'yi muhalefet güçlendiriyor," *Radikal*, July 18, 2007, accessed August 15, 2008, http://www.radikal.com.tr/haber.php?haberno=227199.
93. Interview, *Diyarbakır-Merkez*, September 28, 2007.
94. Ibid.
95. The interviews in *Karşıyaka* took place three months after the elections when the public criticisms on the CHP leader, Baykal were intense.
96. Interview, *Karşıyaka*, October 6, 2007.
97. Interview, *Ümraniye*, October 19, 2007.
98. Ibid.

6   Explaining the Variance in Intraparty Authoritarianism in Turkey

1. The Law on Political Parties (SPK—*Siyasi Partiler Kanunu* No:2820), Article No: 20/9.
2. SPK, Article No: 20/10.
3. Bektaş, *Demokratikleşme Sürecinde Liderler Oligarşisi*, 114.
4. Interview with the executive member of a district party organization in Ankara, August 30, 2007.

5. Adalet ve Kalkınma Partisi, *AK Parti Tüzüğü* [AK Party Constitution], Article 31, accessed March 31, 2009, http://www.akparti.org.tr/tuzuk.asp?dizin =193&hangisi=2.
6. Interview with the AKP District party chair, *Diyarbakır-Merkez*, September 28, 2007.
7. Ibid.
8. Interview, *Diyarbakır-merkez*, September 28, 2007.
9. Interview, *Diyarbakır-merkez*, September 30, 2007.
10. Interview, *Ümraniye*, October 17, 2007.
11. Ibid.
12. Ibid.
13. Ibid.
14. Interview, *Tarsus*, October 9, 2007.
15. Ibid.
16. Ibid.
17. Interview, *Karşıyaka*, October 5, 2007.
18. Interview, *Karşıyaka*, October 6, 2007.
19. Interview, *Karşıyaka*, October 5, 2007.
20. Interview, *Karşıyaka*, October 6, 2007.
21. Interview, *Karşıyaka*, October 5, 2007.
22. Interview, *Tarsus*, October 10, 2007.
23. Ibid.
24. Interview, *Diyarbakır-Merkez*, September 28, 2007.
25. Ibid.
26. Ibid.
27. Interview, *Ümraniye*, October 19, 2007.
28. Ibid.
29. Milliyetçi Hareket Partisi, *MHP Parti Tüzüğü* [The MHP Constitution, Article No: 18/1, accessed April 3, 2009, http://www.mhp.org.tr/kitaplar /mhp_parti_tuzugu_2009_opt.pdf.
30. Interview, *Karşıyaka*, October 6, 2007.
31. Ibid.
32. Interview, *Diyarbakır*, September 26, 2007.
33. Interview, *Diyarbakır-Merkez*, September 26, 2007.
34. Interview, *Diyarbakır-Merkez*, September 29, 2007.
35. Interview, *Tarsus*, October 10, 2007.
36. Ibid.
37. Ibid.
38. Interview, *Ümraniye*, October 18, 2007.
39. Interview, *Ümraniye*, October 16, 2007.
40. Interview, *Ümraniye*, October 18, 2007.
41. Interview, *Karşıyaka*, October 5, 2007.
42. IIbid.
43. Interview, *Diyarbakır-Merkez*, September 28, 2007.
44. Ibid.
45. Ibid.

46. Interview, *Ümraniye*, October 17, 2007.
47. Interviews, *Ümraniye*, October 17–18, 2007.
48. Interview, *Tarsus*, October 8, 2007.
49. Ibid.
50. The party leaders from the moderate wing, Ahmet Türk and Aysel Tuğluk, were replaced by Nurettin Demirtaş and Emine Ayna from the radical wing in the national convention that took place in October 2007. However, since Demirtaş was arrested shortly after the election, Türk returned back to the party's top leadership sharing it with Emine Ayna.
51. The division is based on whether the Kurdish question ought to be solved through establishing an autonomous Kurdish region or through maintaining the democratic rights of the Kurds living in Turkey.
52. Interview, *Karşıyaka*, October 6, 2007.
53. Ibid.
54. Interview, *Tarsus*, October 8, 2007.
55. Ibid.
56. Interview, *Diyarbakır-Merkez*, September 28, 2007.
57. Interview, *Diyarbakır-Merkez*, September 29, 2007.
58. Ibid.
59. Ibid.
60. Interview with the AKP district women's wing member, *Ümraniye*, October 17, 2007.
61. Interview with the AKP district board member, *Ümraniye*, October 17, 2007.
62. Interview with the AKP district party activist, *Ümraniye*, October 17, 2007.
63. Interview with the AKP district youth-wing member, *Ümraniye*, October 17, 2007.
64. Interview, *Ümraniye*, October 17, 2007.
65. Interview, *Karşıyaka*, October 6, 2007.
66. Ibid.
67. Interview, *Karşıyaka*, October 5, 2007.
68. Interview, *Karşıyaka*, October 6, 2007.
69. Interview, *Karşıyaka*, October 6, 2007.
70. Interview, *Karşıyaka*, October 6, 2007.
71. Interview, *Tarsus*, October 10, 2007.
72. Ibid.
73. Ibid.
74. Interview, *Tarsus*, October 8, 2007.
75. Ibid.
76. Ibid.
77. Ibid.
78. Ibid.
79. Interview, *Karşıyaka*, October 5, 2007.
80. Interview, *Karşıyaka*, October 6, 2007.
81. Interview, *Karşıyaka*, October 6, 2007.
82. Interview, *Ümraniye*, October 17, 2007.

83. Ibid.
84. Ibid.
85. Interview *Diyarbakır-Merkez*, September 28, 2007.
86. Ibid.
87. Harmel and Janda, "An Integrated Theory of Party Goals and Party Change," 1994; Janda and Colman, "Formalizing and Testing Duverger's Theories on Political Parties." 1998; Koelble, "Economic Theories of Organization and the Politics of Institutional Design," 1996
88. Interview, *Diyarbakır-Merkez*, September 29, 2007.
89. Interview conducted in *Diyarbakır-Merkez*, 27 September, 2007.
90. Ibid.
91. Interview conducted in *Diyarbakır-Merkez*, 29 September, 2007.
92. Ibid.
93. Interviews with the district party chair and the district executive board member, *Tarsus*, October 10, 2007. The content of the contradiction between the MHP municipality in Tarsus and the MHP central party organization was not revealed during the interviews.
94. Interview, *Ümraniye*, October, 18, 2007.
95. Interview, *Karşıyaka*, October, 6, 2007.
96. In fact, in 2009 local elections, the CHP gained 71 percent of the votes whereas the AKP had only 17 percent. Source: İhlas Haber Ajansı, *Seçim 2009*, accessed August 15, 2009, http://secim.iha.com.tr.
97. Interview, *Karşıyaka*, October 6, 2007.
98. KONDA, "Sandığın İçindekini ne Belirledi?"
99. Mansur Çelik, "Muhaliflerden Sert Çıkış: Siyaseti Bırak," *Milliyet*, July 25, 2007, accessed April 2, 2008, http://www.milliyet.com.tr/2007/07/25/siyaset/siy03.html
100. Interview, *Diyarbakır*, September 29, 2007.
101. Ibid.
102. Interview, *Ümraniye*, October 19, 2007.
103. "CHP Ege Örgütleri Ayaklandı," *Yeniasır Gazetesi*, October 5, 2007, 6.

Conclusions, Implications, Future Studies

1. It is, in fact, internal party democracy; which is the symmetrical opposition of intraparty authoritarianism that usually received attention in the field. Several studies discussed its impact on democratic regimes (for instance, Schattschneider, *Party Government*; APSA, *Toward a More Responsible Two-Party System*; MacPherson, *Life and Times of Liberal Democracy*; Ware, *Logic of Party Democracy*; Duverger, *Political Parties*; Teorell, "A Deliberative Defense"; and Scarrow, *Implementing Intra-party Democracy*.
2. See for instance Katz and Mair, "Changing Models"; Mair and Biezen, "Party Membership"; Koole, "Cadre, Catch-All or Cartel?"; Kitschelt, "Citizens,

Politicians, and Party Cartelization"; Katz, "The Problem of Candidate Selection"; Biezen, *Political Parties in New Democracie*; and Biezen, "On the Theory and Practice of Party Formation."

3. Biezen, *Political Parties in New Democracies*; Dalton and Wattenberg, *Parties without Partisans*; Gunther and Diamond "Species of Political Parties"; Gunther, Montero, and Linz, *Political Parties*; and Kostelecky, *Political Parties after Communism*; Szczerbiak *Poles Together?*

4. The distinction between ideational and material interests is derived from the body of literature on motivations of party activists (some examples are Costantini and King, "The Motives of Political Party Activists"; Eldersveld, *Political Parties*; Clark and Wilson, "Incentive Systems"; and Roback, "Motivation for Activism.")

5. Carter, "Identifying Causality."

6. Emerson, "Power-Dependence relations," 34–38.

7. Moe, "The New Economics of Organization"; and Pierre and Peters, *Governance, Politics, and the State*, 17–18.

8. Müller, "Political Parties in Parliamentary Democracies"; Kitschelt, "Citizens, Politicians, and Party Cartelization"; Katz, "Party in Democratic Theory," 36; and Carty and Cross, "Can Stratarchically Organized Parties be Democratic?" 94.

9. Brehm and Gates, "Donut Shops and Speed Traps"; and Jones, "Bounded Rationality."

10. Emerson, "Power-Dependence Relations"; Blau, *Exchange and Power*; and Baldwin, "Power Analysis and World Politics."

11. Emerson, "Power-Dependence Relations."

12. Lukes, *Power*, 24–25.

13. Galbraith, "Power and Organization," 215.

14. See for instance the reports TESAV [Toplumsal, Ekonomik, Siyasal Araştırmalar Vakfı], *Siyasi Partiler ve Demokrasi Sempozyumu: 17 Haziran 2005* (Ankara: TESAV); TESAV, *Siyasi Partiler ve Seçim Kaunlarında Değişiklik Önerileri Sempozyumu: 18–19 Şubat 2005* (Ankara: TESAV, 2005); TOBB [Türkiye Odalar ve Borsalar Birliği] ; and *Siyasi Partiler ve Seçim Kanunları Önerisi* (Ankara: TOBB, 2000).

15. Mansur Çelik, "Muhaliflerden Sert Çıkış: Siyaseti Bırak."

16. Mansur Çelik, "Yenilginin Sorumlusu Bulundu," Milliyet, August 3, 2007, accessed April 8, 2008, http://www.milliyet.com.tr/2007/08/03/siyaset/siy03.html

17. "Baykal için 'Geri Dön' Mitingi" NTVMSNBC, May 15, 2010, accessed February 15, 2011, http://www.ntvmsnbc.com/id/25095122/

18. "CHP'de Tarihi Kurultay," Habertürk, May 22, 2011, accessed February 15, 2011, http://www.haberturk.com/gundem/haber/516912-chpde-tarihi-kurultay.

19. Mahmut Övür, "Önseçim CHP'de 11 Nisan Depremini Engelledi," Sabah, April 5, 2011, accessed May 2, 2011, http://www.sabah.com.tr/Yazarlar/ovur/2011/04/05/onsecim-chp-11-nisan-depremini-engelledi.

20. Scott Mainwaring and Timothy Scully, eds., *Building Democratic Institutions: Party Systems in Latin America* (Stanford: Stanford University Press, 1995).

21. Freedom House, "Freedom in the World," accessed August 10, 2009,http://www.freedomhouse.org/template.cfm?page=363&year=2009

22. Timothy R. Scully, "Reconstituting Party Politics in Chile," in *Building Democratic Institutions: Party Systems in Latin America*, ed. Scott Mainwaring et al. (Stanford: Stanford University Press, 1995), 126.

23. Ibid., 127.

24. Omar Sanchez, "Transformation and Decay: The De-Institutionalisation of Party Systems in South America," *Third World Quarterly* 29 (2008): 315–337.

25. Weingast, "Congressional Bureaucratic System," 153; and Seth Goldstein, "Party Leaders, Power and Change," *Party Politics* 8 (2002): 327–348.

Bibliography

Acar, Feride. "Turgut Özal: Pious Agent of Liberal Transformation." In *Political Leaders and Democracy in Turkey*, edited by Metin Heper and Sabri Sayarı, 163–180. Lexington Books, 2002.

Aldrich, Howard E. "Organizational Boundaries and Interorganizational Conflict." In *Organizational Systems*, edited by Frank Baker, 379–393. Homewood: Irving-Dorsey, 1973.

Adalet ve Kalkınma Partisi. *AK Parti Tüzüğü* [The AK Party Constitution]. Accessed March 31, 2009. http://www.akparti.org.tr/tuzuk.asp?dizin=193&hangisi=2.

Aksoy, Ergun. "Erdoğan parti içinde 'balans ayarı' yaptı." *Sabah*, June 6, 2007. Accessed August 2, 2008. http://arsiv.sabah.com.tr/2007/06/06/haber,9C1530 5F27D347BD9B008E683B543B3E.html

Albayrak, Mustafa. *Türk Siyasi Tarihinde Demokrat Parti*. Ankara: Phoenix Yayınları, 2004.

APSA [American Political Science Association] Committee on Political Parties. *Toward a More Responsible Two-Party System*. New York: Rinehart, 1950.

Arat, Yeşim. "Süleyman Demirel: National Will and Beyond" In *Political Leaders and Democracy in Turkey*, edited by Metin Heper and Sabri Sayarı, 87–106. Lexington Books, 2002.

Arıkan, Burak E. "The Programme of the Nationalist Action Party: An Iron Hand in a Velvet Glove?" *Middle Eastern Studies* 34, no. 4 (1998):120–134.

Arklan, Ümit. "Siyasal Liderlikte Karizma Olgusu: Recep Tayyip Erdoğan Örneğinde Teorik ve Uygulamalı Bir Çalışma." *Selçuk Üniversitesi Sosyal Bilimler Enstitüsü Dergisi* 16 (2006): 45–65.

Ayan, Pelin. "Authoritarian Party Structures in Turkey: A Comparison of the Republican People's Party and the Justice and Development Party." *Turkish Studies* 11, no. 2 (2010): 197–215.

Ayata, Ayşe Güneş. "Class and Clientelism in the Republican People's Party." In *Turkish State, Turkish Society*, edited by Nükhet Sirman and Andrew Finkel, 159–184. London: Routledge, 1990.

Ayata, Ayşe Güneş. *CHP Örgüt ve İdeoloji*. Ankara: Gündoğan Yayınları, 1992.

———. "The Republican People's Party." *Turkish Studies* 3, no. 1 (2002): 102–121.

Ayata, Sencer. "Patronage, Party and State: the Politicization of Islam in Turkey." *Middle East Journal* 50, no. 1 (1996): 40–56.

Ayata, Sencer and Ayşe Güneş Ayata. "The Center-Left Parties in Turkey." *Turkish Studies* 8, no. 2 (2007): 211–232.

Bachrach, Peter and Morton S. Baratz. "Two Faces of Power." *The American Political Science Review* 56, no. 4 (1962): 947–952.

Baldwin, David. "Power Analysis and World Politics: New Trends versus Old Tendencies." *World Politics* 31, no. 2 (1979):161–194.

Bales, Robert F. *Interaction Process Analysis: A Method for the Study of Small Groups.* Cambridge, MA: Addison-Wesley, 1950.

Bass, Bernard M. *Leadership and Performance Beyond Expectations.* New York: Free Press, 1985.

Bektaş, Arsev. *Demokratikleşme Sürecinde Liderler Oligarşisi: CHP ve AP (1961–1981).* İstanbul: Bağlam Yayıncılık, 1993.

Biezen, Ingrid van. "On the Internal Balance of Party Power: Party Organizations in New Democracies." *Party Politics* 6 (2000): 395–418.

———. *Political Parties in New Democracies: Party Organization in Southern and East-Central Europe.* London: Palgrave Macmillan, 2003.

———. "On the Theory and Practice of Party Formation and Adaptation in New Democracies." *European Journal of Political Research* 44 (2005):147–174.

Bila, Hikmet. *CHP 1919 –1999.* İstanbul: Doğan Kitapçılık, 1999.

Bille, Lars. "Democratizing a Democratic Procedure: Myth or Reality?: Candidate Selection in Western European Parties, 1960–1990." *Party Politics* 7 (2001): 363–380.

Blau, Peter M. *Exchange and Power in Social Life.* New York: John Wiley and Sons, 1964.

Blau Peter M. and M. W. Meyer. *Bureaucracy in Modern Society.* New York: Random House, 1956.

Blyth, Mark and Richard S. Katz. "From Catch-All Politics to Cartelization: The Political Economy of the Cartel Party." *West European Politics* 28, no. 1 (2005): 33–60.

Boland, Vincent. "AKP'yi muhalefet güçlendiriyor." *Radikal,* July 18, 2007. Accessed August 15, 2008. http://www.radikal.com.tr/haber.php?haberno=227199.

Bolleyer, Nicole. "Inside the Cartel Party: Party Organization in Government and Opposition." *Political Studies* 57, no.3 (2009): 559–579.

Bora, Tanıl. "Nationalist Discourses in Turkey." *South Atlantic Quarterly* 102, no. 2/3 (2003): 433–451.

Bosuter, Kudret. *Türk Siyasi Partiler Sisteminde Parti İçi Demokrasi.* Ankara: Ulusal Basımevi, 1969.

Brehm, John and Scott Gates. "Donut Shops and Speed Traps: Evaluating Models of Supervision on Police Behavior." *American Journal of Political Science* 37 (1993): 555–581.

Burns, James M. *Leadership.* New York: Harper & Row, 1978.

Çarkoğlu, Ali, Tarhan Erdem, Mehmet Kabasakal, and Ömer F. Gençkaya. *Siyasi Partilerde Reform.* İstanbul: TESEV Yayınları, 2000.

Çarkoğlu, Ali and Melvin J. Hinich. "A Spatial Analysis of Turkish Party Preferences." *Electoral Studies* 25, no. 2 (2006): 369–392.

Çarkoğlu, Ali. "The Nature of the Left-Right Ideological Self-Placement in the Turkish Context." *Turkish Studies* 8, no. 2 (2007): 253–271.

Carter, Caitriona A. "Identifying Causality in Public Institutional Change: The Adaptation of the National Assembly for Wales to the European Union." *Public Administration* 86, no. 2 (2008): 345–361.

Carty, R. Kenneth and William Cross. "Can Stratarchically Organized Parties be Democratic? The Canadian Case." *Journal of Elections, Public Opinion and Parties* 16, no. 2 (2006): 93–114.

Çelik, Mansur. "Muhaliflerden Sert Çıkış: Siyaseti Bırak." *Milliyet.* July 25, 2007. Accessed April 2, 2008. http://www.milliyet.com.tr/2007/07/25/siyaset/siy03.html

Çelik, Mansur. "Yenilginin Sorumlusu Bulundu." *Milliyet.* August 3, 2007. Accessed April 8, 2008. http://www.milliyet.com.tr/2007/08/03/siyaset/siy03.html.

Çınar, Alev and Ergun Özbudun. "Mesut Yılmaz: From Özal's Shadow to Mediator." In *Political Leaders and Democracy in Turkey,* edited by Metin Heper and Sabri Sayarı, 181–198. Lexington Books, 2002.

Cizre, Ümit, ed. *Secular and Islamic Politics in Turkey: The Making of the Justice and Development Party.* London: Routledge, 2008.

Clark, Peter and James Q. Wilson. "Incentive Systems: A Theory of Organization." *Administrative Science Quarterly* 6 (1961): 129-166.

Collier, Ruth B. and David Collier. *Shaping the Political Arena: Critical Junctures, the Labor Movement and Regime Dynamics in Latin America.* Princeton: Princeton University Press, 1991.

Conway, M. Margaret and Frank B. Feigert. "Incentives and Task Performance Among Party Precinct Workers." *Western Political Quarterly* 27 (1974): 693–709.

Coşar, Simten and Aylin Özman. "Centre-right Politics in Turkey after the November 2002 General Election: Neoliberalism with a Muslim Face." *Contemporary Politics* 10, no. 1 (2004): 57–74.

Costantini, Edmond and Joel King. "The Motives of Political Party Activists: A Factor-Analytic Exploration." *Political Behavior* 6, no. 1 (1984): 79–93.

Cox, Gary W. and Matthew D. McCubbins. *Legislative Leviathan: Party Government in the House.* Berkeley: University of California Press, 1993.

Cross, William and Andre Blais. "Who Selects the Party Leader?" *Party Politics* (2011). Accessed February 10, 2011. doi:10.1177/1354068810382935.

Dağı, İhsan D. "The Justice and Development Party: Identity, Politics, and Human Rights Discourse in the Search for Security and Legitimacy." In *The Emergence of a New Turkey: Democracy and the AK Parti,* edited by M. Hakan Yavuz. Salt Lake City: University of Utah Press, 2006.

Dahl, Robert. "The Concept of Power." *Behavioral Science* 2 (1957): 201–215.

Dahl, Robert. *Who Governs? Democracy and Power in an American City.* New Haven: Yale University Press, 1961.

———. *Polyarchy: Participation and Opposition.* New Haven: Yale University Press, 1971.

———. *Modern Political Analysis.* 3rd ed. NJ: Prentice Hall, 1976.

———. "Power as the Control of Behavior." In *Power,* edited by Steven Lukes, 37–55. New York: New York University Press, 1986.

Dalton, Russell J. and Martin P. Wattenberg, eds. *Parties without Partisans: Political Change in Advanced Industrial Democracies.* Oxford: Oxford University Press, 2000.

De Grand, Alexander. "Giolitti and the Socialists." In *Italian Socialism*, edited by Spencer M. Di Scala, 23–37. Amherst: University of Massachusetts Press, 1996.

Demir, Eyyüp. *Yasal Kürtler.* Istanbul: Tevn Yayınları, 2005.

Demokratik Toplum Partisi. *DTP Program ve Tüzüğü* [The DTP Program and Constitution]. Ankara, 2005.

Detterbeck, Klaus. "Cartel Parties in Western Europe?" *Party Politics* 11 (2005): 173–191.

Dodd, C. H. *Democracy and Development in Turkey.* Walkington: Eothen Press, 1979.

———. "Ataturk and Political Parties." In *Political Parties and Democracy in Turkey,* edited by Metin Heper and Jacop M. Landau, 24–42. London: Tauris, 1991.

Doğan, Erhan. "The Historical and Discursive Roots of the Justice and Development Party's EU Stance." *Turkish Studies* 6, no. 3 (2005): 421–437.

Gilles Dorronsoro and Elise Massicard. "Being a Member of Parliament in Contemporary Turkey." *European Journal of Turkish Studies* 3 (2005). Accessed February 28, 2010. http://ejts.revues.org/index502.html.

Downs, Anthony. *An Economic Theory of Democracy.* New York: Harper, 1957.

Durukan, Namık. "DTP 'şahinler'in kanatları altında." *Milliyet,* November 10, 2007. Accessed April 15, 2008. http://www.milliyet.com.tr/2007/11/10/siyaset/siy08.html

Durukan, Namık. "DTP, kalelerinde oy kaybına uğradı." *Milliyet,* July 31, 2007. Accessed February 5, 2009. http://www.milliyet.com.tr/2007/07/31/siyaset/siy14.html

Duverger, Maurice. *Political Parties.* London: Methuen, 1963.

Eckstein, Harry. "Case Study and Theory in Political Science." In *Handbook of Political Science,* edited by Fred I. Greenstein and Nelson W. Polsby. Reading, MA: Addison-Wesley, 1975.

Eldersveld, Samuel J. *Political Parties: A Behavioral Analysis.* Chicago: MacNally, 1964.

Emerson Richard M. "Power-Dependence Relations." *American Sociological Review* 27 (1962): 31–40.

Enyedi, Zsolt. "Party Politics in Post-Communist Transition." In *Handbook of Political Parties,* edited by Richard Katz and William Crotty, 228–238. London: Sage Publications, 2006.

Enyedi, Zsolt and Lukas Linek. "Searching for the Right Organization: Ideology and Party Structure in East-Central Europe." *Party Politics* 14, no. 4 (2008): 455–477.

Epstein, Leon D. *Political Parties in Western Democracies.* New Brunswick, NJ: Transaction Books, 1982.

Eroğul, Cem. *Demokrat Parti (Tarihi ve İdeolojisi).* Ankara: SBF Yayınları, 1970. Freedom House.

"Freedom in the World." Accessed August 10, 2009. http://www.freedomhouse
.org/template.cfm?page=363&year=2009

Frey, Frederick W. *The Turkish Political Elite*. Cambridge: The M.I.T. Press, 1965.

Frohlich, Norman, Joe A. Oppenheimer, and Oran R. Young. *Political Leadership and Collective Goods*. Princeton: Princeton University Press, 1971.

Galbraith, John Kenneth. "Power and Organization." In *Power*, edited by Steven Lukes, 211–228. New York: New York University Press, 1986.

Gauja, Anika. "The Pitfalls of Participatory Democracy: A Study of the Australian Democrats' GST." *Australian Journal of Political Science* 40, no. 1 (2005): 71–85.

Gençkaya, Ömer F. "The Turkish Constitutional Court and Dissolution of Political Parties: Comparative Perspectives." In *Suna Kili'ye Armağan: Cumhuriyet'e Adanan Bir Yasam*, 165–84. Istanbul: Bogaziçi University Publications, 1998.

———. "Siyasetin Finansmanı ve Siyasi Partiler." *ASOMEDYA*, October 2002.

———. "Turkey." *KAS Democracy Report: Parties and Democracy*. Bonn: Bouvier Verlag, 2007.

George, Alexander L. and Andrew Bennett. *Case Studies and Theory Development in the Social Sciences*. Cambridge, MA: MIT Press, 2005.

Gerth, Hans. "The Nazi Party: Its Leadership and Composition." *The American Journal of Sociology* 45, no. 4 (1940): 517–541.

Geyikdağı, Mehmet Yaşar. *Political Parties in Turkey: The Role of Islam*. New York: Praeger, 1984.

Goldstein, Seth. "Party Leaders, Power and Change." *Party Politics* 8, no. 3 (2002): 327–348.

Güney, Aylin. "The People's Democracy Party." *Turkish Studies* 3, no. 1 (2002): 122–137.

Gunther, Richard, J.R. Montero, and Juan J. Linz, eds. *Political parties: Old concepts and new challenges*. Oxford: Oxford University Press, 2002.

Gunther, Richard and Larry Diamond. "Species of Political Parties: A New Typology." *Party Politics* 9, no. 2 (2003): 167–199.

Gunther, Richard and Anthony Mughan. eds. *Democracy and the Media: A Comparative Perspective*. Cambridge and New York: Cambridge University Press, 2000.

Hall, Peter A. and Rosemary C. R. Taylor. "Political Science and the Three New Institutionalisms." *Political Studies* 44 (1996): 936–957.

Hancock, M. Donald. "Sweden." In *Western European Party Systems: Trends and Prospects*, edited by Peter H. Merkl, 185–204. New York: Free Press, 1980.

Hakyemez, Yusuf Ş. and Birol Akgün. "Limitations On The Freedom Of Political Parties In Turkey And The Jurisdiction Of The European Court Of Human Rights." *Mediterranean Politics* 7, no. 2 (2002): 54–78.

Harmel, Robert and Kenneth Janda. "An Integrated Theory of Party Goals and Party Change." *Journal of Theoretical Politics* 6 (1994): 259–287.

Havel, Vaclav. "Anti-political parties." In *Democracy and Civil Society*, edited by John Keane, 391–398. London: Verso, 1988.

Hemphill, John K., and A. E. Coons "Development of the Leader Behavior Description Questionnaire." In *Leader Behavior: Its Description and Measurement*, edited by Ralph M. Stogdill and Alvin E. Coons, 6–38. Columbus: Bureau of Business Research, Ohio State University, 1957.

Heper, Metin. *The State Tradition in Turkey.* Walkington: Eothen, 1985.

———. "Strong State as a Problem for the Consolidation of Democracy: Turkey and Germany Compared." *Comparative Political Studies* 25 (1992): 169–194.

———. "Turgut Özal's Presidency: Crisis and the Glimmerings of Consensus." In *Politics in the Third Turkish Republic,* edited by Metin Heper and Ahmet Evin. Boulder, CO: Westview Press, 1994.

———. *İsmet İnönü: The Making of a Turkish Statesman.* Leiden: Brill Publications, 1998.

———. "İsmet İnönü: A Rationalistic Democrat" In *Political Leaders and Democracy in Turkey,* edited by Metin Heper and Sabri Sayarı, 25–44. Lexington Books, 2002.

———. "The Justice and Development Party Government and the Military in Turkey." *Turkish Studies* 6 (2005): 215–231.

Heper, Metin, ed. *The State and Public Bureaucracies: A Comparative Perspective.* New York: Greenwood Press, 1987.

Heper, Metin and Sabri Sayarı, eds. *Political Leaders and Democracy in Turkey.* Lanham MD: Lexington Books, 2002.

Heper, Metin and Şule Toktaş. "Islam, Democracy, and Modernity in Contemporary Turkey: The Case of Recep Tayyip Erdoğan." *Muslim World* 93, no. 2 (2003): 157–185.

Heper, Metin and Başak İnce. "Devlet Bahçeli and 'Far Right' Politics in Turkey, 1999–2002." *Middle Eastern Studies* 42, no. 6 (2006): 873–888.

Higley, John and Richard Gunther. *Elites and Democratic Consolidation in Latin America and Southern Europe.* New York: Cambridge University Press, 1991.

Hitlin, Robert A. and John S. Jackson. "Amateur and Professional Politicians." *Journal of Politics* 39 (1977): 786–793.

Hoftstetter, Richard C. "Organizational Activists: The Bases of Participation in Amateur and Professional Groups." *American Politics Quarterly* 1 (1973): 244–276.

Hopkin, Jonathan. "Bringing the Members Back In?: Democratizing Candidate Selection in Britain and Spain." *Party Politics* 10, no. 6 (2001): 343–361.

Howell, Jane M. and Bruce J. Avolio. "Transformational Leadership, Transactional Leadership, Loss of Control, and Support for Innovation." *Journal of Applied Psychology* 78 (1993): 891–902.

Howlett Michael and M. Ramesh. "The Policy Effects of Internationationalization: A Subsystem Adjustment Analysis of Policy Change." *Journal of Comparative Policy Analysis* 4 (2002): 31–55.

İflazoğlu, Nazif. "Çizilen vekiller sordu: Gerekçeniz ne?" *Radikal,* June 15, 2007. Accessed August 2, 2008, http://www.radikal.com.tr/haber.php?haberno =224192.

İnsel, Ahmet. "AKP and Normalizing Democracy in Turkey." *South Atlantic Quarterly* 102, no. 2/3 (2003): 293–308.

Irwin, Galen A. "The Netherlands." In *Western European Party Systems: Trends and Prospects,* edited by Peter H. Merkl, 161–184. New York: Free Press, 1980.

Janda, Kenneth and Desmond S. King. "Formalizing and Testing Duverger's Theories on Political Parties." *Comparative Political Studies* 18 (1985): 139–169.

Janda, Kenneth and Tyler Colman. "Effects of Party Organization on Performance during the 'Golden Age' of Parties." *Political Studies* 46 (1998): 611–632.

Jang, Ji-Hyang. "Taming Political Islamists by Islamic Capital: The Passions and Interests in Turkish Islamic Society." PhD diss., University of Austin at Texas, 2005. ProQuest (AAT 3203533).

Jones, Bryan D. "Bounded Rationality and Political Science: Lessons from Public Administration and Public Policy." *Journal of Public Administration Research and Theory* 13, no. 4 (2003): 395–412.

Jouvenel, Bertrand. *On Power: The Natural History of its Growth.* London: Batchworth Press, 1952.

Jupp, James. *Political Parties.* London: Routledge & Kegan Paul, 1968.

Kabasakal, Mehmet. *Türkiye'de Siyasal Parti Örgütlenmesi 1908–1960.* İstanbul: Tekin Yayınevi, 1991.

Kalaycıoğlu, Ersin. "Elections and Party Preferences in Turkey: Changes and Continuities in the 1990s." *Comparative Political Studies* 27, no. 3 (1994): 402–424.

Kalaycıoğlu, Ersin. "Attitudinal Orientation to Party Organizations in Turkey in the 2000s." *Turkish Studies* 9, no. 2 (2008): 297–316.

Karakuş, Abdullah. "Ilımlılar listede." *Milliyet,* June 7, 2007. Accessed August 2, 2008. http://www.milliyet.com.tr/2007/06/07/siyaset/axsiy03.html.

Karpat, Kemal H. *Turkey's Politics. The Transition to a Multi-Party System.* Princeton: Princeton University Press, 1959.

Karpat, Kemal. H. "Society, Economics and Politics in Contemporary Turkey." *World Politics* 17 (1964): 50–74.

Karpat, Kemal H. "The Republican People's Party 1923–1945." In *Political Parties and Democracy in Turkey,* edited by Metin Heper and Jacob M. Landau, 42–64. London: Tauris, 1991.

Katz, Richard S. "Party as Linkage: A Vestigial Function." *European Journal of Political Research* 18, no. 1 (1990): 143-161.

———. "The Problem of Candidate Selection and Models of Party Democracy." *Party Politics* 7 (2001): 277–96.

———. "Party in Democratic Theory." In *Handbook of Political Parties,* edited by Richard Katz and William Crotty, 34–36. London: Sage Publications, 2006.

Katz, Richard S., Peter Mair, Luciano Bardi, Lars Bille, Kris Deschouwer, David Farrell, Ruud Koole, Leonardo Morlino, Wolfgang Müller, Jon Pierre, Thomas Poguntke, Jan Sundberg, Lars Svasand, Hella van de Velde, Paul Webb, and Anders Widfeldt.. "The Membership of Political Parties in European Democracies, 1960–1990." *European Journal of Political Research* 22 (1992): 329–345.

Katz, Richard S. and Peter Mair. "The Evolution of Party Organizations in Europe: The Three Faces of Party Organization." *American Review of Politics* 14 (1993): 593–617.

———. "Changing Models of Party Organization and Party Democracy: The Emergence of the Cartel Party" *Party Politics* 1, no. 1 (1995.): 5–28.

Katz, Richard S. and Peter Mair. "Cadre, Catch-all or Cartel? A Rejoinder." *Party Politics* 2 (1996): 525–34.

———. "Party Organization, Party Democracy and the Emergence of the Cartel Party." In *Party System Change: Approaches and Interpretations*, edited by Peter Mair, 93–119. Oxford University Press, 1997.

———. "The Ascendancy of the Party in Public Office: Party Organizational Change in Twentieth-century Democracies." In *Political Parties: Old Concepts and New Challenges*, edited by Richard Gunther, J. Montero, and Juan J. Linz, 113–135. Oxford: Oxford University Press, 2002.

Katzenstein, Peter J. *The Culture of National Security: Norms and Identity in World Politics*. New York: Columbia University Press, 1996.

Keohane, Robert O. *After Hegemony: Cooperation and Discord in the World Political Economy*. Princeton: Princeton University Press, 1984.

Key, V. O. Jr. *Politics, Parties, and Pressure Groups*. New York: Crowell, 1964.

Kiewiet. Roderick D. and Matthew D. McCubbins. *The Logic of Delegation: Congressional Parties and the Appropriations Process*. Chicago: University of Chicago Press, 1991.

Kili, Suna. *1960–1975 Dönemi CHP'de Gelişmeler, Siyasal Bilimler Açısından Bir İnceleme*. İstanbul: Boğaziçi Üniversitesi Yayınevi, 1976.

Kinross, Lord. *Atatürk: A Biography of Mustafa Kemal, Father of Modern Turkey*. New York: William Morrow and Company, 1965.

Kirchheimer, Otto. "The Transformation of the Western European Party Systems." In *Political Parties and Political Development*, edited by Myron Weiner and Joseph LaPalombara. Princeton: Princeton University Press, 1966.

Kitschelt, Herbert. *The Logics of Party Formation. Ecological Politics in Belgium and West Germany*. Ithaca, NY and London: Cornell University Press, 1989.

———. "Citizens, Politicians, and Party Cartelization: Political Representation and State Failure in Post-Industrial Democracies." *European Journal of Political Research* 37, no. 2 (2000): 149–179.

Kitschelt, Herbert and Anthony J. McGann. *The Radical Right in Western Europe: A Comparative Analysis*. Ann Arbour: University of Michigan Press, 1997.

Klotz, Audie. *Norms in International Relations: The Struggle Against Apartheid*. Ithaca and London: Cornell University Press, 1995.

Koelble, Thomas. "Economic Theories of Organization and the Politics of Institutional Design." *Party Politics* 2, no. 2 (1996): 251–263.

KONDA Research Company. "Sandığın İcindekini Ne Belirledi?" *Research Report* (2007). Accessed April 10, 2008. http://www.konda.com.tr/tr/raporlar.php.

Kooiman, Jan, and Martin Van Vliet. "Governance and Public Management." In *Managing Public Organizations: Lessons from Contemporary European Experience*, edited by K. Eliassen and Jan Kooiman, 58–72. Sage: London: 1993.

Koole, Ruud. "Cadre, Catch-all or Cartel? A Comment on the Notion of the Cartel Party." *Party Politics* 2 (1996): 507–524.

Kopecky Petr. "Developing party organizations in East-Central Europe: What type of party is likely to emerge?" *Party Politics* 1, no. 4 (1995): 515–534.

Kostelecky, Tomas. *Political Parties after Communism: Developments in East-Central Europe*. Baltimore, MD: Johns Hopkins University Press, 2002.

Krasner, Stephen. "Approaches to the State: Alternative Conceptions and Historical Dynamics." *Comparative Politics* 16, no. 2 (1984): 223–246.

Krouwell, Andre. "Party Models." In *Handbook of Political Parties*, edited by Richard Katz and William Crotty, 228–238. London: Sage Publications, 2006.

Laffont, Jean-Jacques and David Martimort. *The Theory of Incentives: The Principal-Agent Model*. Princeton, NJ: Princeton University Press, 2002.

Laswell, Harold D. and Abraham Kaplan. *Power and Society: A Framework for Political Enquiry*. New Haven: Yale University Press, 1950.

Laver, Michael J. *The Politics of Private Desires*. Harmondsworth, Eng.: Penguin, 1981.

———. *Private desires, political action*. London: Sage, 1997.

Lawson, Kay. "When Linkage Fails" In *When Parties Fail: Emerging Alternative Organizations*, edited by Kay Lawson and Peter H. Merkl, 13–38. Princeton, NJ: Princeton University Press, 1988.

Leach, Darcy K. "The Iron Law of What Again? Conceptualizing Oligarchy Across Organizational Forms." *Sociological Theory* 23, no. 3 (2005): 312–337.

LeDuc, Lawrence. "Democratizing Party Leadership Selection." *Party Politics* 7 (2001): 323–341.

Lewin, Kurtand Robert Lippitt. "An Experimental Approach to the Study of Autocracy and Democracy: A Preliminary nNote." *Sociometry* 1 (1938): 292–300.

Lewis, Paul G. "Party Funding in Post-Communist East-Central Europe." In *Funding Democratization*, edited by Peter Burnell and Alan Ware, 137–157. Manchester: Manchester University Press, 1998.

Lijphart, Arend. "The Comparable-Cases Strategy in Comparative Research." *Comparative Political Studies* 8 (1975): 158–77.

Likert, Rensis. *New Patterns of Management*. New York: McGraw-Hill, 1961.

Linz, Juan. *The Breakdown of Democratic Regimes: Crisis, Breakdown, and Reequilibrium*. Baltimore, MD: John Hopkins University Press, 1978.

Lipset, Seymour Martin and Stein Rokkan. "Cleavage Structure, Party Systems, and Voter Alignments: An Introduction." In *Party Systems and Voter Alignments*, edited by Seymour Martin Lipset and Stein Rokkan, 1–64. New York: Free Press, 1967.

Lukes, Steven. *Power: A Radical View*. London: Macmillan Press, 1974.

Macfie, Al. *Atatürk*. Longman: London, 1994.

Macpherson, C. B. *The Life and Times of Liberal Democracy*. Oxford: Oxford University Press, 1977.

March, James G. and Johan P. Olsen. *Rediscovering Institutions*. New York: Free Press, 1989.

Mainwaring, Scott and Timothy Scully, eds. *Building Democratic Institutions: Party Systems in Latin America*. Stanford: Stanford University Press, 1995.

Mair, Peter. "Continuity, Change and the Vulnerability of Party." *West European Politics* 12 (1989): 169–187.

———. "Party Organizations: From Civil Society to the State." In *How Parties Organize: Change and Adaptation in Party Organizations in Western*

Democracies, edited by Richard Katz and Peter Mair, 1–23. London: Sage Publications, 1994.

Mair, Peter and Ingrid van Biezen. "Party Membership in Twenty European Democracies, 1980–2000." *Party Politics* 7 (2001): 5–21.

Mango, Andrew. *Atatürk: The Biography of the Founder of Modern Turkey*. New York: Overlook, 2000.

Mardin, Şerif. "Center-Periphery Relations: A Key to Turkish Politics?" *Daedalus* 102 (1973): 169–190.

May, John. "Opinion Structure of Political Parties: The Special Law of Curvilinear Disparity." *Political Studies* 21, no. 2 (1973): 135–151.

McCubbins, Matthew, Roger Noll, and Barry R. Weingast. "Administrative Procedures as Instruments of Political Control." *Journal of Law, Economics, and Organization* 3 (1987): 243–277.

McCubbins, Matthew D. and Thomas Schwartz. "Congressional Oversight Overlooked: Police Patrols versus Fire Alarms." *American Journal of Political Science* 28 (1984): 16–79.

Michels, Robert. *Political Parties: A Sociological Study of the Oligarchical Tendencies of Modern Democracies*. New York: Dover Publications, 1959.

Miller, Penny M., Malcolm E. Jewell, and Lee Sigelman. "Reconsidering a Typology of Incentives Among Campaign Activists: A Research Note." *Western Political Quarterly* 40, September (1987): 519–526.

Milliyetçi Hareket Partisi. *MHP Parti Tüzüğü* [The MHP Constitution]. Accessed April 3, 2009. http://www.mhp.org.tr/kitaplar/mhp_parti_tuzugu_2009 _opt.pdf.

Moe, Terry M. "The New Economics of Organization." *American Journal of Political Science* 28, no. 4 (1984): 739–777.

Müller, Wolfgang C. "Political Parties in Parliamentary Democracies: Making Delegation and Accountability Work." *European Journal of Political Research* 37 (2000): 309–333.

Müller, Wolfgang C. and Kaare Strom. *Policy, Office or Votes? How Political Parties in Western Europe make Hard Decisions*. Cambridge: Cambridge University Press, 1999.

Mutlu, Servet. "Ethnic Kurds in Turkey: a Demographic Study." *International Journal of Middle East Studies* 28, no. 4 (1996): 517–541.

Neumann, Sigmund. "Towards a Comparative Study of Political Parties." In *Modern Political Parties. Approaches to Comparative Politics*, edited by Sigmund Neumann, 395–421. Chicago, IL: University of Chicago Press, 1956.

Neuman, William L. *Social Research Methods: Qualitative and Quantitative Approaches*. 2nd ed. Boston: Allyn and Bacon, 1994.

Niskanen, William A. *Bureaucracy and Representative Government*. Chicago: Aldine, 1972.

Nohrstedt, Daniel. "The Politics of Crisis Policymaking: Chernobyl and Swedish Nuclear Energy Policy." *Policy Studies Journal* 36, no. 2 (2008): 257–278.

O'Donnell, Guillermo and Philippe Schmitter. *Transitions from Authoritarian Rule: Tentative Conclusions about Uncertain Democracies*. Baltimore: Johns Hopkins University, 1986.

Olson, Mancur. *The Logic of Collective Action*. Cambridge, MA: Harvard University Press, 1965.

Organization for Security and Cooperation in Europe / Office for Democratic Institutions and Human Rights (OSCE/ODIHR). *Election Assessment Mission Report: Republic of Turkey Early Parliamentary Elections 22 July 2007.* Warsaw, November 27, 2007.

Ostrogorski, Mosei. *Democracy and the Organization of Political Parties.* New York: Macmillan, 1902.

Özbudun, Ergun. *Siyasal Partiler.* Ankara: Sosyal Bilimler Derneği, 1974.

———. "The Nature of the Kemalist Regime." In *Atatürk: Founder of a Modern State,* edited by Ali Kazancıgil and Ergun Özbudun, 79–102. London: C. Hurst & Company, 1981.

———. "Parties and the Party System." In *Contemporary Turkish Politics: Challenges to Democratic Consolidation,* edited by Ergun Özbudun, 73–103. Boulder, London: Lynne Rienner Publishers, 2000.

———. "The Institutional Decline of Parties in Turkey." In *Political Parties and Democracy,* edited by Larry Diamond and Richard Gunther, 238–265. Baltimore and London: The Johns Hopkins University Press, 2001.

———. "From Political Islam to Conservative Democracy: The Case of the Justice and Development Party in Turkey." *South European Society and Politics* 11, no. 3–4 (2006): 543–557.

Övür, Mahmut. "Önseçim CHP'de 11 Nisan Depremini Engelledi." *Sabah.* April 5, 2011. Accessed May 2, 2011. http://www.sabah.com.tr/Yazarlar/ovur/2011/04/05/onsecim-chpde-11-nisan-depremini-engelledi.

Öymen, Altan. "Gizli Oylamanın Temelindeki "Apaçık Oylama"" *Radikal,* 29 April 2008. Accessed April 21 2009. http://www.radikal.com.tr/haber.php?haberno=254294

Panebianco, Angelo. *Political Parties: Organization and Power.* Cambridge: Cambridge University Press, 1988.

Pareto, Vilfredo. *The Rise and Fall of the Elites: An Application of Theoretical Sociology.* New York: Arno Press, 1979.

Parsons, Talcott. "Power and the Social System." In *Power,* edited by Steven Lukes, 94–143. New York University Press: New York, 1986.

Pateman Carole. *Participation and Democratic Theory.* Cambridge: Cambridge University Press, 1970.

Pennings, Paul and Reuven Y. Hazan. "Democratizing Candidate Selection: Causes and Consequences." *Party Politics* 7 (2001): 267–276.

Piattoni, Simona, ed. *Clientelism, Interests, and Democratic Representation: The European Experience in Historical and Comparative Perspective.* Cambridge: Cambridge University Press, 2001.

Pierre, Jon and B. Guy Peters. *Governance, Politics, and the State.* St. Martin's Press: New York, 2000.

Pollack, Mark. "Delegation, Agency, and Agenda Setting in the European Community." *International Organization* 50, no. 1 (1997): 99–134.

Polsby, Nelson W. *Consequences of Party Reform.* New York: Oxford University Press, 1983.

Quinn, Thomas. "Electing the Leader: The British Labour Party's Electoral College." *The Journal of Politics and International Relations* 6, no. 3 (2004): 333–352.

Ragin, Charles. *The Comparative Method: Moving Beyond Qualitative and Quantitative Strategies.* Berkeley: University of California Press, 1987.

Rahat, Gideon and Reuven Y. Hazan. "Candidate Selection Methods: An Analytical Framework." *Party Politics* 7 (2001): 297–322.

Rahat, Gideon. "Candidate Selection: The Choice Before the Choice." *Journal of Democracy* 18, no. 1 (2007): 157–170.

Randall, Vicky and Lars Svasand. "Party Institutionalization in New Democracies." *Party Politics* 8, no. 1 (2002): 5–29.

Rhodes, R. A.W. "The New Governance: Governing without Government," *Political Studies* 44, no. 4 (1996): 652–667.

Roback, Thomas H. "Amateurs and Professionals: Delegates to the 1972 Republican National Convention." *Journal of Politics* 37, no. 2 (1975): 436–468.

———. "Motivation for Activism Among Republican National. Convention Delegates: Continuity and Change, 1972–1976." *Journal of Politics* 42 (1980): 181–201.

Rogow, Arnold A. and Harold D. Laswell. "The Definition of Corruption." In *Political Corruption: Readings in Comparative Analysis,* edited by Arnold J. Heidenheimer. New York: Holt, Rinehart and Winstan, 1970.

Ross, Steven. "The Economic Theory of Agency: The Principal's Problem." *American Economic Review* 63, no. 2 (1973): 134–139.

Rubin, Barry and Metin Heper, eds. *Political Parties in Turkey.* London: Cass, 2002.

Rubin, Barry. "Introduction—Turkey's Political Parties: A Remarkably Important Issue." In *Political Parties in Turkey,* edited by Barry Rubin and Metin Heper, 1–3. London: Cass, 2002.

Rubin, Herbert J. *Applied Social Research.* Columbus, OH: Charles E. Merrill, 1983.

Rubin, Herbert J. and Irene S. Rubin. *Qualitative Interviewing: The Art of Hearing Data.* California: Sage Publications, 1995.

Russell, Bertrand. "The Forms of Power." In *Power,* edited by Steven Lukes, 19–27. New York: New York University Press, 1986.

Russell, Meg. *Building New Labour: The Politics of Party Organisation.* Basingstoke: Palgrave Macmillan, 2005.

Rustow, Dankwart. "The Development of Parties in Turkey." In *Political Parties and Political Development,* edited by Joseph La Palombara and Myron Weiner, 107–136. New Jersey: Princeton University Press, 1966.

Salisbury, Robert H. "An Exchange Theory of Interest Groups." *Midwest Journal of Political Science* 13 (1969): 1–32.

Sanchez, Omar. "Transformation and Decay: the De-Institutionalisation of Party Systems in South America." *Third World Quarterly* 29, no. 2 (2008): 315–337.

Sappington, David E. M. "Incentives in Principal-Agent Relationships." *Journal of Economic Perspectives* 5, no. 2 (1991): 45–66.

Sarigil, Zeki. "Paths are What Actors Make of Them." *Critical Policy Studies* 3, no. 1 (2009): 121–140.

Sayarı, Sabri. "Aspects of Party Organization in Turkey." *The Middle East Journal* 30, no. 2 (1976): 187–199.

———. "Political Patronage in Turkey." In *Patrons and Clients in Mediterranean Societies*, edited by Ernest Gellner and John Waterbury, 103–113. London: Duckworth, 1977.

———. "Introduction." In *Political Leaders and Democracy in Turkey*, edited by Metin Heper and Sabri Sayarı, 1–7. Lanham MD: Lexington Books, 2002.

———. "Adnan Menderes: Between Democratic and Authoritarian Populism." In *Political Leaders and Democracy in Turkey*, edited by Metin Heper and Sabri Sayarı, 65–85. Lanham MD: Lexington Books, 2002.

———. "Towards A New Turkish Party System?" *Turkish Studies* 8, no. 2 (2007): 197–210.

Scarrow, Susan. *Parties and their Members: Organizing for Victory in Britain and Germany*. Oxford: Oxford University Press, 1996.

———. "Parties and the Expansion of Direct Democracy. Who Benefits?" *Party Politics* 5, no. 3 (1999): 341–362.

———. "Parties without Members? Party Organization in a Changing Electoral Environment." In *Parties Without Partisans: Political Change in Advanced Industrial Democracies*, edited by Russell Dalton and Martin Wattenberg, 79–101. Oxford: Oxford University Press, 2000.

———. Implementing *Intra-Party Democracy*. New York: NDI, 2005.

Schattschneider, Elmer E. *Party Government*. New York: Farrar and Rinehart, 1942.

Schmitt, Herman and Soren Holmberg. "Political Parties in Decline?" In *Citizens and the State*, edited by Hans-Dieter Klingemann and Dieter Fuchs, 95–133. Oxford: Oxford University Press, 1995.

Schmitter, Philippe. "Parties Are Not What They Once Were." In *Political Parties and Democracy*, edited by Larry Diamond and Richard Gunther, 67–89. Baltimore: Johns Hopkins University Press, 2001.

Schüler, Harald. *Türkiye'de Sosyal Demokrasi: Particilik, Hemşehrilik, Alevilik*. Translated by Yılmaz Tonbul. İstanbul, İletişim Yayınları, 1998.

Scully, Timothy R. "Reconstituting Party Politics in Chile." In *Building Democratic Institutions: Party Systems in Latin America*, edited by Scott Mainwaring and Timothy R. Scully, 100–137. Stanford: Stanford University Press, 1995.

Seyd, Patrick. "New Parties / New Politics: A Case Study of the British Labour Party." *Party Politics* 5, no. 3 (1999): 383–407.

Shamir, Boas; Robert J. House and Michael B. Arthur. "The Motivational Effects of Charismatic: A Self-Concept Based Theory." *Organizational Science* 4 (1993): 577–594.

Shefter, Martin. *Political Parties and the State: The American Historical Experience*. Princeton: Princeton University Press, 1994.

Shepsle, Kenneth A. and Mark S. Bonchek. *Analyzing Politics: Rationality, Behavior, and Institutions*. New York: W. W. Norton, 1997.

Sherwood, W. B. "The Rise of the Justice Party in Turkey." *World Politics* 20 (1967): 54–65.

Simonton, D. K. *Psychology, Science, and History: An Introduction to Historiometry.* New Haven, CT: Yale University Press, 1991.

Somer, Murat. "Turkey's Kurdish Conflict: Changing Context, and Domestic and Regional Implications." *Middle East Journal* 58, no. 2 (2004): 235–253.

Songer, Donald R., Jeffrey A. Segal, and Charles M. Cameron. "The Hierarchy of Justice: Testing a Principal-Agent Model of Supreme Court-Circuit Court Interactions." *American Journal of Political Science* 38, no. 3 (1994): 673–696.

Soule, John W. and James W. Clarke. "Amateurs and Professionals: A Study of Delegates to the 1968 Democratic National Convention." *American Political Science Review* 64 (1970): 888–898.

Spence, Michael and Richard Zeckhauser. "Insurance, Information and Individual Action." *American Economic Review* 61, no. 2 (1971): 380–387.

Stoker, Gerry. "Governance as Theory: Five Propositions." *International Social Science Journal* 50, no. 155 (1998): 17–28.

Streeck, Wolfgang and Kathleen Thelen. "Introduction: Institutional Change in Advanced Political Economies." In *Beyond Continuity: Institutional Change in Advanced Political Economies*, edited by Wolfgang Streeck and Kathleen Thelen, 1–39. Oxford: Oxford University Press, 2005.

Strom, Kaare. "A Behavioral Theory of Competitive Political Parties." *American Journal of Political Science* 34 (1990): 565–598.

Sunar, İlkay and Sabri Sayarı. "Democracy in Turkey: Problems and Prospects." In *Transitions From Authoritarian Rule: Experiences in Southern Europe and Latin America*, edited by Guillermo O'Donnell, Philippe C. Schmitter, and Laurence Whitehead, 165–187. Baltimore: The Johns Hopkins University Press, 1986.

Szczerbiak, Aleks. *Poles together? The Emergence and Development of Political Parties in Post-cCommunist Poland.* Budapest: Central European University, 2001.

Tachau, Frank. "Bülent Ecevit: From Idealist to Pragmatist." In *Political Leaders and Democracy in Turkey*, edited by Metin Heper and Sabri Sayarı, 107–125. Lexington Books, 2002.

Teorell, Jan. "A Deliberative Defence of Intra-Party Democracy." *Party Politics* 5, no. 3 (1999): 363–382.

TESAV [Toplumsal, Ekonomik, Siyasal Araştırmalar Vakfı] *Siyasi Partiler ve Demokrasi Sempozyumu: 17 Haziran 2005.* Ankara: TESAV, 2005.

TESAV [Toplumsal, Ekonomik, Siyasal Araştırmalar Vakfı] *Siyasi Partiler ve Seçim Kaunlarinda Değişiklik Önerileri Sempozyumu: 18–19 Şubat 2005.* Ankara: TESAV, 2005.

TOBB [Türkiye Odalar ve Borsalar Birliği]. *Siyasi Partiler ve Seçim KanunlarıÖnerisi.* Ankara: TOBB, 2000.

Toka, Gabor. "Political Parties and Democratic Consolidation in East Central Europe." In *Consolidating the Third Wave Democracies: Themes and Perspectives*, edited by Larry Diamond, Marc F. Plattner, Yun-han Chu, and Hung-mao Tien, 93–134. Baltimore, MD: John Hopkins University Press, 1997.

Toker, Metin. *İsmet Paşayla 10 Yıl 1954–1964.* İstanbul: Akis Yayınları, 1969.

Tosun, Tanju and Gülgün E. Tosun. "Voter Preferences in Izmir from the November 3, 2002 to the July 22, 2007 Elections: Has the Election Map Altered?" *Turkish Studies* 9, no. 2 (2008): 247–295.

Turan, İlter. "Political Parties and the Party System in Post-1983 Turkey." In *State, Democracy and the Military: Turkey in the 1980s*, edited by Metin Heper and Ahmet Evin, 63–80. Berlin: W. de Gruyter, 1988.

———. "Old Soldiers Never Die: The Republican People's Party of Turkey." *South European Society and Politics* 11, no. 3–4 (2006): 559–578.

Verdier, Daniel. "The Politics of Public Aid to Private Industry: The Role of Policy Networks." *Comparative Political Studies* 28, no. 1 (1995): 2–42.

Vroom, Victor H. and Philip W. Yetton. *Leadership and Decision-Making*. Pittsburgh, PA: University of Pittsburgh Press, 1973.

Yanık, Murat. *Parti İçi Demokrasi: Parti Disiplini, Lider Sultası, Partilerde Oligarşik Yapı, Siyasal Yozlaşma, E-demokrasi, E-devlet, E-parti*. İstanbul: Beta, 2002.

Ware, Alan. *The Logic of Party Democracy*. London: Macmillan, 1979.

———. *Political Parties: Electoral Change and Structural Response*. NewYork: Basil Blackwell, 1987.

———. *Political Parties and Party Systems*. Oxford: Oxford University Press, 1996.

Watts, Nicole F. "Allies and Enemies: Pro-Kurdish Parties in Turkish politics, 1990–1994." *International Journal of Middle East Studies* 31, no. 4 (1999): 631–656.

———. "Activists in Office: Pro-Kurdish Contentions Politics in Turkey." *Ethnopolitics* 5, no. 2 (2006): 125–144.

Weber, Max. *Economy and Society*. Translated by Guenther Roth and Claus Wittich. New York: Bedminster Press, 1968.

———. *Law in Economy and Society*. Cambridge: Harvard University Press, 1954.

Weingast, Barry R. and Mark J. Moran "Bureaucratic Discretion or Congressional Control? Regulatory Policymaking by the Federal Trade Commission." *The Journal of Political Economy* 91, no. 5 (1983): 765–800.

Weingast, Barry R. "The Congressional Bureaucratic System: A Principal-Agent Perspective." *Public Choice* 44 (1984): 147–88.

Wendt, Alexander. "On Constitution and Causation in International Relations." *Review of International Studies* 24 (1998): 101–118.

———. *Social Theory of International Politics*. Cambridge: Cambridge University Press, 1999.

White, Jenny B. *Islamist Mobilization in Turkey: A Study of Vernacular Politics*. Seattle: University of Washington Press, 2003.

Wildavsky, Aaron. "The Goldwater Phenomenon: Purists, Politicians, and the Two–Party System." *Review of Politics* 27 (1965): 386–413.

Williams, Russell Alan. "Exogenous Shocks in Subsystem Adjustment and Policy Change: The Credit Crunch and Canadian Banking Regulation." *Journal of Public Policy* 29, no. 1 (2009): 29–53.

Wilson, James Q. ed. *The Politics of Regulation*. New York: Basic Books, 1980.

Wilson, Frank L. "The Center-Right at the End of the Century." In *The European Center-Right at the End of the Twentieth Century*, edited by Frank L. Wilson. Basingstoke: Macmillan, 1998.

Wittman, Donald A. "Parties as Utility Maximizers." *American Political Science Review* 67 (1973): 490–98.

Yıldırım, Ergün, Hüsamettin İnaç and Hayrettin Özler. "A Sociological Representation of the Justice and Development Party: Is It a Political Design or a Political Becoming?" *Turkish Studies* 8, no. 1 (2007): 5–24.

Young, Oran R. "Interdependencies in World Politics." *International Journal* 24 (1969): 726–750.

Index